Lord High Executioner

*London-born Thomas Rowlandson (1756–1827) made several drawings
and paintings of executions. Like many of his fellow citizens, he found it
difficult to miss a good hanging. This execution, dated 1803, makes use of
the same hangman that appears in the hanging of Mary Evans at York in
1799 (see page 92).*

LORD HIGH EXECUTIONER

*An Unashamed Look at Hangmen,
Headsmen, and Their Kind*

HOWARD ENGEL

Robson Books

To Kildare Dobbs
and David Mason

This edition published in 1998 by Robson Books Ltd
First published in Great Britain in 1997 by Robson Books Ltd,
Bolsover House, 5-6 Clipstone Street, London W1P 8LE

Reprinted 1998

British Library Cataloguing in Publication Data
A catalogue record for this title is available from the British
Library

ISBN 1 86105 159 X (pbk)
ISBN 1 86105 096 8 (cased)

Text design: Peter Maher

Printed in Great Britain by St Edmundsbury Press Ltd, Bury
St Edmunds, Suffolk.

Contents

Acknowledgments

There are a great many people to whom I owe my thanks, people who have helped me with one aspect of the work or another. Among them I would like to thank Kildare Dobbs, David Mason, Scott Tyrer, Dominique Roydon, Bill Gladstone, Gerald Owen, Eric Wright, Diane Francis, John Fraser, Vittorio Frigerio, Prof. Jim Jackson (Trinity College, Dublin), Martin L. Friedland, John M. Beattie, Jerry G. E. Bentley, Jack McLeod, Carolyn Strange, Rona Abramovitch, Hubert de Santana, Dudley Witney, James Carley, David Stafford, Jeanne Canizzo, Meg Taylor, Archie Campbell, Jonathan Freedman, Elizabeth Legge, Asa Zatz, Douglas Fetherling, the Greek Tourist Bureau, the staff of the Conan Doyle Room at the Metro Toronto Public Library, and many other individuals and institutions, whose names, for the moment, are stuck in my failing memory, for their help and encouragement throughout this project.

I would like to thank Frank W. Anderson, the author of *Hanging in Canada*, for the clippings from the *Manitoba Free Press* (1899 and 1900) and correspondence with the author in 1972. I owe a similar debt to Prof. Michael Millgate for sending me clippings and chapbooks relating to the execution of Martha Brown at Dorchester in 1856.

My wife, Janet Hamilton, who has encouraged and sustained me, also deserves my thanks, as do my agent, Beverley Slopen, and Anna Porter and Cynthia Good, the publishers, respectively, of my non-fiction and of my fiction, without whom I would be a drag on the remaining social services of this country. Throughout the process of the making of this book they have at various times noted the fact that I have become a glutton for punishment.

Preface

Edward L. Greenspan, QC

Howard Engel won the 1984 Arthur Ellis Award for his Benny Cooperman mystery series. Perhaps it was intrigue with the name of this prize that led him to write a book on executioners. Arthur Ellis, of course, was Canada's most notorious hangman. He is reputed to have hanged six hundred people, making him this country's worst serial killer.

Why would an award for crime fiction be named after an executioner? Because an effective executioner is a great artist. Executioners require the ready eye, steady hand, and cool, calculating, swift mind of an artist. Being poorly paid, they practice art for art's sake. In early times, they played the lead role in a bloodthirsty spectacle of sovereign power. Later, their object was to dispatch the condemned with as little fuss and mess as possible.

Different countries developed distinct styles of execution. The English excelled at "drop" hanging, while the Americans invented the Wild West "jerk 'em up" method. The Americans were also the architects of the "Death House," which featured the electric chair, the gas chamber, and the lethal injection. For sheer depravity, however, it is difficult to match the medieval European method of disposing of condemned women: stitch them into a sack with an ape, a poisonous snake, a dog, and a cockerel, and fling them into a pond to drown. Variety is the spice of life—and death.

Howard Engel's passionate curiosity has produced a feast for the reader. With his celebrated gift for narrative, he describes executions throughout the ages, many of which are stranger than fiction: the condemned thief who steals from the chaplain on his way to the gallows; the former executioner who is himself executed; the condemned woman who turns her execution into a fashion statement and an outlet for repressed Victorian passions. A lover of words, Engel injects his work with literary quotations and allusions, puns and etymological references.

Yet *Lord High Executioner* explodes the myth of the noble execution, in which a condemned person goes bravely to meet his or her maker. In fact, executions are often breathtaking in their clumsiness. Bloody, smelly indignities inevitably result. Reading stories of botched executions, in which heads and limbs refuse to separate from bodies, and physical functions refuse to quit, I began to think that the body itself could conspire with the mind and soul to revolt against the cruelty of execution.

Most executioners appear to have avoided moral headaches about the death penalty by focusing on deadly details: How far must the condemned drop in order to break the neck but avoid decapitation? How long must a person be left in a gas chamber to ensure asphyxiation? How can the condemned be brought to the gallows without the difficulty of having them climb stairs? How can a woman's modesty be guarded as she dangles lifelessly from a rope?

We learn that in the end, however, most executioners could not escape the ghosts of their victims; many sank into a drunken, nasty, and brutish existence. Some "stuck their necks out" when they retired, renouncing the death penalty. Others tried the lecture circuit. Most simply wanted to sink into obscurity. Arthur Ellis, who had used a pseudonym as an executioner, reverted to his real name. In a great feat of humanity, Ellis said, upon reflecting on his life as an executioner, "Hanging belongs to a past age. I am strongly in favour of the electric chair."

I have always fervently opposed capital punishment. To me it is a cruel, barbaric, brutal, useless act that fails to deter crime. It is state-sanctioned vengeance, and even the worst murderer does not release the state from its obligation to respect the dignity of life, for the state does not honor the victim by emulating the killer. Capital punishment is, at its essence, different from all other forms of punishment by being ultimate, completely irrevocable, irreparable, and final. It is beyond correction.

I believe that the death penalty is administered for no reason other than a deep hatred of the individual and an abiding thirst for revenge. I would hate to live in a state that I did not believe was any better than a murderer. Although Howard Engel appears to share this view, *Lord High Executioner* is not a polemic, nor even an argument against the death penalty. It is simply a portrait, like Oscar Wilde's *Picture of Dorian Grey*, that shows the toll evil wages on its practitioners. And that is why this book is an invaluable addition to death-penalty literature, and a superb read for anyone with an interest in history, crime and punishment, law, literature, and the mysteries of life and death.

Introduction

Behold the Lord High Executioner
A personage of noble rank and title—
A dignified and potent officer,
Whose functions are particularly vital!
Defer, defer,
To the Lord High Executioner!

—W. S. GILBERT

By and large, executioners have not been personages of noble rank and title. In fact almost every society has counted them among the lowest of the low. True, there have been dynasties of headsmen in France and hangmen in Britain, a kind of parallel aristocracy where the first-born inherited the mantle of office from his father along with a certain dignity that goes with it, but most executioners have come from the same ranks as the criminals they executed and the policemen who enforced the laws—that is to say, from the lower-middle and working classes. Their functions may have been vital—few more so—but they were hardly dignified officers of the court. Pariahs, every one of them.

Logically, a case can be made for the social acceptance of the functionary who carries out the sentence of death. He is, after all, merely an extension of the law courts. If no one condemns or stigmatizes a hanging judge, why should the technician who carries out the law be shunned? In *The Mikado*, Pooh Bah, the portly Lord High Everything Else, explains how it is that the status of executioner stands so high in the town of Titipu:

> . . . Our logical Mikado, seeing no moral difference between the dignified judge who condemns a criminal to die, and the industrious mechanic who carries out the sentence, has rolled the two offices into one, and every judge is now his own executioner.

That may have been all very well for the town of Titipu and the topsy-turvy world of Gilbert and Sullivan, but in the world beyond operetta there are claims to be made for the executioner as an important functionary in the legal system. Honest hangmen have for centuries resented being looked down upon by the rest of society. After all, many thought of themselves as the benefactors of society.

The question of whether the public has a right to treat the hangman as an outcast was actually contested in a court of law. It was a judge, not a jury, who had to decide the question. The *English Law Journal* of 28 July 1926 describes the case of a man who, arriving in Norwich on the eve of an execution, was taken by a bystander for the hangman and thrown into a duck pond by the mob that quickly collected. All the while, the first irate citizen shouted: "You are Jack Ketch!" The mob echoed: "You are Jack Ketch, the hangman!" Let me allow Louis Blake Duff to take up the story at this point:

> The victim consulted his lawyer and decided to sue the man who had called him the hangman. The defence claimed the allegation could not possibly be defamatory.
>
> "The executioner," said the defence lawyer, "is a public official, necessary to the security of the State, and it is no more a libel to describe a man as a hangman than to say he is a judge."
>
> The judge listened to this argument and in the very teeth of it awarded damages. So the outrageous prejudice against the hangman has invaded even the bench whose faithful necessary servant he is. To say the least, it is hardly sporting.

Hangmen and headsmen have been in the back of our minds for hundreds of years. They are the bogeymen of our worst nightmares, the shape of our darkest fears. They stalk the subconscious in thick leather boots carrying with them the bloodstained tools of their deadly mystery. They repel and revolt us, and, against all rationality, attract and fascinate us. They have been closest to the line between life and death. The mystery and majesty of the law have been condensed into these appalling shapes. They stand at the entrance to the dungeons of our worst dreams, beckoning with their hands: "Come with me." The executioner is at once hated and feared, and yet he may go where no man may go. He is wrapped up in our primitive selves, personifying the atavism that lives deep within all of us. To understand ourselves, it is important to face the irrational, the phobic, the taboos of the society that created this unpleasant stand-in for everyman.

In our reading, the executioner often stands just offstage in the wings. Like the *deus ex machina* of the drama, the headsman casts a long shadow through fiction. For instance, it is impossible to fully understand Dickens, Thackeray, and Hardy without seeing the mark of the gallows on their work.

At the same time, executioners have added to the lore of language: Derrick, a hangman from the early seventeenth century, who operated upon the legendary gallows at Tyburn, gave his name to a device for hoisting heavy objects. Jack Ketch, towards the end of the century, gave his name to the whole breed of hangmen. His very name became synonymous with "executioner." Of him his wife is reported to have said:

> ... Any bungler might put a man to death, but only her husband knew how to make a gentleman die sweetly.

The crusade against capital punishment is a distinguished and long one. Throughout history there have always been a few farsighted people who were ready to lead that crusade. But it was only in the nineteenth century that signs of improvement began to appear. In Britain, the Bloody Code—the ever-growing catalogue of crimes which brought the death sentence—was trimmed of many capital offenses, and the forms of execution were consolidated: in Britain, the gallows; in France, the guillotine. The spirit of reform was in the air, of course, but sometimes it turned up in odd places. Turning the pages of Punch, the satirical magazine published in London, one finds short squibs aimed at the hangman—who in the traditional Punch and Judy show, you will remember, ends up on his own gallows. This squib is from the end of 1849:

The Gibbet Cure

> It may seem astonishing that there should exist, in this nineteenth century, such a folly as that instanced in the following paragraph, extracted from the *Boston [Lincolnshire, England] Herald:*—
>
> "SUPERSTITION.—On Friday last a respectable looking female, afflicted with a wen in the neck, applied at Lincoln Castle, after the execution of WARD, for leave to see the body, with a view of curing her disease; the request was very properly refused."
>
> It may, however, be questioned whether a man hanged is not as likely to remove a wen as to put an end to murder. The remedy has been long enough tried for the latter complaint, but without success.

In this book about our recorded legal merchants of death, I have dealt with the whole tribe of hangmen and headsmen, not leaving out the likes of Robert G. Elliott, the official executioner of New York, who "hurled into eternity three hundred and eighty-seven occupants of the electric chair." In some places around the world, the names of the executioners have not been recorded. Like the dog that failed to bark in the Sir Arthur Conan Doyle story, this too is highly significant.

This book is offered as an inspection of the men—and women!—who

The touch of a hanged man's hand was said to be a sure cure for warts, wens, and other blemishes, but, as Douglas Jerrold noted in Punch, *hanging was supposed to cure murder, and that didn't work either. This 1828 print depicts an incident in 1814, when several women tried out "the gallows cure."*

have done our dirty work for us. It is presented as a close-up look at the ritual of killing in the public's name. In it I have tried to illustrate with what courage, or lack of it, many of the famous of history shuffled off this mortal coil before their time. I have examined what the agents of death thought of their craft, their victims, and themselves.

I am a strong believer in abolition, but for the most part I have tried to keep that out of the text. It is not totally possible to remove my own feelings about the subject, and I cannot assume a god-like neutrality which I do not own. My biases and opinions show throughout the book. They lend a flavor. To write with absolute neutrality would be like trying to run a car in neutral: it won't go. But this book is not intended as a sociological, or even psychological, tome; it is literary and curious.

As a writer of fiction, I recognize that books feed on books, that new books are begotten from older ones. In this, my first attempt at non-fiction, I feel as though I am standing upon the heap of books I have been feasting upon. Not only have I consulted books directly in the way of my inquiry, but I have dabbled far afield, finding useful items that I have incorporated into my manuscript. A list of the books I have consulted is to be found at the end of this book.

When Albert Pierrepoint appeared before the British Royal Commission on Capital Punishment in 1949, he told the chairman, Sir Ernest Gowers, that in England at that time the position of executioner was a hereditary job. He was the third in his family to hold the position—his father, his uncle, and himself. "It's in the family, really," he said.

In this book, I would like to introduce you to "the family."

CHAPTER ONE

Marking Out the Territory

Yet within three days shall Pharaoh lift up thy head from off thee, and shall hang thee on a tree; and the birds shall eat thy flesh from off thee . . .

—GENESIS, XL, 19

When Pharaoh of old hanged his chief baker, he pardoned his butler, just as the imprisoned Joseph had predicted. A fat lot of good it did for the young Hebrew who had interpreted their dreams. He was left behind in the prison house until Pharaoh himself had troubling dreams.

This is the first biblical reference to capital punishment and perhaps a good place to begin this study of headsmen, hangmen, and their ilk. On the face of it, it seems simple enough: the baker was hanged and the butler was restored to his place, serving the Egyptian king his cup. But it is not quite as clear as it looks. Although the text says that Pharaoh hanged his baker, it also says that he would "lift up thy head from off thee," which sounds more like the sword or ax than the rope. Does it mean that the baker suffered beheading as well as hanging? With a severed neck one should at least be safe from hanging. It seems more likely that the baker's corpse was exposed in public, hanging from a tree, suspended by some part of him other than his neck until "the birds shall eat thy flesh from off thee." With this interpretation it would appear that the exposure of hanging dead bodies—as a warning to other would-be wrongdoers, as a warning to strangers, as a measure of the terrible power of Pharaoh—was an established practice before hanging in its usual sense was introduced.

Although the Bible speaks of Pharaoh hanging his baker, it should be said that there is no suggestion that the king-god did the work himself. The times were primitive to be sure, but the more sophisticated times of Caligula in early Imperial Rome, and Vlad the Impaler, in fifteenth-century Transylvania, were yet to come.

The Babylonian ruler Hammurabi put together the earliest surviving code of laws around 2100 B.C. He had them written on a diorite shaft eight feet high, placed where all could see and wonder at it. "An eye for an eye, a tooth for a tooth" was the gist of it, with paternal care offered to the widow and orphan. But there were peculiarities. For instance, if a builder was

Vlad the Impaler, who inspired Bram Stoker's Dracula, *relished lingering death for the victims of his persecutions. In these he rarely played favorites, treating all classes, religions, and crimes equally. He stopped giving Eastern Europe a bad name only when he was finally felled by an assassin.*

convicted of negligence in constructing a house that collapsed, killing the buyer's son, it was the builder's son's life that was forfeited to the law, not the builder's. Such a view is farther from our thinking than "the eye for an eye" concept; it robs the characters involved of their uniqueness, their individuality, rather in the way that God's taking Job's children is not precisely addressed by giving him replacements. The Code of Hammurabi was an enlightened code for its time, but its harsher provisions gave the official executioners ample work for their blades.

Exodus and the rest of the Five Books of Moses made improvements on the Code of Hammurabi, but it still wasn't an executioner's holiday.

> . . . Behold also, the gallows fifty cubits high, which Haman had made for Mordecai, who had spoken good for the king, standeth in the house of Haman. Then the King said, Hang him thereon. So they hanged Haman on the gallows that he had prepared for Mordecai. Then was the king's wrath pacified.
>
> —ESTHER VII, 9 AND 10

This reporting of King Ahasuerus's decisive dealing with Haman is clearer than the description of the death of Pharaoh's baker. The king issued an order and it was obeyed. It was singularly appropriate, since Haman built the gallows to be revenged upon his arch-enemy, Mordecai, the queen's cousin and stepfather. He had intended also to wipe out all of the Jews in Persia because Mordecai refused to do him reverence. (It must be remembered that in those days Persia and its 127 provinces ran from India to Ethiopia. No mean kingdom, as St. Paul might have observed.) The king's vengeance, it is worth noting, embraced Haman's ten sons, who also perished on the gallows. We must assume that they were deeply involved in Haman's plotting and also shared the guilt of the planned genocide. Unfortunately, the story speaks of a scheming wife, Zeresh, not sons. It does rather leave an unpleasant aftertaste once this Turkish delight of a story has been swallowed. Perhaps once a gallows has been set up, there is a tendency to keep it operating. An empty gallows might become a symbol of social flaccidity, imperial meltdown, and judicial *laissez-faire.*

The state has always exercised power over the individual. That, some think, is what the state is for. In the Bible, few get off with a warning. Take Haman's poor sons, for example. One of the ways in which the state, be it king, sultan, or emperor, exercised this authority was through terror. There is nothing like a few dangling bodies outside the citadel to remind the newcomer that one transgresses civil and criminal law at one's peril. There is a story somewhere about European travelers being cast away on a strange and foreign shore. When they see bodies dangling from a gibbet, instead of turning around and heading back into the breakers, they thank their lucky stars and embrace one another warmly, for they've landed in a Christian country.

In the twenty-second book of the *Odyssey*, Homer describes what must be the most ancient formal description of an execution by hanging. The hangman, the first whose name has come down to us, was Telemachus, the son of Ulysses, who executed Penelope's twelve faithless handmaidens. Telemachus may have been a figure in fiction, but so much of Homer has been discovered to have some parallels in history, I have included his treatment of the faithless handmaidens. Here is the passage in a translation by William Cowper:

> . . . leading forth
> The women next, they shut them close between
> The lofty wall and scullery, narrow, straight,
> And dreadful, whence no prisoner might escape.
> Then, prudent, thus Telemachus advised:

    The death of honour would I never grant
To criminals like these, who poured contempt
On mine and on my mother's head, and lay
By night enfolded in the suitors' arms.
    He said, and noosing a strong galley rope
To a huge column, led the cord around
The spacious dome, suspended so aloft,
That none with quivering feet might reach the floor.
As when a flight of doves entering the copse,
Or broad-winged thrushes, strike against the net
Within; ill rest, entangled, there they find;
So they, suspended by the neck, expired
All in one line together. Death abhorred!
With restless feet awhile they beat the air,
Then ceased.

In the library at Trinity College, Dublin, is a treatise, *On Hanging* (1866), by a Victorian fellow of the college, the Reverend Samuel Haughton, M.D., F.R.S. (1821–1897). In it he argues at great length how Telemachus was able to dispatch a dozen women on a cable suspended at both ends. He found, through the use of mathematics that are beyond my technical means to display and my mathematical ability to fathom, that if Telemachus suspended one end of his cable from a high pillar; tied slip-knots in the cable for nooses; and then, with help, hoisted the women aloft by pulling on the other end of the rope which had been passed over another high point, it could not be done. The force needed to lift the handmaids in a group was lacking. Homer never claimed to have test-driven every part of his book. Haughton goes on to say that if the youthful hangman attached a dozen noosed ropes from the suspended cable, then it would be possible. Here is what the polymath Haughton concludes:

> The ship-rope, with one end fastened to the pillar, was carried around the vaulted dome of the kitchen and made fast upon itself; from this rope were then suspended smaller ropes with slipknots or nooses, which were passed round the necks of the women, who must have been lifted up one by one for the purpose, so as to swing clear of the ground. The simile of fieldfares [thrushes] and wood-pigeons [doves] caught in nooses hanging from a rope stretched from tree to tree, and placed in the passage to their roost, seems rather to favour the second interpretation . . . as if the women hung, like Bluebeard's wives, "tit tat toe, all in a row!"

Dr. Haughton's scholarship was given not only to tidying up minute points of physics in the classics, but also to research into the brakes of railway trains, the physiological properties of nicotine and strychnia, the Baltic sea-louse, polarized light on polished surfaces, the velocity of rifle bullets, the muscular anatomy of the leg of the crocodile, climate, tides, urine in human beings, and the distortion of fossils through slaty cleavage. He also wrote about the long drop, which transformed the old practice of hanging from being a tumble and a kick to the modern practice of giving the victim a sudden drop of some distance which either breaks the neck outright or at least dislocates vertebrae, which is almost as good. The Irish invented the long drop, which, in time, crossed the Irish Sea to England, where it was picked up by William Marwood and his successors.

In order to get another grasp on the questions surrounding an execution, let me leap more than two thousand years away from Ithaca and Ulysses' happy reunion with his family, to the all-but-forgotten death of Julia Murdoch, in Toronto, Upper Canada. This case, not extraordinary in any way, except for the people involved, will be used as a paradigm of what this book is concerned with. On 14 December 1837, while the restless province of Upper Canada was getting ready to participate in or resist a rebellion in favor of democratic institutions, and Lower Canada was about to launch a similar grassroots insurrection, but in French, Toronto legally hanged a young woman named Julia Murdoch for having murdered her mistress. It was only when Julia began selling silver spoons that her nursing of the invalid Mrs. Harriet Henry was questioned. When the body was examined, arsenic was found and Julia was immediately arrested. At her trial, she maintained her innocence in spite of evidence that she had mixed the poison in a dish of fish she served her patient. I found her story buried in the hundreds of pages of John Ross Robertson's *Landmarks of Toronto*.

> The murderess was a woman about 21 years of age, unmarried . . . and
> well thought of by the family. . . . The day before her execution she stated
> that she considered the dreadful circumstances in which she was placed
> as a merciful arrangement of Divine Providence for the purpose of lead-
> ing her to a true repentance of her misimprovement of early religious
> advantages.

By that, I suppose she meant that being condemned to death had led her back onto the goodly paths of righteousness and that a timely repentance would bring her all the joys of eternal bliss—"after a few short years of harmonious torture in Purgatory," as Brendan Behan used to say, although I don't suppose that Purgatory played a big part in Julia Murdoch's theology.

The mention of Brendan Behan was not without guile. In his play *The Quare Fellow*, the warder, Regan, has a conversation with the prison visitor, Mr. Healy, on the night of a hanging in an Irish prison:

Healy: I can't see how society could exist without hanging. Don't you believe in it?

Regan: Well, I've seen such a lot of it, sir, that I suppose familiarity breeds contempt. But do I believe in it? Well, it works. I've never seen the fellow that could go out and drink a pint afterwards. You mean we kill people to stop other people killing other people?

Healy: And because they have killed other people.

Regan: Oh sir, we never mention that part of it in the business. That'd be revenge.

Healy: But we give a condemned man every spiritual facility. I venture to say that some of them die holier deaths than if they had finished their natural span.

Regan: But that's not our reason for hanging them, sir. We don't advertise 'Commit a murder and die a happy death'. You want to be very careful in what you're saying, sir, or you'll have them all at it. They take religion very seriously in this country, sir.

Healy: The fact remains, the condemned man does get a priest and the Sacraments, more than his victim got maybe.

Regan: Well, sir, maybe it would be more of a deterrent if we gave them no priest and no Sacrament.

Behan based this play about what happens to a prison population when a hanging takes place on his own experiences in Mountjoy Prison. The "quare fellow" told Brendan the night before he was *topped*, "I will be praying for you in Heaven tonight."

Let's return to the execution of Julia Murdoch in Toronto in December 1837.

. . . The day of execution was cold, snow on the ground, and the scaffold was erected on Toronto Street, where now stands the York Chambers, near the old jail. . . . *The Christian Guardian* of that date says that the utmost decorum marked the conduct of the vast assemblage of persons who witnessed the fatal result. "It was, however, exceedingly revolting," says the *Guardian*, "to see among the spectators a number of females." On the day of her execution fully four thousand people congregated about the jail yard, a large proportion of them being women and children. . . .

Whenever one reads an account of a public execution, whether it is in Beijing or Tripoli, Tyburn or the Place de la Révolution, the reporter is shocked and amazed at the number of women and children who have come to look. Dickens himself said it. Maybe it was expected of him. Writers were always shocked and amazed that one-half of the population should show the same morbid curiosity as the other.

Let us go back to poor Julia Murdoch where we left her on her way to a Toronto scaffold, with four thousand curious spectators of both sexes and all ages waiting to see the fatal outcome.

> . . . She readily submitted to be pinioned. . . . The prisoner was dreadfully agitated, and as she walked to the gallows leaned for support on her spiritual comforter's arm. When she arrived at the platform she appeared to regain her courage, and after prayer had been offered up she knelt on the trap-door, and was hurried into eternity. . . .

Kneeling on the trap seems to have been a North American phenomenon. I can't recall an Englishman going to his death in that position, unless he was being beheaded. From a religious point of view, it would appear to be an excellent way to leave this world, but in Britain, even preachers, like the celebrated Dr. Dodd condemned for forgery, on the point of death at Tyburn or Newgate, preferred to stand. It might have had something to do with the amount of slack in the rope. It would appear, in the case of Julia Murdoch at least, that there was no shortage. Giving people enough rope is not only a figure of speech.

Earlier, I referred to the excellent Reverend Samuel Haughton, the Victorian polymath, who used mathematics to settle problems in Homer. In his paper *On Hanging*, he demonstrates, with impressive use of mathematical calculations, the science of neck-breaking. With the unfortunate Julia having just been turned off, this might be a good place to discuss what happens. With a short drop, death comes from asphyxia, caused by stoppage of the windpipe, or apoplexy, caused by pressure on the jugular vein. With a long drop, death comes about through a shock to the medulla oblongata, caused by fracture of the vertebral column. As Haughton explains:

> In the [cases of the short drop], death is preceded by convulsions, lasting from five to forty-five minutes, which are caused by the cessation of the supply of arterial blood to the muscles. In the [case of the long drop], death is instantaneous and painless, and is unaccompanied by any convulsive movement whatever.

From the time of William Marwood, the English hangman, the job has been trying to calculate how the latter alternative could be managed. The variables are the weight and height of the prisoner and the length of the drop, which is controlled by the length of the rope. With a large range in heights and weights, the correct drop for one will not do for another. Each of us has a correct drop. It is personal to each of us. Like a fingerprint or credit card, it is not transferable.

The trick, of course, is trying to figure out the scientifically perfect drop for everyone requiring one. Unfortunately, it is not a purely scientific question. Two men may possess the same height and weight, but one of them might be young, muscular, and active, and the other old, flabby, and sedentary. The hangman must make a judgement. Should he give men and women of similar heights and weights the same drop? The hangman has to make a judgement. If he is conservative by nature, there is a chance of asphyxiation with convulsions; if he is too liberal, the head may be torn off. From a medical point of view, a decapitation is fast and painless, but it fails on aesthetics and decorum. A decapitation is messy, discredits the hangman, and gives the whole prison service and the justice system itself a black eye.

Here is Haughton's formula for a perfect hanging, guaranteed to give a clean break, or at least a dislocation:

> Divide the weight of the patient in pounds into 2,240, and the quotient will give the length of the long drop in feet. For example, a criminal weighing 160 pounds should be allowed [a] 14 feet drop.

Haughton suggests that if it is inconvenient to provide a drop that long, and a lighter person would require even more space to fall through, shot or heavy weights should be affixed to the legs of the patient. This was in fact done with very light victims.

A word of caution: Dr. Haughton's long drops are very long indeed. I cannot in all conscience recommend them. His suggestion of using a standard shock of 2,240 foot-pounds was amended in 1888 in Britain. The figure used there was 1,260 foot-pounds, and this force too was changed again, in 1913, to include another factor. Although it was prepared on a slightly different principle, let me insert here the table that English executioner James Berry developed after an earlier one led to some professional embarrassment.

A HANDY GUIDE FOR HANGMEN

SCALE SHOWING THE STRIKING FORCE OF FALLING BODIES AT DIFFERENT DISTANCES.												
Distance Falling in Feet	8 Stone	9 Stone	10 Stone	11 Stone	12 Stone	13 Stone	14 Stone	15 Stone	16 Stone	17 Stone	18 Stone	19 Stone
Zero	Cw. Qr. lb.	Cw. Qr. lb.	Cw. Qr. lb.	Cw. Qr. lb.	Cw. Qr. lb.	Cw. Qr. lb.	Cw. Qr. lb.	Cw. Qr. lb.	Cw. Qr. lb.	Cw. Qr. lb.	Cw. Qr. lb.	Cw. Qr. lb.
1 Ft.	8 0 0	9 0 0	10 0 0	11 0 0	12 0 0	13 0 0	14 0 0	15 0 0	16 0 0	17 0 0	18 0 0	19 0 0
2 ,,	11 1 15	12 2 23	14 0 14	15 2 4	16 3 22	18 1 12	19 3 2	21 0 21	22 2 11	24 0 1	25 1 19	26 3 9
3 ,,	13 3 16	15 2 15	17 1 14	19 0 12	20 3 11	22 2 9	24 1 8	26 0 7	27 3 5	29 2 4	31 1 2	33 0 1
4 ,,	16 0 0	18 0 0	20 0 0	22 0 0	24 0 0	26 0 0	28 0 0	30 0 0	32 0 0	34 0 0	36 0 0	40 0 0
5 ,,	17 2 11	19 3 5	22 0 0	24 0 22	26 1 16	28 2 11	30 3 5	33 0 0	35 0 22	37 0 16	39 2 11	41 3 15
6 ,,	19 2 11	22 0 5	24 2 0	26 3 22	29 1 16	31 3 11	34 1 5	36 3 0	39 0 22	41 2 16	44 0 11	46 2 5
7 ,,	21 0 22	23 3 11	26 2 0	29 0 16	31 3 5	34 1 22	37 0 11	39 3 0	42 1 16	45 0 5	47 2 22	50 1 11
8 ,,	22 2 22	25 2 4	28 1 14	31 0 23	34 0 5	36 3 15	39 2 25	42 2 7	45 1 16	48 0 26	51 0 8	53 3 18
9 ,,	24 0 11	27 0 12	30 0 14	33 0 23	36 0 16	39 0 18	42 0 19	45 0 21	48 0 22	51 0 23	54 0 25	57 0 26
10 ,,	25 1 5	28 1 23	31 2 14	34 3 4	37 3 22	41 0 12	44 1 2	47 1 21	50 2 11	53 3 1	56 3 19	60 0 9

RULE—Take the weight of the Client in Stones and look down the column of weights until you reach the figure nearest to 24 cwt. [hundred-weight], and the figure in the left hand column will be the Drop.

The prisoner's height comes into the matter when it is time to cut the rope and make a noose. A tall client will need less rope than a short one to drop the same distance. By calculating the total length of the drop and subtracting the height of the prisoner, you have the length of rope needed from the surface of the scaffold down. The distance from the beam to the floor gives you the rest of the length.

Although we do not know his name, we shall hope that the hangman who ushered Julia Murdoch into the next world knew his business. You will notice in this account that the hangman's presence is only implied. We don't get a picture of him standing there. "She readily submitted to be pinioned. . . ." The hangman must have been there to do the job, but the writer keeps him far from the event, as though he were not there at all. His appearance may have been wondered at by the crowd, but it is his disappearance from the written account that makes me wonder. Is this woman hanging herself? Is she alone, kneeling on the trap, high above the crowd with its abundance of women and children? Where are the other functionaries? Are we in a dream, a nightmare where things are done but where there are no doers? There is a spiritual comforter, a prop for her last moments as he supports her to the gallows. Any decent spiritual support should involve the practical as well as the metaphysical. When prayers are offered up, without a direct reference to who it was who was offering them up, or who it was who was hurrying Julia into eternity, the narrative takes on a ghostly appearance. Many years after this, when hangings were first being done without the gentlemen of the press in attendance, the Home Office in London instructed governors of Her Majesty's Prisons to pull a veil over these things:

> . . . no record should be taken as to the number of seconds, and if pressed for details of this kind the Governor should say he cannot give them, as he did not time the proceeds [*sic*] but "a very short interval elapsed", or some general expression of opinion to the same effect. . . .

It is also suggested that any reference to the manner in which the sentence was carried out should be brief, without detail, such as: ". . . it was carried out expeditiously and without a hitch . . . ," which, one might say, John Ross Robertson seems to have anticipated by nearly one hundred years. In his version, Julia arrives "at the platform" and is "hurried into eternity" in the same sentence.

I have wandered some distance from the square on Toronto Street, near the old jail, where Julia Murdoch leaned for religious support upon the arm of her spiritual adviser. The clergy was there for Julia and for most other customers of Jack Ketch, and Ned Dennis, and all of the honest tradesmen to follow them. The state seemed to be aware that at the moment of execution the culprit separates into two parts: the earthly remains and the immortal soul. It is a complicated business, and however dark the deed for which the condemned prisoner is about to suffer, the state recognizes that there is a point beyond its jurisdiction where the Church takes over. In some Catholic countries, where hanging is or was practiced, the death hoods placed over the heads of the prisoners have a hole cut in them to allow the soul to escape the cotton confines and begin winging its way back to the Creator who gave it.

In the story of Julia Murdoch, there is no mention of the medical profession; yet it was usual for a doctor to be standing by on these melancholy occasions to declare that the prisoner was dead. In Julia's day, the presence of a surgeon was no more suspect than the prayer book of the spiritual adviser. Indeed, in modern times, it was always assumed that the attending physician played his role as an act of charity. But he was part of the execution team. He played his part just as the guards strapping the unfortunate criminal into the embrace of the electric chair were playing theirs. The Reverend Samuel Haughton recalled the execution of a man who had had a tracheotomy some years previous to his execution; and such was the ignorance of those who conducted the hanging, that he was dropped through a short height quite insufficient to injure the spinal cord, and breathed with ease through the aperture in the trachea, suffering horrible tortures, until relieved by the *humanity* [italics mine] of the surgeon of the jail, who closed with his finger the aperture through which he breathed, and so completed the clumsy work of the hangman.

The anomaly of this, the contradiction to the Hippocratic oath sworn by all medical men, was somehow unchallenged until the coming of the lethal injection. This form of execution seemed to demand more from the medical profession than it cared to give. Before, they had only to announce when a pulse could no longer be heard; now, they were being asked to pick a vein, open it, and see that an injection of deadly poisons went into the arm of the condemned. The doctors refused to play. But had they already passed that point? When a doctor, holding the limp wrist of a suspended body, said that he could still hear a pulse, the execution continued. His voice could have stopped it. It is probably playing theoretical games to dissect the role of the doctor at the place of execution, and I'm reminded of Brendan Behan's philosophical warder in *The Quare Fellow*. The withholding of sacraments and priests might be more of a deterrent to crime than having them on tap. Having a "physician in attendance" tends to remove the barbaric realities of an execution. He makes it palatable for the multitude.

In this chapter, I've used poor Julia Murdoch as a typical example and have wandered away from her story to explore the role of executions in general, and the role of the executioner in particular. Her case was typical of most of the people who suffered for their crimes: they had the misfortune to be born in their own times and not our—in this respect—more enlightened times. Today, Mary Jones, hanged for a minor theft, would be on welfare, not dragged to Tyburn with a babe at her breast. In Britain, Jack Ketch and his kind have been paid off and retired. The last of them has just died after keeping a pub, raising rabbits, or growing geraniums for the last decade or two. As it should be.

In Canada, the hangman has been on furlough since December 1962. Once exiled on 13 August 1964, the hangman has never been invited back to Britain. In the United States he was banished and then recalled after a hiatus of a dozen years. There the executioner is still a busy man, and we will come to him in due course.

CHAPTER TWO

The Road to Tyburn

"You're a kind of artist, I suppose—eh!" said Mr Tappertit.
"Yes," rejoined Dennis; "yes—I may call myself an artist—a
fancy workman—art improves natur'—that's my motto."

—DENNIS THE HANGMAN
IN *BARNABY RUDGE* BY CHARLES DICKENS

John Price was a hangman. He followed in the footsteps of the original Jack Ketch. That means he was adept with both ax and rope. The block served for political crimes, such as came out of the troubles in Scotland; the noose served most other felonies, from murder to shoplifting. The stake was still in use until 1790. Price would have done his share of whipping and branding as well. He was a well-known figure outside Newgate and along the long road through Holborn and Oxford Street to Tyburn. This was well west of the city, at what is known as Marble Arch today. A small plaque marks the fatal spot, for those brave enough to risk modern traffic to look for it. Here stood the infamous triangular gallows: three mighty beams of oak supported by a like number of uprights. At Tyburn, John Price could tie a tippet as nice as you please and turn off one, two, three, four, five, six, seven, eight gallows birds from each of the three crossbars of the Deadly Never-Green, Tyburn's Triple Tree. Twenty-four could ride the three-legged mare at once. And John Price was the factotum who made the felons piss when they couldn't whistle, take a leap in the dark, ride a horse foaled by an acorn.

Price was a Londoner, born about 1677. His father had been killed in Tangiers when Johnny was only seven. As a youth he learned the rag trade, which in those days *was* the rag trade not *haute couture*, which he practiced until he was pressed into the navy. This is where he learned about ropes and knots and rum. From there he became hangman for London and Middlesex, a not very skillful practitioner of a function that demanded very little in the way of craft.

The public and officialdom alike were blind, deaf, and dumb to the sufferings of his victims. The spectacle was all, and, of course, the edifying examples provided the fruits for further crime. Pickpockets and other petty hoodlums worked the crowd around Tyburn, missing much of the moral lesson being enacted for their benefit. If there were reformers in Britain, they were not looking at the gallows in Price's day. The idea that horror corrupts was unknown in 1700. The parade to Tyburn Fair served a useful social purpose: those who saw the lawless turned off would go and sin no more. That was the philosophy, and the nation remained blind to its fallacy for another hundred and fifty years.

Although Price had plenty of practice in his craft—the cavalcade to Tyburn was increasing as the list of capital crimes enacted for the protection of British citizens and their property grew longer—there is no sign that he improved in his calling. He also missed the message that his trade was supposed to broadcast. Of the hundreds of the condemned who started out from Newgate with him, he was the sole survivor. Price must have felt himself grown immortal, he outlived so many of his traveling companions. Perhaps a kind of hubris set in which made him complaisant, and led him at last through debt and prison to the prisoner's dock. Coming home drunk in Moorfields one moonless night, he met his nemesis, Elizabeth White, an apple seller. Perhaps he misunderstood her profession. Anyway, by whim or design, he was on her. But Mrs. White was not going to be had by every drunken ruffian in London. She put up a fight, which enraged Price, who began to batter her unmercifully. The watch, alerted by her screams, took him into custody. Despite her injuries, she was able to describe what had happened before she died four days later. Price was condemned to death and afterwards to be hung in chains on the last day of May 1718.

As a token that Price's crime was considered especially vile, the gallows had been erected in Bunhill Fields, close to the scene of the crime and, today, to the Old Street underground station. Price was sent thither from Newgate in a cart, heading east for a change. (The expression "gone west," as a euphemism for dying, came from the drive west from Newgate to Tyburn.) He was a game one, but nearly stupefied with drink, which could be found anywhere in the prison for such a good cause. A hanging was a celebration of a kind, a celebration of life for the living and a send-off in style for the victim. The nubbing cove, as the hangman was called by the street loafers and pickpockets, was the master of ceremonies, even though a beadle sat astride his horse and the ordinary (chaplain) from Newgate offered the consolations of religion. According to the latter, Price stubbornly refused to confess his crime before they left the prison, but did so on the gallows, where he cautioned the huge crowd to take warning by his example.

In 1820, the Cato Street Conspirators were the last to be hanged, drawn, and quartered. But this drawing of an imagined dance around a Maypole with the severed heads displayed harks back more to London Bridge under the Tudors, when heads affrighted new arrivals to London.

Price was not the first hangman to have been hanged, nor the last. But his fate serves as a useful introduction to this functionary who served the forces of law and order in Britain at a time when both law and order were rather different from what they are today. The eighteenth century may have given us the Enlightenment, but the life of the mind and the supremacy of reason were born out of a dungheap of social ills that can scarcely be imagined. Picture, if you can, a place where dead bodies hanging in chains and cut-off legs, arms, and heads stuck on spikes at the outskirts of cities, rather the way the emblems of service clubs are now, were among the common-places of daily life. It was a rare criminal brought to the gallows who hadn't made his way through the crowd to see others executed on some earlier, happier day. Many in the condemned hold at Newgate thought that hanging was too good for the likes of themselves.

The bravest tried to make a good end. They dressed for the occasion, wore nosegays, distributed alms to the poor, bought drinks along the way for their friends, and, at the last, made a ringing, flippant speech about a short life and a merry one. When all was ready, and if they had nerve enough, they then flung themselves off the hangman's ladder, which rested against the gallows. Some jumped out of the cart before the hangman could do his job. The rest stood on the tailgate of the cart and waited for the hangman to start up the horse and leave them kicking in the air. Jumping off the hangman's ladder may have improved the chances of an easier death, but it didn't take much to produce something better than the slow onset of death at Tyburn.

Traditionally, highwaymen died game. Men like "Sixteen-String" Jack Rann flirted with the ladies as they went down Holborn. He won his Tyburn tippet as a bridal cull on Watling Street. Jack always cut a fashionable figure in the pleasure-gardens of Bagnigge Wells, where he promenaded with his mistress, Miss Roach; in front of Henry Fielding's brother, Sir John, at Bow Street; at Tyburn itself, where he came with the bright blades of his day to watch the show. He came at last to Tyburn in 1774 *as* the show, with a nosegay and a quip. His end was marked not only in the usual way, with the hawking of Last Dying Speech and Confessions of Sixteen-String Jack Rann, but with a "flash ballad" that was written and circulated some time after Jack had stepped into the air:

Farewell ye rooks, fairwell ye plains,
> No more Miss Roach will on you reign.
Your sighs and tears are all in vain.
> We part but ne'er shall meet again.

I wish I was a country girl
> My cows to milk, my lambs to tell;
And love I'd never took in hand,
> I'd never parted with Jack Ran.

Fellow highwayman Jack Sheppard, who had astonished everybody by escaping from Newgate four times, made a good end trying to astonish everybody with another hairbreadth escape, which was foiled by a cautious jailer who discovered a hidden penknife in Sheppard's pocket. He was twenty-two at the time of his death and a mighty loss to the ladies who came in droves to see him suffer.

Jonathan Wild, who was the model for Peachum in Gay's *The Beggar's Opera*, earned his reputation as a thief-taker, or prototype policeman, but was in fact in league with the underworld, acting as a fence and running what we would call a protection racket. He was in the end taken to Tyburn, wearing a nightshirt, ready for the grave. On the way, Wild picked the pocket of the ordinary, the chaplain who saw prisoners through their last agonies. This last theft brought some embarrassment to the Reverend Thomas Purney. It was a corkscrew.

Just as Wild was turned off, he grabbed the body of the man standing next to him so that the force of both their falls would be absorbed by the one neck. The stratagem failed and Wild went off to his grave with the others.

Jonathan Swift caught the temper of the times when he wrote "Clever Tom Clinch, Going to Be Hanged," in 1727, which, oddly enough, is the year of Bach's great *St. Matthew Passion.*

As Clever Tom Clinch, while the rabble was bawling,
Rode stately through Holborn, to die in his calling;
He stopped at the *George* for a bottle of sack,
And promised to pay for it when he came back.
His waistcoat and stockings and breeches were white,
His cap had a new cherry ribbon to tie't.
The maids to the doors and the balconies ran,
And said, "Lack-a-day, he's a proper young man!"
But, as from the windows the ladies he spied,
Like a beau in the box, he bowed low on each side!
And when his last speech the loud hawkers did cry
He swore from his cart "It was all a damn'd lie!"
The hangman for pardon fell down on his knee;
Tom gave him a kick in the guts for his fee:
Then said, "I must speak to the people a little;
But I'll see you all damn'd before I will whittle!
My honest friend Wild (may he long hold his place)
He lengthen'd my life with a whole year of grace.
Take courage, dear comrades, and be not afraid,
Nor slip this occasion to follow your trade.
My conscience is clear, and my spirits are calm,
And thus I go off without prayer-book or psalm."
Then follow the practice of clever Tom Clinch,
Who hung like a hero, and never would flinch.

Like beer and tea, sprouts and plum duff, hanging suited England. Englishmen understood the gallows as they understood iron, brick, and railways. But the noose wasn't native to this sceptered isle. It was imported by invading Anglo-Saxons. You might say that the gallows and the cross arrived in Britain about the same time. The ax and block were well established by then, a Roman legacy like straight roads and high walls facing Scotland. The first executioner we hear about was the Roman soldier, around A.D. 303, who beheaded St. Alban and turned him into a martyr with a stroke of his short blade.

Brian Bailey talks about these early days in his *Hangmen of England*:

William the Conqueror was extremely sparing in his use of the death penalty, inflicting it only on conspirators against his rule, but Henry I reintroduced it for murder and other crimes, including theft, and there

Jonathan Wild, who acted as an informer and "thief-taker general" before London had real constables, was also a major fence or receiver of stolen goods. He came at last to the gallows after sending many of his old customers thither before him. He was the prototype of Peacham in John Gay's The Beggar's Opera.

are several mentions of hanging sentences by local manorial lords during the early Norman period, most notably the instance in 1124 recorded in the *Anglo-Saxon Chronicle*, when Ralph Basset "held a court of the king's thanes at Hundehoh in Leicestershire, and hanged there more thieves than ever before: forty-four of them in all were dispatched in no time, and six had their eyes put out and were castrated."

Who did this castrating and eye-gouging has not come down to us in any detail. Generally speaking, the lord of the manor let his bailiffs attend to such things, delegating a local ne'er-do-well who had assisted before. According to Bailey, there was a law in force in Kent at the time of Henry VII that if a prosecutor could not find someone to execute the sentence of the law upon a felon, he was obliged to do it himself or face prison.

An executioner named Cratwell—we have only his surname—served during the reign of Henry VIII and was kept busy by him on both block

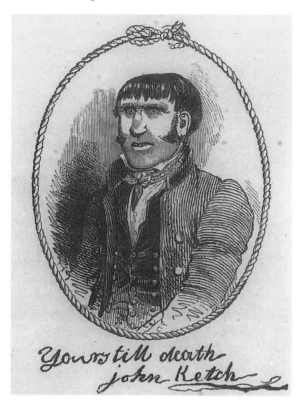

*Yours till death
john Ketch*

Wreathed in a noose, the face of Jack Ketch leaps out at the beholder. Drawn from his imagination by Joseph Meadows in 1836, 150 years after Ketch's death, it so caught the public fancy that the face was copied in woodcuts and engravings to show the face not of justice, but of criminal types.

and gallows, until he mounted the ladder himself for stealing from a booth at Bartholomew Fair. Cratwell must have been missed on the job, because all the Tudors had need of the services of a small army of headsmen and hangmen. And with the complications of changing religious orthodoxies, it was hard to keep up with the burnings in Smithfield, Tyburn, and elsewhere. Foxe's *History of the Acts and Monuments of the Church*, popularly known as *Foxe's Book of Martyrs*, is, as George IV might have observed, a damned fat book, and it recounts the groans and sufferings of only one side of the religious question. Hangmen, Papist and Protestant, had to deal with all comers or face the consequences. A headsman needs to suspend his religious curiosity, as Edward Gibbon did, at an early age, if he plans on getting on in his trade.

The first executioner whose name has stuck in the imagination of succeeding generations was Jack Ketch. His became the generic name for hangman right down to our own time. Although his name has lasted down the years, his ineptness has happily been forgotten by almost everyone. Historians are less fortunate. Although they can discover little about the early years of Richard Jacquett or John Catch, who became Jack

Ketch, his last years on the job were memorable enough. In 1683 he appeared on the scaffold erected at Lincoln's Inn Fields to execute Lord William Russell, the son of the Duke of Bedford, who was implicated in the Rye House plot to assassinate King Charles II. Lord Russell gave Ketch ten guineas to dispatch him quickly, but the first stroke of his ax only hurt him. Lord Russell turned his head to the headsman and said sharply to him: "You dog, did I give you ten guineas to use me so inhumanly?" Ketch lifted his ax and struck again and again and again before the head was severed. It was said that he had been bribed to do his work badly in order that Lord Russell should not escape without pain. The amount mentioned was twenty pounds. If that is so, Jack Ketch earned more than most in London that day. When faced with this story, Ketch denied it, blaming his poor workmanship on Lord Russell's inability to keep his head still on the block.

Two years later, the Duke of Monmouth mounted the scaffold at Tower Hill for being part of the same plot that implicated Lord Russell and for leading an unsuccessful insurrection to replace James II on the throne of England with himself. When he saw Jack Ketch, he handed him a purse. "Here are six guineas for you. Pray do your business well: don't serve me as you did my Lord Russell. I have heard you struck him three or four times." He then gave his servant, who was standing by, more gold coins to be handed over only if Ketch performed well.

"If you strike me twice," Monmouth said, "I cannot promise not to stir." He then kneeled before the block, but in a moment he was on his feet again. "Prithee, let me feel the ax." He tried the edge with his finger and said to Ketch, with some truth judging from what followed, "I fear it is not sharp enough." He kneeled again and placed his head once more on the block and dropped a handkerchief when he was ready to die. Once again Jack Ketch was not up to the job. He lifted the ax, turned it around in the air, and brought it down, smashing into the block, but only wounding the duke slightly. Monmouth gave the headsman a sharp look, then resumed his position. Two more blows and the head was still attached to its body. Ketch threw down the ax and cried out, "God damn me, I cannot do it! My heart fails me!"

"Take up the ax, man!" ordered the sheriff, who was ultimately responsible for carrying out the death sentence, "Take up the ax!" Meanwhile the crowd was shaking fists at Ketch and shouting, "Fling him over the rails!" Ketch raised the ax two more times, but still the head had not fallen. Ketch used a knife to finish the job, and then narrowly escaped being lynched by the mob that came to watch an execution but was made witness to butchery instead.

What Ketch lacked in skill, or even pride in his craft, he made up for in the frequency of his appearances during the years of the Popish Plot and immediately afterwards. The plot had been a fabrication of a disgraced Anglican cleric, Titus Oates, who invented the story which was all too readily believed by people who should have known better. According to Oates, the Catholics were about to assassinate King Charles II, seize the throne, murder all Protestants in their beds, and burn London to the ground. For two years Titus Oates was a hero, and Catholics everywhere were persecuted. When his deception was discovered, and Oates was found guilty of perjury, he was not sentenced to death, as he would have been if he had been caught shoplifting, but condemned to be put in the pillory and flogged to within an inch of his life. First he was whipped at the rear of a cart from Aldgate to Newgate. Two days later the flogging was repeated from Newgate to Tyburn. When Jack Ketch got finished with him, there was precious little life left, but what there was was put in prison. After the Glorious Revolution in 1688, Oates was freed and given a pension for life.

The loathsome Judge Jeffreys and the Bloody Assizes also kept Ketch busy following the collapse of Monmouth's rising. This time it was a persecution by Catholics against Protestants. In Dorset, 74 were hanged; in Somerset, 233 were hanged, drawn, and quartered. The politician, essayist, and historian Lord Macaulay observed in his *History of England*:

> At every spot where two roads met, on every market-place, on every
> green of every large village which had furnished Monmouth with sol-
> diers, ironed corpses clattering in the wind, or heads and quarters stuck
> on poles poisoned the air, and made the traveller sick with horror.

Ketch appears to have been a consummate politician, since he managed to execute both Protestants and Catholics in turn without ruffling official feathers. But it couldn't last forever. Jack had spent some time in the Marshalsea prison for debt around 1649, and he was sent to Bridewell in 1686 for insulting the sheriff. His replacement, one Pascha Rose, a butcher by trade, was hardly installed in office when he was himself hanged for burglary. The sheriff swallowed his pride and fetched Ketch out of Bridewell and sat him again athwart the three strong arms of the Deadly Never-Green at Tyburn. Not long after his vindication, Jack Ketch was taken from us. Whether it was the plague or drink that took him, we don't know. The only thing that we know of a certainty is that he was buried in

The brutality of a hanging is made to look comic or quaint in these old woodcuts. Similarly, the dexterity of the headsman was seldom as on the mark in real life as is depicted in this scene of ritualized savagery.

Clerkenwell. We also know the date of this because of the following nota-tion. A man named Johnson was whipped in London in the first days of December 1686, "but civilly used by the new hangman, Jack Ketch being buried two days before."

The name "Jack Ketch" stuck to every executioner in Britain for cen-turies afterwards. So hated was he that, from that time onward, the hang-man was a creature to be shunned by all but the most lowly. He was even kidnapped as a character into the traditional Punch and Judy show. Although the crafty Mr. Punch murders his wife and baby, he also outwits the hangman, Jack Ketch, into hanging himself.

Both Jack Ketch and his immediate predecessor, Dun, styled themselves "squire," which was a fair leap up the social ladder from their fellow hang-men. It is believed that this honorary distinction was bestowed upon the executioners of important, well-born state criminals. The usual crime was high treason. Dun's predecessor, Gregory Brandon, was so busy taking off the heads of the nobility that he was granted a coat of arms.

Brian Bailey reminds us that the bulk of Jack Ketch's working time was spent on the gallows, where far more men and women perished for ordi-nary crimes than ever mounted a scaffold on Tower Hill for treason. Further, there were many executed for witchcraft at this time, as the century moved to its close. In Scotland, witches were burned at the stake. In England, they were hanged. The last "witch" hanged in England was Alice

"*Thou shalt not suffer a witch to live,*" says the Bible, and seeking out witches became a mania in the seventeenth century. The Salem hangings at the end of the century were anticipated in good measure by persecutions in central Europe and Britain. The last witch to hang in England was Alice Molland, at Exeter in 1684, a decade before the devil came to Massachusetts.

Molland, who went to the gallows in Exeter in 1685. This was just seven years before the great American witch hunt in Salem, Massachusetts.

Scottish law and legal practice have always differed from the English, since Scotland was a separate nation until the two countries were officially united under James I. In Scotland heretics were burned with witches, adulterers, coiners, or, as we would say, counterfeiters, women found guilty of treason, as well as those sentenced for incest and bestiality. David Hume gives some examples of this: Lady Glamyss was burned for treason in 1537; James and Agnes Bonnar for incest and adultery in 1570; Euphan Mackelzean for a combination of sorcery and treason in 1591—his sentence was "to be burned quick to the death"; in 1630, Michael Erskine for sodomy; in 1670, Major Weir for incest and bestiality; and, in 1702, Thomas Fotheringham for bestiality alone.

In practice, the hangman saw to it that the victim was strangled before the fire was well begun, but this was a difficult operation that often ended badly for the victim. Even the great jurist Sir William Blackstone, uncharacteristically boasting of the British system, says:

The humanity of the English nation has authorized, by a tacit consent, an almost general mitigation of such part of these judgments as savour of torture or cruelty: there being very few instances (and those accidental or by negligence) of any person's being embowelled or burned till previously deprived of sensation by strangling.

Whether or not the "almost general mitigation" might make the occasional lapses "cruel and unusual" I will leave to legal theorists. As an instance of the hit-or-miss quality of this mitigation, take the case of Catherine Hayes, who was burned on 9 May 1726 for petty, or petit, treason, that is, murdering her husband. This account is taken from the *Newgate Calendar*:

> When the wretched woman had finished her devotions, an iron chain was put around her body, with which she was fixed to a stake near the gallows. On these occasions, when women are burnt for petit treason, it is customary to strangle them, by means of a rope passed round the neck, and pulled by the executioner; so that they are dead before the flames reach the body. But this woman was literally burnt alive; for the executioner letting go the rope sooner than usual, the fire burnt fiercely round her. . . .

There was discussion at the time about whether this cruel death was cruel by accident or design. The *Newgate Calendar* says this:

> . . . that the flames reaching the hands of the executioner, he was compelled to let go the rope for his own safety. . . .

At least five heretics are being burned at the stake in this 1483 engraving from Schwarzenburg, Switzerland. Changes in religious thinking created martyrs to all factions.

Burnings were carried out in various parts of Britain, often following a witch-hunt. Pitch or tar was sometimes smeared on the living prisoner prior to setting the fire. Some of the martyrs who perished in the flames for their faith, whether that was Protestant or Catholic, carried bundles of gunpowder with them to the stake, on the principle that, once the flames exploded the powder, they would be past the worst of their struggles.

The last recorded burning in Britain took place on 18 March 1789, when a woman named Christian Murphy, alias Christian Bowman, was burned at the stake outside Newgate Prison in London.

"She was a decent looking woman," according to an anonymous contemporary report, "about thirty years of age. She behaved with great decency, but was much shocked at the dreadful punishment she was to undergo. . . ." Christian Bowman or Murphy was a coiner, as were those executed with her. Of course, the men were hanged. Coining counted as a kind of treason, since it was the king's coins that were being clipped, or counterfeited. Henceforth women found guilty of coining and petit treason would join their male associates in crime on the gallows.

It is difficult to think of capital punishment in any context without considering the support that organized religion brought to it. The churches supported moral, godly behavior; along with the wealthy and empowered classes, they deplored crime, violence, unauthorized sex, and perversion. They also came down hard on alternative orthodoxies, as seen in the religious wars and the crackdowns throughout history on heresy, witchcraft, and sorcery.

At the same time, the churches supported condemned criminals on the way to their deaths, exhorting them to accept salvation, repent their sins, and forgive their enemies. The ordinaries of Newgate sustained thousands of delinquents on the road to Tyburn. But if they and the churches they represented—not only in Britain but in Europe, America, and elsewhere as well—had not been so convinced of a hereafter, of eternal bliss as well as damnation and hell's fires, the courts might not have been so confident in their judgements of death. With all of our civilization and the knowledge that history has given us, we appear to have advanced very little in the nearly four thousand years since the writing of the Book of Exodus.

The Church of St. Sepulchre stands close to Newgate, where its bell loudly counts away the hours. St. Sepulchre's connection with Newgate was more than mere propinquity. The vicar of that church was one of the first Protestant martyrs, for he was burned as a heretic at Smithfield in 1555.

John Rogers, the vicar of St. Sepulchre's Church near Newgate, died a martyr's death during the religious persecutions in Europe. It is not without irony that the bellman from his church, beginning in 1612, started exhorting prisoners lying under the death sentence at Newgate to repent.

Prior to his execution, he lay in Newgate, confined with thieves and murderers. He was exhorted to repent his heresy as he was drawn on a hurdle to die at the stake. Donald Rumbelow, in his book *The Triple Tree*, pointed out the irony that after this event it was the bellman from St. Sepulchre who tolled his handbell and warned the condemned that the judgement was upon them. The night before every hanging day and again the next morning, the bellman would solemnly call:

All ye that in the condemned hold doth lie,
Prepare ye, for tomorrow you shall die.
Watch and pray, the hour is drawing near.
That you before the Almighty must appear;
Examine well yourselves, in time repent,
That you may not to eternal flames be sent;
And when St. Sepulchre's Bell in the morning tolls,
The Lord above have mercy on your souls.
PAST 12 O'CLOCK

To the condemned of Newgate, religion was represented by the ordinary chaplains, who preached sermons that were intended to bring the lost sheep back into the fold. But while their spirits were salvageable, their bodies had to go to heaven by way of Tyburn. In many cases the ordinaries were laughed at by the condemned; their experience of the good and bad things of life being so different. In some cases the ordinaries were hucksters in their own right: writing up the lives of the condemned to sell to the publishers of broadsides and "last dying confessions." And, of course, occasionally, preachers themselves came to Tyburn to expiate their own crimes.

With this handbell, the bellman of St. Sepulchre's Church rang the knell of the condemned:
". . . And when St. Sepulchre's bell in the morning tolls, The Lord above have mercy on your souls. PAST 12 O'CLOCK."

Take the case of Dr. Samuel Johnson's acquaintance the Reverend William Dodd, whose sermons Horace Walpole and all the great and good and talented people of London went regularly to hear.

Dr. Dodd was in every sense a success. He lived as a man of fashion, a rare situation for a clergyman, and added to his income through the practice of journalism. He wrote books, some fifty of them, poems, pamphlets, theological works, and newspaper articles. For two hundred pounds a year, he also took up tutoring young Philip Stanhope, the son of Lord Chesterfield, he of the letters that took up the generational dispensation of wisdom where Polonius's advice to Laertes left off. Dodd lived like a maharajah, keeping open rooms, entertaining lavishly, and ignoring the mountain of debt he was erecting. When he chose, in a bad moment, to cover some of these with a note bearing the forged signature of his patron, young Stanhope, just to get the creditors off his back and give him time to breathe, he undid himself. The note for £4,300 was discovered. When Dodd was brought before the Lord Mayor at the Guildhall, his patron, taking the high ground, refused to prosecute. But the Lord Mayor, a banker by trade, felt that an example should be made, and sent Dr. Dodd along to the Old Bailey, where it took a jury only ten minutes to find him guilty. From the dock Dr. Dodd spoke well and eloquently and long. His speech had been written for him by Samuel Johnson, who also wrote an appeal to the king. It was a bad week for writers. Dodd was condemned and suffered at Tyburn with some dignity, attempting to console a fellow sufferer himself and cutting out the Newgate ordinary who tried to interfere. He was driven to the place of execution in a coach, his head resting in the lap of his elderly father, who came to help sustain him in the great agony he now had to undergo. When the coach arrived, he took leave of his father and joined the other malefactor in the traditional cart under one beam of the triangular gallows. Henry Angelo, a fencing master, saw and recorded what he witnessed.

> Every visage expressed sadness; it appeared, indeed, a day of universal calamity. . . . Thousands sobbed aloud, and many women swooned at the sight. . . . [Dodd's] corpse-like appearance produced an awful picture of human woe. Tens of thousands of hats, which formed a black mass, as the coach advanced, were taken off simultaneously. . . . [The crowd's] silence added to the awfulness of the scene.

There is a story that friends of the doctor planned to revive him after he was turned off. Perhaps it was to this end that Dodd whispered to Ned Dennis, the hangman, at the last moment, and why Dennis tried to steady the clergyman's legs when he had been turned off. Perhaps Dennis had been bribed to make his noose so it would not throttle his patient. As soon as the body was cut down, it was rushed to the house of a surgeon, who tried to revive it with "air mixed with 'volatile alkali' . . . pumped into the Doctor's lungs by a double-bellows." Peppermint water, horseradish juice, and essences of turpentine were introduced, but all to no avail. Dodd was dead, as was young Joseph Harris, the fifteen-year-old boy hanged with him, for whom there was no outcry, no letter to the king. Harris had robbed a stagecoach of two half-guineas and a few shillings.

London was expanding. Tyburn, once out in the country, then in the suburbs, was now within a growing metropolis. In 1600 London numbered about 200,000 inhabitants. By 1750 that figure had risen to around 700,000. Traffic was thickening along the narrow streets between Newgate and Tyburn. Property in the neighborhood, once only of use to the likes of Mother Proctor, who rented out a grandstand to the regulars and casual visitors to Tyburn Fair, began to be developed along the New (Marylebone) Road, Edgware Road, and Bryanston Street. There is something about a gallows at the corner that keeps lowering property values; and so, the gallows, which had stood there from 1220 to 1783, had to go. On hearing of this, Dr. Samuel Johnson, ever a conservative in these matters, protested:

> Tyburn itself is not safe from the fury of innovation. Executions are intended to draw spectators; if they do not, they do not answer their purpose. The old method was most satisfactory to all parties; the public was gratified by a procession, the criminal supported by it. Why is all this to be swept away?

First it was moved to Bethnal Green, east-northeast of Newgate, and then to the square in front of Newgate itself. But the end of Tyburn Fair did not represent anything more than the successful lobbying of property developers. There was no change in official opinion about what the nature of public executions ought to be.

There were those, of course, who wanted an end to it; Bernard Mandeville and Henry Fielding were two who wrote against the iniquities of Tyburn.

> The day appointed by law [wrote Mandeville] for the thief's shame is the day of glory in his own opinion.

In other words he believed that every thief and murderer on his way to execution became a hero in the opinion of the admiring crowd. In this, Polly Peachum, in Gay's *The Beggar's Opera*, concurs:

> . . . methinks I see him already in the cart, sweeter and more lovely than the nosegay in his hand!—I hear the crowd extolling his resolution and intrepidity!—What volleys of sighs are sent from the windows of Holborn, that so comely a youth should be brought to disgrace!—I see him at the tree! . . .
> The whole circle are in tears!—even butchers weep!—Jack Ketch himself hesitates to perform his duty, and would be glad to lose his fee, by a reprieve. . . .

Samuel Johnson saw the removal of the gallows in 1783 as a rite of passage for our civilization. He was pessimistic about the outcome. And he agreed with Mandeville that a relationship was built up between the crowd and the condemned. But where Mandeville disapproved, Johnson thought it was only just. Johnson's idea of the crowd supporting the condemned along the way to Tyburn and at the place of execution itself was elaborated by Adam Smith some time later:

> A brave man is not rendered contemptible by being brought to the scaffold. The sympathy of the spectators supports him, and saves him from that shame, that consciousness that his misery is felt by himself only, which is of all sentiments the most insupportable. . . . He has no suspicion that his situation is the object of contempt or derision to any body, and he can, with propriety assume the air, not only of perfect serenity, but of triumph and exaltation.

Both of these views, Johnson's and Smith's, suggest that the majority of those who suffered at Tyburn proved their case; that they acted as bravely as Tom Clinch in the Jonathan Swift poem. V. A. C. Gatrell, in his *The Hanging Tree*, disputes this version of the reality with some vigor:

> While public executions lasted, many knew that outward bravado did not speak for a felt reality, and that the powdered wig, Holland shirt, gloves, and nosegays which some flaunted on their last journey was the only resort they had to "meliorate the terrible thoughts of the meagre tyrant Death" [as one unsigned broadside put it]. The man who did contrive to conduct himself bravely was often actually drunk out of his mind. . . .

Even Macheath's dependence on strong drink cannot support him in the end. Almost his last words, as he is overwhelmed by wives, offspring, and the overturning of "strict poetical justice," are:

> Oh leave me to thought! I fear! I doubt!
> I tremble! I droop!—See my courage is out.
> (He turns up an empty bottle.)

Gatrell continues to make his argument that few die well on the gallows, in spite of the traditions of bravado and nonchalance on the part of the condemned. He argues that this is the only role left for the condemned to play, but often they are not up to the part:

> If drunkenness gave the game away, so did the demands of the imperilled body. For everyone who died boldly, forgotten numbers died expelling urine and feces, sharing kinship in this with the greatest (Marie Antoinette had to squat on the Conciergerie cobbles when she saw her waiting tumbril). Surgeons anatomizing hanged bodies would complain that their effluvia "rendered the room quite offensive". Most wretches had

already betrayed their terror in the dark silence of the condemned cell. Here on the eve of execution the attempted suicides would take place, like that of the deranged Bousfield who in 1856 tried to burn himself to death in the condemned cell's fire and had to be taken to the scaffold next morning bandaged like a mummy. The gentleman highwayman McLean, adulated by the crowd in 1750, "is so little a hero," Walpole wrote, that in private "he cries and begs". Paul Lewis became abject when he knew he was to be hanged. Holloway and Haggerty spent the night before their deaths in dejection and prayer, and Haggerty was "deeply affected" on the scaffold, mounting it with "an unsteady step and pale countenance". Women wailed frightfully as they were sentenced to death: "The agitation and cries of the two women were too shocking for description, particularly of her [the coiner Phoebe Harris] who was to be burnt." In Newgate's condemned cells in 1804 the forger Anne Hurle was "several times deprived of sensation and supposed to be dead". Eliza Fenning in 1815 died bravely enough, but she had broken down at the condemned sermon.

The condemned cell in Newgate Prison, where hundreds passed their last night on earth. Leaving here, the condemned felon walked along Birdcage Walk, perhaps over his own freshly dug grave, to the gallows. Newer prisons placed the condemned cell as close as possible to the execution shed.

THE CONDEMNED CELL IN NEWGATE PRISON
From *Old and New London*, Cassell, 1897

Most victims of the gallows, both at Tyburn and in front of the Debtors' Door at Newgate, did not die well. It is true that around them swirled the throng making a holiday of their suffering, but their catcalls, their shouts of support, their lively vigor, did little to sustain the condemned for more than a moment or two. Most were so far gone in the contemplation of their deaths that even the ordinary from Newgate couldn't reach them. Some couldn't even stand. A pirate hanged with four of his fellows in 1865 was so distraught that he had to be seated in a chair before being turned off. Others had to be held up by the hangman and the ordinary under the beam of the gallows.

It should be noted here that a good hanging requires the cooperation of the patient. He must "toe the line," which happens to be the origin of that useful phrase; he must stand by himself while the final adjustments are made. Someone being electrocuted, gassed, injected, garotted, and even guillotined may collapse at the last moment with no "harm" done to the completion of the execution. Even with his head on the block, the victim of the headsman may relax the powers that have sustained him thus far. But the hangman requires the consciousness of his victim. Probably if fewer had stood tall and straight, if more had drooped in utter dejection, the obscenity of hanging might have disappeared sooner.

In 1759 Tyburn Tree was cut down and then turned into beer-butt stands for casks and barrels in the cellar of a nearby public house, The Carpenters' Arms. The structure, which had inspired so much drinking and rowdiness since the twelfth century, continued to support further quaffing and drinking long after the crowds had shifted to Newgate and the hangings there. Still, for another quarter-century executions continued at the old location, but on structures that could be set up when required and removed afterwards. One scaffold had a short drop of eighteen inches or so built into it, but, in fact, it was no great improvement on the cart and horse. In 1783, the last executions took place, and Tyburn drifted into British folklore along with Robin Hood, and King Arthur and his Round Table. Thereafter, Newgate became the principal place of execution in the cities of London and Westminster.

Newgate proved Dr. Johnson wrong. The crowd, saved from the long ride or walk westward, made holiday in the same old way in front of the Debtors' Door. Here the shape of the gallows was different, but the drama was unaltered. The New Drop made it modern, scientific. The nearness to the center of London swelled the crowds. Those who couldn't waste half a day trekking to Tyburn could arrange to get away long enough from work

This two-beamed gallows with a collapsible platform was an improvement on Tyburn's "triple tree." Set up before the Debtors' Door at Newgate, it demonstrated the "New Drop" weekly, drawing crowds to the City that used to have to make their way to what is now Marble Arch.

to take in a multiple hanging. In fact, the hour the hangings were scheduled would allow most people to pass in front of Newgate on the way to work. But nothing else was changed. Just as many pockets and purses were picked. The same "last dying speeches" were hawked. The same refreshments were peddled in the streets: oranges, apples, hot meat pies! The great moral lesson still eluded the multitude. People still got maimed or killed in the crush when grandstands fell down. Householders nearby rented out windows profitably to the wealthy and socially prominent, who wished to take in the spectacle through their opera glasses. Innovation had not really changed anything.

CHAPTER THREE

The Ugliest of Trades:
The Long-lived Bungler,
William Calcraft

The ugliest of trades have their moments of pleasure. Now, if I were a grave-digger, or even a hangman, there are some people I could work for with a great deal of enjoyment.

—DOUGLAS JERROLD (1803–1857), UGLY TRADES

Douglas Jerrold was one of Britain's leading satirists towards the middle of the nineteenth century. Writing in *Punch*, he was a powerful enemy of capital punishment, who used his wit, irony, and grisly humor in an attempt to send the hangman packing for good. His opposition to the gallows was based upon the firm religious conviction that, since all men must die, it is a sacrilege and a distortion to take a human life.

Jerrold had ample opportunity to see capital punishment in action. Hoisted upon his father's shoulders, young Jerrold might have seen several hangmen at work. He was too young, of course, to remember Tyburn, although his father might have told him tales of the Deadly Never-Green or Three-legged Mare. Hangmen in those days came and went quickly, but he might have seen William Burnskill, the successor to Ned Dennis; or John Langley; or the two Jameses, Batting and Foxen. For a time Thomas Cheshire had the job. "Old Cheese," as he was called, was a brutal drunk, who seemed to enjoy flogging prisoners for minor offenses more than executing others on the scaffold. This closet humanist wore a long snuff-colored greatcoat and was habitually followed everywhere by small boys calling names after him. His wife, Ann, was charged on one occasion for throwing a bunch of these ragamuffins down into a cellar.

Tom Cheshire was quickly discarded by the authorities in favor of William Calcraft, who began his trade in 1829, when Jerrold was in his twenties, and continued for another seventeen years after Jerrold's death in 1857. "Old Cheese" still turned up on the scaffold from time to time, but only as Calcraft's assistant.

Thomas Turlis "turned off" felons like this trembling pair using the cart as the drop. A corner of the famed "triple-tree" of Tyburn can be seen at the right of the picture. Turlis could be found at Tyburn from 1752 until 1771.

Calcraft was born in Baddow, Sussex, near Chelmsford, in 1800, so it is easy to calculate his age at the date of each of his public appearances. A cobbler by trade, he came to London and tried working in a brewery, and then as a butler. At last he tried hawking meat pies:

> Trade was bad for me then. In fact, I could not get anything to do. Being in no way particular what I turned my hand to to earn money, as long as it was honestly come by, I attended the execution of the Quaker Joseph Hunter and sold pies to the people round the scaffold.

He talked to James Foxen and became one of his assistants, which placed him high on the list when Foxen's successor was being sought.

Once installed in office, Calcraft quickly became a well-known public figure both on and off the gallows. While he was not a man of science, not of an inquiring turn of mind, he was still a cut above his predecessors. He was not personally from the criminal classes. True, he did have brushes with the law towards the end of his life, but they were minor compared with the crimes committed by earlier hangmen when not protected by the mask of "government work."

Calcraft wore a "dirty wide-awake hat" on the job ("wide-awake," in the humor of the day, "because it had no *nap*"). He worked comfortably dressed in a shooting jacket. He shunned the wearing of funereal garb with the explanation "I must keep my client in good spirits. Besides, I'm not a parson or an undertaker. . . ." Sometimes he sported a bright blossom in his buttonhole, which worked towards the same end.

In his early life at least, Calcraft was quiet and respectable. He was married, with two sons and a daughter. His hobbies included rabbit-breeding and gardening. Sundays saw him and his family in church, and he often took one of his boys with him when he went around to Newgate to pick up his pay. His local pub was the Tiger, on tiny Devizes Street in Hoxton, where he lived for many years.

Mr. Serjeant Ballantine, who acted as counsel for the celebrated murderers Frederick and Maria Manning in 1849, recalled in his memoir, *Some Experiences of a Barrister's Life* (1882), that "in a past generation" Calcraft was something of a celebrity around the Old Bailey:

> Rarely met with upon festive occasions, he was, nevertheless, accustomed to present himself after dinner on the last day of the sessions. He was a decently dressed, quiet-looking man. Upon his appearance he was presented with a glass of wine. This he drank to the health of his patrons, and expressed with becoming modesty his gratitude for past favours, and his hopes for favours to come.

This sign is ostensibly the one that hung above Calcraft's cobbler's shop in London. It is unlikely, however, that William would have worked long under a sign with the wrong initial before his name.

There is a rare photograph of Calcraft, not in the vigor of his young manhood, but in his comfortable old age. It is a conventional studio portrait with one of the subject's hands at rest on a small table and the other, his left, placed upon his waistcoat, at the spot where heartburn strikes someone as generously built as he was. He wears a full gray beard, tidily pruned, and rather curly dark hair, thinning on top. His dress is formal: frock coat, waistcoat with gold chain, black bow tie. You might take him for an alderman or a merchant. His eyes look steady, though heavy lidded. He is certainly not a man you would withhold your hand from if he offered to shake yours. There are, it must be said, other pictures of Calcraft. Drawings and engravings depict a rather unkempt, scruffy figure.

THE GROANS
OF THE
GALLOWS,
Or the Past and Present
LIFE OF
WILLIAM CALCRAFT,

THE LIVING
Hangman of Newgate.

" The Cross shall displace the Gibbet,
and all will be accomplished." Victor Hugo.

ENTERED AT STATIONERS' HALL.

Taken from the title page of his ghosted autobiography, this portrait represents Calcraft as he looked around 1829, when he succeeded Jack Cheshire, who was called "Old Cheese" by the mob that watched him work.

A rare photograph of William Calcraft in his prime in the mid-nineteenth century.

Calcraft is remembered as having been a bungler. His successor, William Marwood, said:

> Ah! Calcraft came from a family of slow worms. He choked his prisoners to death. . . . He THROTTLED them, but I EXECUTE them.

"Slow" he was: slow to get the prisoner ready, slow to get him through the trap, and slow again in bringing word that the prisoner was dead. A reporter has left this eyewitness account of his incompetence. To be fair to the old strangler, it comes from one of his last public appearances, the year before his retirement.

> . . . The robed priest walked directly in front of the condemned, a bound figure. Next hobbled an aged, palsied, trembling man—Calcraft, the official executioner. At the foot of the fatal tree, Father Bonté offered O'Connor [the condemned man] a crucifix to kiss, which he did with evident devotion. I shuddered as Calcraft placed the rope round the victim's throat and drew it tight. The white-robed priest—last friend of the dying man on earth—read on. A crash! A thud! The end has come! No; the rope flies loosely in the air! What has happened? With a vault Father Bonté sprang into the pit, his priestly vestments flying in the wind. I followed him. Propped up against the wooden partition lay O'Connor,

the broken rope around his neck, and the white cap over his eyes. . . . Seizing my arm with his two pinioned hands he exclaimed: "I stood it bravely, didn't I? You will let me off now, won't you? Let me off, do!" Think of the horror of that appeal! "You will let me off, won't you?" And there was no power to do so. "There to be hanged by the neck until you are dead," was the dread sentence, and the Law must be obeyed. The half-hanged man was supported by warders and taken behind the scaffold, while the other officials hurriedly procured a new rope, and then again he was placed in position. Calcraft pulled the lever, the drop fell, and James O'Connor was dead.

Had Calcraft spent as much time preparing his gear as his successors did, poor O'Connor would not have had to climb out of the pit and face the hangman a second time.

The official executioner for the City of London and Middlesex, William Calcraft, began his bungling in 1829 and remained unimproved in technique for the next forty-five years. Less than two weeks after his appointment was confirmed, Calcraft was called upon to perform publicly for the first time. His debut victim was Esther Hilmer, an unpopular sadistic child-killer. It is highly likely that she was insane. She arrived on the scaffold struggling desperately with her jailers, "wearing only a long black skirt over her nightdress." On the drop the struggle continued in spite of the fact that, after having been dragged from her Newgate bed, she had been thrust into a straitjacket. While the crowd booed and hissed the much distracted murderess, who had to be held under the fatal beam, it cheered the hangman. "Good old Calcraft! Three cheers for the hangman!" the people cried. Meanwhile, Calcraft slipped the noose over Esther's head and covered her face, with some difficulty. He pulled the bolt as quickly as he could. "Good old Calcraft! Hip! Hip! Hurrah!" This was a novelty for London, where the criminals were often popular favorites, and the hangman a creature of derision and abuse.

The New Drop, which, by the time Calcraft inherited it, was new no longer, may have been inspired by a gallows used in Dublin. It had been designed in 1783 by the younger George Dance, of the family of architects closely connected with Newgate for two centuries. It consisted of a high platform, with a collapsible trapdoor, covered in at the sides. The scaffold was reached by mounting a roofed-over set of stairs from within the prison, near the Debtors' Door. The approach of the criminals was masked from the crowd by a wooden screen. The drop was operated by a pin or

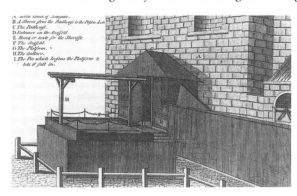

The "New Drop" at Newgate. The innovation is found in the central platform, which collapses downward when a bolt is pulled by the hangman. It made longer drops possible, although Calcraft was initially reluctant to employ them.

bolt which the executioner pulled when all but the condemned were clear of the trap. In the early days, and indeed well into the nineteenth century, there were accidents that tumbled assistant hangmen and others through the drop, when they had not moved clear fast enough.

Dance later amended and improved his design, making the whole engine of destruction portable. Mounted on wheels, it could be rolled into position outside Newgate on a Monday morning, secured in place by wedging rocks under the wheels, and then tucked away until it was needed again the following week. In the first version, two parallel beams ran horizontally over the drop. The twin beams were later replaced by a single one, when the need to execute more than twenty-two at a time occurred less often than the forecasts had indicated.

In the beginning, Calcraft favored a short rope, which gave a short drop. In fact, when the drop fell, only the feet of the condemned prisoners disappeared from sight. Such a drop would hardly break the necks of the condemned, or even render them immediately unconscious. Death on the New Drop in the early years, as at Tyburn, was a strangling matter. In examining old prints and engravings of the New Drop in action, it is difficult to tell whether the drop has fallen or not. The high platform was provided, not for a long drop, but for the convenience of a large crowd of onlookers. In an illustration of the execution of the "Flowery Land" pirates at Newgate in 1864, the five bodies are visible, from their shrouded heads down to the waist. In forty-five years, Calcraft had learned to give his clients more rope. The criminals still did not disappear from view, as they would in a modern hanging, but it was an improvement. So, even Calcraft's short drops, which became notorious only in retrospect, were an improvement over the old arrangements.

In spite of his lack of understanding of the effects of the sudden open-

By 1864, when Calcraft was a decade from his retirement, he was giving longer and more deadly drops to his victims. Here the "Flowery Land" pirates have dropped at least three feet, an improvement, if that's the word, over the scene shown on page 56, where only the feet have vanished from sight.

ing of a trapdoor beneath the feet of the condemned, Calcraft was at least aware that it was now necessary to pinion the lower limbs of the condemned. As a cobbler, it was natural for him to contrive a leather strap for the purpose. Earlier, his clients had sometimes succeeded in getting a foothold on the edge of the scaffold platform after the drop had fallen.

When, a century earlier, Mary Blandy, having ascended five rungs of the ladder that was to serve as a drop, trembled saying, "Gentlemen, do not hang me high, for the sake of decency," the hangman did not think to tie her dress so that she should not be exposed as she hung suspended from a beam slung between two fruit trees. But by the time Calcraft executed Elizabeth Martha Brown at Dorchester in 1856, the practice of securing the legs of men and women about to be hanged was well established. On this occasion, however, according to the reporter from *The Times*, he nearly forgot:

> . . . Having drawn a white cap over the culprit's face, he adjusted the rope around her neck, and retired from the scaffold; he, however, appeared to have forgotten to tie the culprit's dress, and for that purpose reascended the steps. . . .

In his biography of Thomas Hardy, Robert Gittings comments on this execution, which was witnessed by the young, impressionable Hardy from quite close to the gallows:

> . . . Even Calcraft the executioner showed nervousness. Since it was some time since he had executed a woman in public, he forgot to tie her dress so that she should not be exposed as she swung, and had actually to reascend the scaffold to do this. . . .

In one of the several accounts Hardy gave to friends at the end of his life, he says that he watched from the limb of a nearby tree. Hardy stayed to marvel at the marble-like covered face of the hanging woman as she twisted back and forth on the rope "in the misty rain." Others might have been more impressed by her stamina in being able to climb the necessary thirty or more steps to the drop.

Gittings is quite wrong to suggest that the executioner's near blunder was prompted by the fact that the execution was taking place in public. Of course in 1856, and indeed until 1868, all executions were public executions. And while it was understood to be unseemly to have the skirts of a female criminal blowing about her hanging limbs, it was still considered to be proper to leave the bodies of executed criminals of both sexes dangling in the sun, or in the misty rain, as in this case, for at least an hour after the drop was released. Newspaper accounts of this and other executions of the time referred to letting the body hang "the usual time," as though there was no one in England who was unaware of what the usual time was. Invitations of an official or semi-official kind sent out to people of rank or influence used to be worded rather like this: "We hang at eight and breakfast at nine." For instance, in its account of the double hanging of John Bishop and Thomas Williams at London in 1831, *The Times* of 6 December states the following:

> . . . It is an old custom at Newgate for the sheriffs to entertain the under-sheriffs, the chaplain and other friends at breakfast in the prison on the occasion of an execution.

This is the measure of public sensibility in the early and mid-1800s.

One can but wonder at the effect the hanging experience had upon Calcraft. After turning off the notorious couple, the murdering Mannings, Calcraft came down from the gallows looking pale. He was trembling visibly, although in 1849 he was still in mid-career. Upon being asked what was troubling him, he replied in a faltering voice "that he was very nervous that morning, and that he should like to have a mouthful of air." When he left the jail, he exclaimed that he "did not much like hanging a man and his wife."

Charles Dickens himself commented on the hangman's performance. Among the things he said was this: "Mr Calcraft, the hangman (of whom I have some information in reference to this last occasion), should be restrained in his unseemly briskness, in his jokes, his oaths, and his brandy." No one else has suggested that Calcraft was drunk, or even tipsy on the occasion of the execution of the Mannings. I can understand, however, Dickens's complaint about Calcraft's "unseemly briskness." It must be remembered that the author paid ten guineas for the use of a roof and back kitchen windows overlooking the scaffold. After waiting up all night, even with a picnic hamper and sufficient wine, the event was over before it was truly started. There were no replays. The quivering figures could not walk to the scaffold and take their places again. So why not blame it upon the hangman? In working as quickly as he could, he was shortening the earthly pain of the condemned couple; he had no contract to prolong the event for the edification of Charles Dickens and his guests.

While Calcraft looks secure enough in the picture, he was not the holder of a monopoly. Scotland and the north, Lancashire and Yorkshire, still provided their own hangmen when the occasion demanded. It wasn't until the Scots discovered that they had been paying the locally retained man the equivalent of four hundred pounds for every execution for the previous twenty years that they thought better of this arrangement. (There were fewer hangings in Scotland than in England. The Scots never believed in the Bloody Code and began sparing even murderers, while the Sassenachs were still hanging boys who started housefires.)

Calcraft read about his clients in the newspapers of the day, so that he knew whom he was hanging. For instance, when he executed James Greenacre at Newgate for the murder of Hannah Brown, he wore his Sunday best, for Greenacre had been a prosperous tradesman and politician in Southwark, who had entertained members of Parliament and some of the nobility in his condemned cell. Naturally, the hangman appeared in his black frock coat with a gold watchchain hanging across his waistcoat. (When simply flogging minor criminals through the streets, which must be remembered was always part of his job, he wore old clothes.) He would appear to have been non-political in his views, since he executed, or to use the expression of the time, "stitched up," Irish revolutionaries like the "Manchester Martyrs," Larkin, O'Brien, and Allen, or Luddite rioters—

Charles Dickens was part of a crowd of 30,000 in November 1849 when the Mannings were hanged at Horsemonger Lane prison in Surrey. The gallows, shown here in 1809, was raised on the roof of the prison to make sure that as many as possible should witness justice at work.

seven before dinner and seven afterwards—as calmly as he hanged murderers and thieves. More and more he was required to move about the country, officiating in Scotland and Yorkshire.

The story that Calcraft drank persisted through the latter part of his long career. *The Times* of London, for instance, described him in action at the execution of Franz Mueller, a German tailor turned railway robber, who murdered one of the passengers. A vast, rowdy crowd assembled before Newgate to see the hanging. *The Times* said:

> . . . the old hangman slunk again along the drop amid hisses and sneering
> inquiries of what he had had to drink that morning. After failing once to
> cut the rope he made a second attempt more successfully, and the body of
> Mueller disappeared from view. . . .

The unruliness of the spectators went a long way to convincing responsible people that public executions belonged to a bygone and barbaric age. In fact, Calcraft had the distinction of hanging both the last woman and the last man to be publicly executed in Britain: Frances Kidder at Maidstone on 2 April 1868 and Michael Barrett at Newgate on 26 May of the same year. The ending of public executions relieved public opinion. One might parody Lord Macaulay and say that some abolitionists at least hated public hanging, not because it gave pain to the condemned, but because it gave pleasure to the spectators. Dickens and other intellectuals were overjoyed, although the abolitionists continued to work for the complete end of capital punishment. While Calcraft might argue with them about abolition, he was happy that he no longer had to perform with an audience of abusive ruffians on a public scaffold.

From 1868 on, hangings were held inside the walls of prisons. Those attending, besides the official party, tended to be there at the whim of the local sheriffs. There were certainly more invited witnesses in the early

A single beam was substituted for the original two in the revised "New Drop." Two men share the drop with a woman, in what might serve as an illustration of the pathetic end of Elizabeth Fenning in 1815. Here, the drop has already fallen, yet so short were the ropes that the bodies of the condemned remained in full view.

days than later on, and, of course, the press was well represented and felt a keener responsibility to report what no longer could be seen outside prison walls.

The few sketches of the elderly Calcraft that have survived show what time had wrought with him. Brian Bailey, in his *Hangmen of England*, has left this description:

> Calcraft was now an old man. At seventy, he was surly and sinister-looking, with his long hair and beard and his scruffy black attire and fob-chain. He wore a tall hat and had a slouching gait, but this forbidding appearance was sometimes relieved by a rose in his button-hole—he was fond of flowers. His wife had died and he had become even more of an outcast than before, moving house, no longer going to his "local" or meeting his rabbit-fancier friends, and conducting his "business" with a glassy-eyed indifference to everyone around him.

On one occasion when Calcraft had gone to Sheffield to act professionally, a journalist at the prison inquired of one of his assistants, "I wonder if that bloodthirsty scoundrel Calcraft has arrived." A figure in black shuffled from the shadows and acknowledged in a bone-chilling voice, "The bloodthirsty scoundrel is here."

Today we would call Calcraft's existence a "marginal" one, although there were thousands in Britain at the time living as close to the poverty line as he was. It is not surprising that from time to time he had his own scrapes with the law. He was no criminal, but he was sometimes in debt, and one time he was summoned for failing to come to the aid of his seventy-four-year-old mother, Sarah, who was confined in a workhouse. A few years later, in 1869, he was summoned for debt. The magistrate ordered him to pay up within a month or else.

For nearly half a century, Calcraft was, in the public mind at least, *the* hangman in Britain. He had executed more people than anyone before or since. He made a quiet living, had been able to give up shoemaking altogether, and relied upon his "government work" to sustain him. He picked up a little from doing whippings through the streets and floggings in Newgate and elsewhere, and sold off the clothes the condemned wore to their deaths. This last-mentioned "perk" of the trade was as old as the practice of hanging itself. When Madame Tussaud opened her famous wax museum, she created a market for the clothes, keepsakes, pinions, ropes, and hanging hoods that has never been equalled. And there were other markets: Calcraft sold at great profit lengths of rope both to private collectors of morbid curios and to those who thought that hanging ropes were "lucky." In earlier times it was believed that bits of rope and pieces of

William Calcraft was lord of the English gallows from 1829 to 1874, longer than any man before or since. He used to turn up at the end of sessions at the Old Bailey and accept a glass of wine with judges, lawyers, and others in the justice profession.

wood from the gallows itself had miraculous curative powers, comparable to holy relics. Hanging ropes were good for the complexion, it was believed, in the same way that a touch from the hand of a hanged criminal was a cure for warts, wens, and other blemishes to beauty. Calcraft humored the afflicted, although once it proved dangerous. Louis Blake Duff cites the incident in *The County Kerchief*:

> Came to the great executioner a man with a wen on his neck. He had been told that to rub a wen with the hand of one who had been hanged, lo! it would disappear. Said Calcraft, "You may stand on the scaffold and I'll give you a signal." The trap was sprung; the signal was given. The guest on the scaffold, his mind concentrated on the wen, sprang forward, grabbed the now lifeless hand and brought it to the back of his neck for rubbing. The crowd sensed that something sinister was afoot and stormed the scaffold. The writer of the chronicle tells how the hangman got away, how the man with the wen got away, but of the fate of the wen he says never a word.

His last professional appearance was on the scaffold at Newgate, where he hanged James Godwin, a wife-killer, on 25 May 1874. Calcraft was gently forced into retirement. He received a government pension amounting to a guinea a week for the five years remaining to him. His last years and death were recorded in *Life and Recollections of Calcraft the Hangman*.

> He died peacefully at his residence in Poole Street, Hoxton, on Saturday the 13th of December, 1879, in his eightieth year, having resided in the same house over twenty-five years. He used to be a regular attendant at the Church of England, and prior to his death was constantly visited by the clergyman of Hoxton Church. He was buried at Abney Park Cemetery, and leaves behind him a daughter and two sons.
>
> Calcraft was never known to have committed any crime, and he left the world respected by all his personal friends.

William Calcraft, for all his bungling, was a sharp break from the likes of John Price, who was hanged himself, and Ned Dennis, who first used the New Drop at Newgate. While he may have been a terrifying figure to wrongdoers, Calcraft, when seen wandering along the banks of the Grand Union Canal near his home, was not at all frightening. If his shade still walks about the old streets of Hoxton, it hasn't caused a great commotion.

CHAPTER FOUR

A Man of Science:
William Marwood

I'd sooner be by a Serpent stung,
Or hugg'd by a grizzly Bear,
Or crush'd by one of Pickford's Vans,
Or blown into the Air;
I'd sooner be by Marwood hung—
Or slowly fade away,
Than have the least connection
With deceitful Emma Hay.

—MUSIC HALL BALLAD

The identity of Emma Hay is no doubt recorded in some history of that excellent institution, the English music hall. Pickford's vans may still be a menace to London pedestrians. But it is the memory of the executioner, another gentle giant, William Marwood, that is the concern of this chapter. That William Calcraft was a bungler has been said a great deal, but by no one more often than Marwood, his ultimate successor.

Marwood stood unchallenged on the scaffold from 1874 until 1883. He looked down on his predecessors, styled himself as "executioner" rather than "hangman." He was more scientific in his approach to his craft than anyone we have so far encountered. Marwood was also more enterprising. He was one of the modern men of the last quarter of the century. He saved money when traveling on business, for instance, by cashing in his pre-paid second-class railway ticket and traveling third class. In turn he respected his calling sufficiently to leave it better than he found it.

Marwood is remembered as the inventor of the long drop. His clients were not simply strangled, as they had been from time immemorial, but had a good chance of breaking their necks and dying at once, or at least of dislocating vertebrae in the neck, resulting in an instant loss of sensation. In the arts of death, Marwood's name should be honored in the same breath with those of the inventor of the repeating rifle, poison gas, napalm, and the machine gun. In only eight years, from December 1875, his London debut, to September 1883, Marwood brought science into the picture for the first time.

William Marwood, who succeeded to Calcraft's calling, is remembered as the hangman who brought the "long drop" to the "New Drop" at Newgate. He was the first hangman to inquire into the science of falling bodies.

Like Calcraft, William Marwood was also from East Anglia and a cobbler by trade. But where Calcraft left his birthplace to seek his fortune in the British capital, Marwood stayed with his family at home in Horncastle, Lincolnshire, in a small, two-story cottage on Church Lane, next to the cemetery of Holy Trinity Church. Unlike most of the criminals he executed, Marwood never went to see a public execution—neither in his youth nor in his prime. We have no idea where his interest in capital punishment came from and must either guess at his motives or take him as we find him, Cromwellian warts and all.

As a basically humane man, Marwood could not help but sympathize with the victims of Calcraft's plodding inefficiency. In early middle age, he began writing letters to the local sheriffs and prison governors about the need to reform and improve on Calcraft's standard of workmanship. He denounced current practices in the strongest terms, arguing that hanging need not be a long, painful ordeal, odious to look upon and excruciating to endure. By the aid of certain scientific principles, he argued, "instant death" could be meted out on every occasion. Unfortunately, many people in authority believed that "long, painful and excruciating" were exactly what capital punishment called for. They were not in the market for reform. How could instant death improve upon a lingering one as a deterrent?

Whether Marwood was saying that *anyone* could improve on Calcraft, which was almost the literal truth, or that he, personally, should be given a chance to demonstrate what a few scientifically based improvements could do for the name of justice in England, I don't know, and neither do the other biographers I have consulted. At last, in 1871, perhaps to call his bluff, the governor of Lincoln Prison engaged him to perform an execution that would either prove or disprove his claims. There is no record that the criminal involved was consulted in the matter. But, in the event, and on a subsequent occasion, Marwood proved that he could indeed execute without throttling his clients.

The technology of the drop had been developed around 1760, long before Marwood's birth, but it had been insufficiently exploited. The New Drop at Newgate was capable of being used to allow the condemned to fall far enough to break their necks, but it was not in fact used that way until the coming of Marwood, who made it the established practice.

William Marwood was a shoemaker, not a physicist. As far as we know, he had no notion of the writings of the Reverend Dr. Haughton of Trinity College, Dublin, who worked out scientific formulae for breaking necks. He had no training or theoretical grasp of the forces released when falling objects are suddenly brought to a halt. But he could see, as anyone can who has ever dropped a yo-yo to the end of its string, that the greater the fall, the greater the force when the object is arrested at the end of its rope or string. No drop at all, or a short one, ends in a strangulation, a long drop ends in a broken neck, or at least a dislocation, which is almost as good.

Once Calcraft's shoes were empty, the authorities in London were quick to call upon Marwood, whose work was soon being applauded by everyone concerned. The prison governors were happy that the man from Horncastle could dispatch criminals more efficiently than his predecessor, and with more humanity. Marwood was never followed home by gangs of

Ten condemned criminals stand noosed and hooded in front of Newgate. The scaffold was kept within the prison and rolled into place when it was needed. Compare this picture with the one on page 44.

shouting boys as Calcraft and his predecessors had been. He was deemed the "gentleman executioner"; his private notepaper declared:

William Marwood
Executioner
Church Lane, Horncastle, Lincolnshire

This was the age when reformers of all sorts were changing every aspect of English life. The spirits of Elizabeth Fry and John Howard were felt in the land. First the gallows was swept off the street and behind prison walls, and now death could be administered in the twinkling of an eye. No wonder the spirit of the late nineteenth century was so "go ahead," so devoted to progress and industry.

Marwood himself was industrious. First, he improved on the straps that Calcraft had used to pinion the hands and arms of the condemned. As a shoemaker, it was easy for him to experiment with various types of belts, straps, loops, and buckles until he hit upon an arrangement that could be quickly slipped around the wrists and arms of the condemned.

Marwood's chief technical change, apart from his employment of the long drop, was what he did about the hanging rope itself. First, he

Irish prisons often employed a scaffold where the condemned stood on a balcony, the floor of which gave way. A variation of this put the gallows above the prison gate.

improved upon the quality of the rope used. Calcraft had used by prefer-
ence a stiff, one-and-a-half-inch rope, but anything handy would do.
There was little chance that his short ropes would break, since with the
short drops he gave, only the weight of the prisoner had to be supported.
No great force was generated by the falling body. But this would not serve
Marwood's more demanding needs. He used a soft, pliable five-ply Italian
silk hemp rope with a three-quarter-inch diameter.

Marwood developed the modern noose as well. He fixed a metal ring
or "eye" in one end of his rope and brought the other end through it. The
metal "eye," usually made of brass, took the place of a slipknot. At the same
time, it added a heavy metal object exactly at the point where it touched
the prisoner's neck. With a reasonably long drop, the sudden force of the
slack running out would be delivered through this metal "eye" to the neck
of the condemned. Marwood's noose has not been much altered since he
first used it.

The executioner from Horncastle was also concerned about the place-
ment of the noose, so that the metal "eye" could do the most damage. In
most positions, other than towards the front, under the chin, a hanging
rope will be found to have been pulled around to the back of the neck after
the drop. Marwood discovered that when the knot was placed under the
chin or at the corner of the jaw on the left side, the head of the condemned
is thrown back on falling, and a fracture or dislocation occurs. A further
refinement to Marwood's noose was the addition of a leather washer, which
hindered movement of the noose after the hangman's hands settled it.

Over the years and based upon his practical experience and experi-
mentation, Marwood developed a table of weights and drops. A heavy
criminal requires a shorter drop than a light one. A slight figure will
require a longer drop to develop the same killing force that a massive
frame will require. Marwood began his table at 8 stone or 112 pounds. He
couldn't imagine hanging anyone lighter than that. Nor did his table
encourage the hanging of anyone who weighed more than 16 stone or 224
pounds. He allowed a seven-foot drop for his heaviest customers and ten
feet for the lightest. By modern standards these are very long drops indeed
and it is amazing that Marwood did not find that he had decapitated more
than a few of his clients. But, as a later Royal Commission on capital punishment decided, if the hangman must err, let it be on the side of decapitation
rather than strangulation, which is as humane and courageous a decision
as ever came from a committee of any kind.

We have seen, at some length, that William Marwood took pride in his

Hanging ropes, like these made in a South London factory, not only supplied the needs of England, Scotland, Northern Ireland, and Wales, but were exported to the Empire and later to the Commonwealth.

craft and in the expertise he brought to it. To him, it was a mystery in the ancient sense, perhaps almost a priestly function. He told Major Griffiths, a contemporary inspector of prisons, that he took up the work in order to be useful to his generation.

At the same time, while I think the above is true, there is still something inscrutable about Marwood. Calcraft is a simpler case; what you see is what you get. But Marwood, for all his humanity and craftsmanship, remains a partly occluded figure, somewhat in the shadows. Is he not a more chilling personality altogether than his predecessor?

Marwood traveled about Britain and Ireland on professional business. He made suggestions to prison governors about how their apparatus might be improved. He disliked the scaffolds erected in prison yards because of the number of steps the condemned had to climb in order to reach the drop. He suggested the use of ramps and the digging of pits below trap-doors mounted on the same level as the condemned cell. As the number of places in Britain where executions were authorized to be carried out decreased, an improved standard could be detected. And this improvement may be credited to Marwood's influence and persuasive powers.

In a letter to a nervous prison governor, dated 7 June 1879, Marwood replied to some questions about his methods. The letter was printed in facsimile in the *St. Stephen's Review* in 1883. In an unpracticed hand, probably comparable to that of other shoemakers in Britain at the time, he wrote:

> *Sir,*
> in Replie to your Letter of this day i will give you a Compleat Staitment
> for *Executing* a Prisoner—1-Place Pinnion the Prisoner Round the Boady
> and Arms tight—2 Place Bair the Neck—3 Place Take the Prisoner to the
> Drop 4-Place—Place the Prisoner Beneath the Beam to stand Direct
> under the Rope from the Top of the Beam 5-Place strap the Prisoners

Leggs Tight 6 Place Putt on the Cap 7-Place Putt on the Rope Round the
Neck thite. Set the Cap be Free from the Rope to hide the Face angine
Dow in Frunt 8-Place Executioner to go Direct Quick to the *Leaver* Let
Down the Trap *Doors Quick*
No—greas to be Putt on the Rope all Rops to be Well *Tested* before
Execution and all Rops to be kept Dry in good *Auder*
Sir the araingements of the Place of Execution you Can git at HM Prison
Newgate London it wanting 2 Feet Deeper in the Pitt beneath then it is
Perfect say 10 *Feet beneath*
Sir Pleas i thought it would be the Best Way to give you a Clear under-
standing in the araingements of a *Execution* of a *Prisoner*
    to Prevent aney Mistake in the Araingement in the Matter in
Question
Sir i shall be glad to asist you in all improvements
        Sir i Remain your Humble Servant
            Wm Marwood
            Church: Lane—Horncastle Lincolnshire

Marwood, according to Horace Bleackley, was a typical Lincolnshire character with a sturdy figure; rough, ruddy, not unhandsome features; and a
good store of affable, bluff good-humor. Justin Atholl suggests that he was
in appearance not unlike the late Prince Consort, Prince Albert. He wore
an ordinary coat with tails and deep side-pockets. His cravat was always
tidy, although of a somber black, and he tipped a low felt hat at the ladies
in the marketplace.

Under a sign that read "Crown Office," to advertise his official connection with the government, Marwood continued to make and mend shoes
and boots, and to cobble harness and other leather items with straps and
belts. He was universally popular in Horncastle and came to be a celebrity, for local people and strangers alike flocked to his shop to be measured
for a new pair of boots or to examine the hangman's growing collection of
mementoes on display, such as the ropes, clothing, combs, and jewelry
identified with famous clients. He sold most of it as old clothing, but
retained relics from cases of more than passing interest. For a serious collector, like Madame Tussaud, he would part with an item or two, which he
could replace the next time he traveled to Leeds or London on official
business. Marwood was justly proud of his collection. It proved to be one
of the first of the "black museums," rivaling the slower developing one at
Scotland Yard, which boasted the possession not only of hanging ropes

and hoods, but also phrenological plaster casts of the heads of executed criminals. As Dickens tells us in *Great Expectations*, lawyers also made collections of this kind, though perhaps not criminal lawyers; it wouldn't be good for business.

Marwood was proud of showing off the technological improvements that he had introduced. Although he was not in general a vain man, when it came to his craft, he fairly crowed with pride. In describing his work, he assumed the air of a medical specialist on general rounds, pointing out the interesting aspects of his varied operations.

At the same time, he was not blind to his position in the world. While he could boast that he was the "most humane and merciful operator that the world had ever seen," he was able to tell James Berry, who was showing an interest in following in Marwood's footsteps, that there was a stigma attached to the high office of executioner. "My position," he told Berry with emphasis and repetition, "is not a pleasant one. No, it is *not* a pleasant one." One can understand Marwood's warning to young Berry. Becoming an executioner is not a job to be taken up without sober reflection, and the timorous should be discouraged. But, generally speaking, William Marwood, in the decade he ruled the scaffold, had a better time of it than had any of his predecessors. He was less of a public figure than Ned Dennis or William Calcraft. He could move through the streets without being recognized.

The only time he was nearly involved in a riot was on the occasion of a well-advertised public lecture that he gave to a packed hall in Sheffield, just before Christmas 1879. First, he rambled on about religious matters, perhaps Cain and Abel, then he went on to the Irish Question and then to the position of the Queen and the Royal Household. None of this the ticket-holders

A desire to properly recognize the signs of criminality and to understand them gave rise to making casts of the heads of the recently hanged in order to study the bumps on them at leisure. Newgate acquired a collection of these, as did the famed "Black Museum" of Scotland Yard.

had come to hear. As he rambled back to religion, the crowd grew angry. Hecklers interrupted him. They wanted to hear about the lore of the rope and noose, not what they could find in the daily press. The chairman of the meeting tried to restore order by reminding the house that Mr. Marwood was not allowed to disclose "official secrets." The audience went wild. They had been cheated of money that might well have gone towards a Christmas goose or presents for the kiddies on Boxing Day. When it is announced that the hangman is going to give a lecture, the assumption is that he is not going to give a lecture on temperance. Luckily, Marwood escaped unharmed, but his taste for the podium had been seriously damaged.

On the drop or in the condemned cell, Marwood was always confident and assured. When the celebrated Yorkshireman, Charlie Peace, an old lag who spoiled a memorable career in petty crime by killing a policeman, came at last into Marwood's pinions, he used every delaying tactic in the book. He needed time to finish his prayers, he needed a drink, he needed to relieve himself. As Marwood began putting on the white cap, Peace, who was not noted for his church attendance, checked Marwood nodding in the direction of the chaplain reading the prayer for the dead. "Stop a minute," Peace croaked, "I must hear this." There were further delays for Peace to speak to the reporters, punctuated by renewed demands for strong drink, and finally he began to complain about the rope around his neck.

"Oh, it's too tight! It's too tight!"

"Keep still," whispered Marwood, attempting to calm the fellow, "I won't hurt you a bit."

Afterwards, Marwood was quizzed by a curious witness, to whom he replied: "I expected difficulties, because he was such a desperate man, but bless you, my dear sir, he passed away like a summer's eve." This was the most memorable of Marwood's sayings. A slightly different version tries to add the quality of Marwood's speech: "'e parsed hoff like a summer's heve."

The execution of Kate Webster five months later was the end of another celebrated murder mystery. Kate, a brutal Irishwoman living in Richmond, murdered her mistress, dismembered the body and *cooked* the remains, then made up parcels of the pieces wrapped in paper and discarded them in various locations. Although the case was followed by the popular press and the execution was eagerly anticipated, in the event, it appears to have been a routine hanging.

As Marwood was about to execute Charles Shurety at Newgate in 1880, a letter was received marked "On Her Majesty's Service" and "Immediate" on the envelope. Upon opening it the governor of the prison read:

The "penny press" exploited lurid crimes, following trials of celebrated criminals from the dock to the drop, as in this illustrated nightmare, which shows Kate Webster reliving the stages of her crime all the way to the gallows.

49, Rutland Gate

Sir:

From information just brought forward and laid before me, in the name of Her Most Gracious Majesty the Queen, I countermand the order for the execution of Charles Shurety this day. Will communicate further.

I am, sir, your obedient servant,

A. F. Liddell (pro Assheton Cross *in absentia*)

At first the governor was moved to postpone the execution in order to check the letter's provenance. But on further examination, and on the basis of the unusual form of the letter, he decided to continue with the execution on schedule. He didn't want to keep the man waiting in his cell for an hour while the matter was looked into. In those days it would have involved sending a runner to the Home Office in Whitehall. Marwood hanged Shurety on schedule and the governor's decision was confirmed when, some months later, Dr. Caleb C. Whitefoord was convicted of forgery and attempting to obstruct the course of judgement.

On 29 November 1881, in Lewes, Marwood executed Percy Lefroy, who had murdered a passenger on the train to Brighton during the course of a robbery. When questioned about the hanging, Marwood rejected the newspaper accounts that had described Lefroy as being in a serious state of collapse prior to his last walk:

All my eye! The newspapers were wrong. Lefroy meant mischief. If I had not had him by the belt he would have given me a run round the yard.

Of Dr. George Lamson, who came to the rope a year later, Marwood said that he "died like a gentleman." Marwood didn't flinch from executing his betters, but he was always aware of the social differences and the deference due to the well-born or well-educated.

Closer to Marwood in class were "The Invincibles," Irish nationalists responsible for the death in Dublin's Phoenix Park of Lord Cavendish, Chief Secretary of State for Ireland, and Thomas Henry Burke, Permanent Under-Secretary. The condemnation of five of these assassins brought Marwood to Ireland on several occasions during May and June of 1882. Although he was well guarded during his crossing to Kingstown, he enjoyed talking to his fellow passengers on the ferry. There is a story, quoted in *Hangmen of England*, which is to be taken with a grain of salt, that during one of these crossings, Marwood fell into conversation and then a night of convivial drinking with a fellow passenger. A steward, recognizing him on a later crossing, asked after his friend of that memorable night. "Oh," Marwood is supposed to have said, "I just hanged him."

With the exception of his Sheffield lecture, Marwood was a good judge of what the public wanted from him, and, as the anecdote above suggests, he enjoyed pulling people's legs and gilding his fame, especially when he could manage them both together.

In Lincolnshire, he was thought of as a family friend, a benefactor of mankind. There was nothing of the recluse about him. He wore the term "social pariah" with a difference. His appearance was respectable, his dress and grooming never at a loss. And while his fellow townsmen told jokes about him, such jokes savored of good humor rather than dislike or repulsion.

The music halls remembered him as well.

Question: If Pa killed Ma, who'd kill Pa?
Answer: Marwood.

When, two months after the last of the Phoenix Park assassins went to his death, Marwood took to his bed in Horncastle, it was said that "The Invincibles" were being revenged on the sixty-three-year-old hangman. He was told that he had an inflammation of the lungs complicated by jaundice. He died in his Church Lane house on 4 September 1883; a passing marked in all of the British papers. As Horace Bleackley states, his death was seen as "a death in the official family." All of Horncastle turned out for the funeral in Holy Trinity Church and he was buried within view of his little house with the "Crown Office" sign.

In medicine, engineering, and the other professions, one may say as valedictory that the mourned departed member of the profession left it better than he found it. But in the arts of death, what is "better"? William Marwood certainly improved upon his predecessors in speed, efficiency, and humanity. But while a better mousetrap is readily agreed to be a boon to mankind, a better noose and gallows may need to be judged more cautiously.

CHAPTER FIVE

The Reluctant Hangman: James Berry

My brother, sit and think
While yet on earth some hours are left to thee;
Kneel to thy God, who does not from thee shrink,
And lay thy sins on Christ, who died for thee.

—JAMES BERRY

The hangmen in England seem to have been under the protection of St. Crispian, the patron saint of cobblers, shoemakers—and perhaps even shoe salesmen from Bradford, as was James Berry, William Marwood's successor. Unlike William Calcraft, William Marwood, and the martyred saint, cobblers all, Berry was familiar only with the front of the store.

When we think of a hangman of the last part of the last century, if we ever do, it is Berry who probably comes to mind. In the film *Kind Hearts and Coronets*, the hangman played by Miles Malleson, the gentlest of actors, is modeled on him. Malleson even quotes a verse of Berry's to his intended victim before proceeding to more practical matters. Berry left behind rather a lot of poetry written "for these melancholy occasions." Like the epigraph to this chapter, it often proved the most painful part of the proceedings.

Berry was born into a wool-stapler's large family in Heckmondwike, between Huddersfield and Bradford, in Yorkshire in 1852. In school, he learned to write a fine copperplate script, which led to some minor clerking jobs. He was for a time a policeman, and it may have been while he was on the force at Bradford that he first encountered Marwood. It would appear that at the time they knew each other neither knew that their relationship was to become that of master and apprentice. Nor, in fact, did Berry ever work directly with Marwood, although he sometimes claimed to have assisted at the execution of Charlie Peace. Justin Atholl, who has tried in *The Reluctant Hangman* to improve upon the omissions in Berry's own memoir, says:

Berry's friendship with Marwood extended over a period during which they discussed in detail the science of securing instant death by hanging.

Marwood's pride in his occupation was that of a craftsman and —at least so he felt—that of a humanitarian. . . .

Berry bought one of Marwood's slim ropes from him. This purchase may mark the Rubicon in Berry's career, for it ended his term of disinterested curiosity and introduced one of serious study. By 1883, Berry had acquired more rope and pinioning straps from his master, so that when Marwood died, he applied in writing to the Sheriff of London. Unfortunately, so did 1,400 others, some of whom said they would work for nothing. When London chose Bartholomew Binns for the job, the ambitious Berry applied to the magistrates in Edinburgh to be appointed executioner of two murdering poachers. Thus, in March 1884, he presented himself, with a bag full of hanging ropes and pinioning straps, before the prison governor, who quizzed him about every detail of his work. Berry had up to this time never harmed a living soul, although as a policeman he had been involved in a life-or-death struggle with a burglar who was armed with a broken bottle. He wore proof of this battle on his forehead to the end of his days.

The double execution in Edinburgh was a great success, and Berry returned to Bradford with testimonials in his pocket to prove it. In the meantime Bartholomew Binns had not been adding to the dignity of his craft. In Liverpool, he bungled an execution in the old hit-or-miss Calcraft way, which angered the authorities there, and he was found riding in a railway carriage without a ticket, which added to his disgrace. After questions were asked in the House of Lords, he was dismissed and Berry was given the nod.

Why did Berry want to become the official executioner? He admitted that he had "great distaste for the work." In 1884 he was thirty-one and had already left the Bradford constabulary. Here was a man who saw himself slipping off the lower shelf of the middle class into the ranks of a large and bleak working class. He could see that he was never going to "get on" as a shoe salesman; he needed to lift himself out of the ranks he was slowly falling into. The vacancy created by Marwood's death and Binns's disgrace brought him to look upon the position of executioner as his "one chance in life" to better himself.

Berry's next execution was that of Mary Lefley in Lincoln Gaol, May 1884. This execution, his first of a woman, established a repugnance at executing women which dogged him all his days. Berry had hoped that women on the scaffold would show the kind of strength of which he knew

This picture of James Berry (1852–1913) appeared in his published memoir, My Experiences as an Executioner. *Dubbed "the reluctant hangman," he wrote verses to read to his victims. Berry retired when he was only thirty-nine, after a dispute with a prison doctor about the length of a drop, which proved to be a drop too much.*

them capable. In the event, Mary Lefley proved troublesome, and later Mary Britland and Elizabeth Berry (no relation) were carried and cajoled to the drop, out of their minds with fear and horror, while Berry did "the necessary." Of Mary Britland, for instance, a reporter wrote, that while Berry slipped the white cap over her head and fixed the noose around her neck, Mary uttered a cry "such as one might expect at the actual separation of body and spirit through mortal terror."

Berry never worried about the guilt or innocence of his clients. For him, in the early years at least, it was enough that they had been found guilty in a proper court of law. If mistakes were being made—and he came to believe that Mary Lefley was innocent—it was none of his business.

His successes with these difficult clients gave him courage to experiment further in the science of sudden death. He had Marwood's rough table of drops from the beginning, and worked out a table of his own that modified his predecessor's long drops. In its earliest form, it looked like this:

14 stones	....	8 ft. 0 in.
13½ ,,	....	8 ,, 2 ,,
13 ,,	....	8 ,, 4 ,,
12½ ,,	....	8 ,, 6 ,,
12 ,,	....	8 ,, 8 ,,
11½ ,,	....	8 ,, 10 ,,
11 ,,	....	9 ,, 0 ,,
10½ ,,	....	9 ,, 2 ,,
10 ,,	....	9 ,, 4 ,,
9½ ,,	....	9 ,, 6 ,,
9 ,,	....	9 ,, 8 ,,
8½ ,,	....	9 ,, 10 ,,
8 ,,	....	10 ,, 0 ,,

"Taking a man of 14 stones [196 pounds] as a basis, and giving him a drop of 8 ft . . . I calculated that every half-stone [7 pounds] lighter weight would require a two-inch longer drop . . ." wrote James Berry of his early table of drops.

Later on, when he had had more experience, he developed this further, including the weights of people heavier than in the early version. This table has been altered but little since that time.

SCALE SHOWING THE STRIKING FORCE OF FALLING BODIES AT DIFFERENT DISTANCES.

Distance Falling in Feet	8 Stone	9 Stone	10 Stone	11 Stone	12 Stone	13 Stone	14 Stone	15 Stone	16 Stone	17 Stone	18 Stone	19 Stone
Zero	Cw. Qr. lb.	Cw. Qr. lb.	Cw. Qr. lb.	Cw. Qr. lb.	Cw. Qr. lb.	Cw. Qr. lb.	Cw. Qr. lb.	Cw. Qr. lb.	Cw. Qr. lb.	Cw. Qr. lb.	Cw. Qr. lb.	Cw. Qr. lb.
1 Ft.	8 0 0	9 0 0	10 0 0	11 0 0	12 0 0	13 0 0	14 0 0	15 0 0	16 0 0	17 0 0	18 0 0	19 0 0
2 ,,	11 1 15	12 2 23	14 0 14	15 2 4	16 3 22	18 1 12	19 3 2	21 0 21	22 2 11	24 0 1	25 1 19	26 3 9
3 ,,	13 3 16	15 2 15	17 1 14	19 0 12	20 3 11	22 2 9	24 1 8	26 0 7	27 3 5	29 2 4	31 1 2	33 0 1
4 ,,	16 0 0	18 0 0	20 0 0	22 0 0	24 0 0	26 0 0	28 0 0	30 0 0	32 0 0	34 0 0	36 0 0	40 0 0
5 ,,	17 2 11	19 3 5	22 0 0	24 0 22	26 1 16	28 2 11	30 3 5	33 0 0	35 0 22	37 0 16	39 2 11	41 3 15
6 ,,	19 2 11	22 0 5	24 2 0	26 3 22	29 1 16	31 3 11	34 1 5	36 3 0	39 0 22	41 2 16	44 0 11	46 2 5
7 ,,	21 0 22	23 3 11	26 2 0	29 0 16	31 3 5	34 1 22	37 0 11	39 3 0	42 1 16	45 0 5	47 2 22	50 1 11
8 ,,	22 2 22	25 2 4	28 1 14	31 0 23	34 0 5	36 3 15	39 2 25	42 2 7	45 1 16	48 0 26	51 0 8	53 3 18
9 ,,	24 0 11	27 0 12	30 0 14	33 0 23	36 0 16	39 0 18	42 0 19	45 0 21	48 0 22	51 0 23	54 0 25	57 0 26
10 ,,	25 1 5	28 1 23	31 2 14	34 3 4	37 3 22	41 0 12	44 1 2	47 1 21	50 2 11	53 3 1	56 3 19	60 0 9

In its final form, Berry's "ready reckoner" of drops looked like this. With only slight modification, it remained the standard for many years.

Berry's easy-to-read scale could turn up the right drop for all the people he was likely to meet professionally. Once the weight of his client was known, it could be located on the table. Moving his finger down the column, he would stop at the striking force he was looking for and by moving his finger to the left, he found the length of drop that would provide such a force. After that, it was only a matter of removing the approximate height of the condemned from the length of rope he needed to give a particular drop. With a pencil and a piece of paper, you will be able to work out Berry's plans for yourself.

In his memoir, written near the end of his professional career, Berry stated that it took him only three minutes from when he entered the condemned cell to what he called the "finish of life's greatest tragedy for the doomed man." He goes on:

I enter the cell punctually at three minutes to eight. When we enter the condemned cell the chaplain is already there, and he has been for some time. The attendants who have watched through the convict's last night on earth are also present. At my appearance the convict takes leave of his attendants to whom he generally gives some small token or keepsake, and I at once proceed to pinion his arms. As soon as the pinioning is done a procession is formed.

On the way from the cell to the scaffold the chaplain reads the service for the burial of the dead, and as the procession moves, I place the white cap upon the head of the convict. Just as we reach the scaffold I pull the cap over his eyes. Then I place the convict under the beam, pinion his legs just below the knees, adjust the rope, pull the bolt and the trap falls. Death is instantaneous.

So Berry reported. It may have happened this way on many occasions, but Berry was forgetting that he often slowed up the proceedings himself with a recitation of the sort of verse that has already been referred to. He would also delay things by quizzing the criminal about his crime as he slipped the pinions around him. Berry slept better afterwards if the prisoner confessed his guilt on his way to the scaffold. As a non-conformist lay preacher, Berry also looked for some indication of repentance as well. He was not above suggesting to some hard cases that there was still time enough to alter the drop in order to give his client a more disagreeable death. This was bluff, of course, and the officials took a dim view of it. Once in Cork, the governor or under-sheriff had to interrupt the dialogue between the condemned man and his executioner in order to move the procession towards the gallows. Elsewhere, Berry was invited by the authorities to try to winkle a confession out of his victim. Faced with his executioner, many a condemned man told more than he had in court. One man named William Henry Bury, who was hanged in 1889, the year following the five Jack the Ripper murders in Whitechapel, was suspected of being the Ripper by the police. He said to Berry, "I suppose you think you are clever to hang *me*," which only added fuel to the speculation.

Berry believed that a bond connected the hangman and his victim. It excluded all others in the "official party." They were each dependant upon the other: the hangman for the victim's cooperation and steadiness, the victim upon the executioner's skill and speed. If such a relationship existed, it would be an extremely intimate one. This was the victim's last human contact; Berry's the last face he would ever see. "They don't tell lies to the hangman," he said many times.

Dr. Philip Henry Eustace Cross, the poisoner, a former army doctor, and one of the most conceited and foolish of all the professional men ever brought to the scaffold, may serve as a good example of those few clients who resisted Berry's approach. Dr. Cross refused to speak to Berry, treating him like a pesky tradesman of no account. Still, they engaged in one of the more curious mute battles that was ever waged on the gallows. Berry believed, with Marwood, that a man should never be hanged facing east. Cross stood on the drop confronting the officials in the party, facing east. Berry asked Dr. Cross to turn around. When the condemned man did not move, Berry turned him around himself. To everybody's astonishment, Dr. Cross turned around again. Again Berry turned the pinioned figure around, and again the doctor returned to his original position. If the governor had not interfered, they might be at it yet. Berry dropped him through and quickly left the prison before the inquest could be convened. Without Berry, the inquest was adjourned. The Irish authorities wrote to Berry demanding that he return to give his evidence. Berry replied that he never attended inquests and that he would return only for a payment of ten pounds and expenses. No one was willing to pay this, and that is why at this late date Dr. Philip Henry Eustace Cross is still officially among the living, there never having been a death certificate issued.

On the other hand, no one could have been more forthright and co-operative than Mary Eleanor Wheeler, better-known to history as Mrs. Pearcy. With typical indifference to what was happening outside the Prison Service, the Home Office had scheduled her execution to occur two days before Christmas 1890. Totally unsentimental, the Home Office appears to have ignored the holiday mood, as well as the feelings of the condemned who would not live to see the festive day. Mrs. Pearcy, who had murdered her lover's wife and infant daughter, seemed not at all upset by the fact that she was to die on 23 December. "Was that the executioner?" she asked her wardresses, when Berry was measuring her for the drop through the judas hole in her cell door. "He is in good time, isn't he? Is it usual for him to arrive on the Saturday for the Monday?" Such sangfroid was unusual in Berry's experience. On the Monday morning, Mrs. Pearcy shook hands with the hangman and said, when asked if she had any last words, "The sentence was just, but some of the evidence was false." Marveling at her calm acceptance of death only moments away, Berry approached her.

"If you are ready, madam, I will get these straps round you."

Berry, who disliked the term "hangman," believed that "executioner" possessed the required dignity and had calling cards printed accordingly. This one featured a maidenhair fern motif.

"I am quite ready, Mr. Berry," she replied. And then a moment later, "I need no one to assist me. I can walk by myself and there is no need for you [the wardresses] to come." Upon being assured that they would gladly walk the short distance with her, she said, "Oh, well, if you don't mind coming, I shall be glad to have you." Then, quite calmly they all marched into the execution shed, where Berry never executed a braver subject, man or woman.

Berry was much relieved when a prisoner was respited at the last minute. Although a reprieve meant that he would lose the better part of his fee, he was always on the side of life. Like everyone else, he had his theories about Home Office sensitivities. He could never understand why people who committed murder in a fit of passion should be executed, when, had they killed themselves immediately after the crime, the coroner's jury would have found them guilty of suicide while temporarily insane. If insane in the one instance, why not in the other?

In February 1885, Berry took the train to Exeter to hang John Lee, a footman, convicted of brutally murdering his employer. It was said that Lee's earlier "trouble" with the law told against him. Nevertheless, on the morning of Monday, 23 February 1885, Berry took Lee to the drop and attended to him just as he has described above. In this case, however, the trapdoors did not open under Lee's pinioned legs. The lever was pushed, nothing happened. Berry stomped upon the drop. There was no movement. The warders tried to kick and stomp the trapdoors into falling according to the judgement of the law. Nothing happened. Lee was taken off the trap and removed to a nearby room while Berry and the others tried to operate the lever again. With the condemned man's weight off the drop, the trapdoors fell normally. Berry tested the scaffold twice before the prisoner was returned to the chalk mark where the two leaves of the trap came together. Again and again, and yet once again, the execution was attempted and failed. With the weight of the prisoner, the drop refused to fall. At last the Home Office respited Lee, and Berry was sent packing. The

```
                    119

┌──────────┐   Bradford,................................189
│ QUOTB    │          YORKS.
│ No. .....│
└──────────┘

  Sir,

        I beg leave to state in reply to your letter

of the ................................................. that I

am prepared to undertake the execution you name of

_____

at ....................... on the..............................

      I also beg leave to state that my terms are as

follows: £10 for the execution, £5 if the condemned

is reprieved, together with all travelling expenses.

      Awaiting your reply,

              I am, Sir,

                    Your obedient Servant,

                          James Berry.

  The High Sheriff,

      for the County of.........................................
```

James Berry used this printed form when dealing with sheriffs. It gave his terms "and left no opening for mistake or misunderstanding." His "travelling expenses" were understood to include a second-class return railway ticket and cab fare from Bradford to the place of execution. If he was not lodged in the jail, he expected that his hotel bill would be paid.

executioner was paid his full fee, but was never able to free his mind from thinking of Lee, whom the papers at once dubbed: THE MAN THEY COULD NOT HANG.

If Lee was innocent, Berry never believed it, even though he learned from the warders that Lee told them quite calmly that he would not die that day. Berry knew that he had hanged several people who were more innocent than Lee. Berry also became involved in trying to explain the physical phenomenon of why the drop worked when the trap was weightless but failed to function when the weight of the condemned was added. If Berry learned anything from this terrible experience, which unnerved many strong men, it was to test the scaffold in future with a weight upon the drop. He made it his practice thereafter to test the drop with a bag of cement or sand approximating the weight of the prisoner and to leave the sack suspended on the rope overnight to get the stretch out of it. As for John Lee, he served his life sentence, about twenty years, and upon his release went to live in the United States, where he died in his late sixties.

On the last day of November 1885, Berry hanged Robert Goodale at Norwich Castle. Goodale, who was a heavy man at two hundred pounds, went through the trap to instant death. The story was over for Goodale and no one could have wished him a speedier end. Unfortunately, he was not hanged; he was decapitated. For James Berry, all hell broke loose and a long shadow was cast on his career and livelihood. A committee in the House of Lords was set up under the chairmanship of Lord Aberdare to look into all aspects of judicial hanging. It heard from leading authorities both practical and medical about the best way of insuring instant death without a hitch, if possible. The medical people contradicted one another, confusing everybody. What emerged was the theory that if the knot were placed under the ear of the condemned, a greater drop was required than if the knot were placed under the chin of the prisoner. And with a shorter drop, the chances of the Goodale accident repeating itself were reduced.

Where he could, Berry tried to improve familiar practice. For instance, he advocated having the drop on the same level as the condemned cell. This shortened the last walk of the condemned and overcame any reluctance on the part of the prisoner to mount the scaffold steps, where it was often a battle royal to bring him to the top. This new form of scaffold was built so that the drop opened up into a pit, or cellar, that the hangman and doctor could reach by stairs leading down into it. Here the body hung until it was cut down to be prepared for the inquest, or hauled up through the open trap by tackle supplied by the prison engineer for the purpose. In many places, the pit was just that, a dark, squalid brick-lined shaft with a stepladder at the bottom.

Berry also invented clips that caught the falling leaves of the trapdoor and held them tightly until they were released for resetting. That prevented injury to the prisoner during his fatal drop as well as damage to the suspended corpse. The falling of the drop could be heard all over the prisons of Britain and Ireland. There was no attempt to muffle the sound until much closer to our own day when sensibilities also questioned the traditional tolling of bells at eight o'clock on the morning of an execution and the hoisting of a black flag on top of the prison at the moment of the execution. It is with the raising of a black flag at the end of *Tess of the d'Urbervilles* that Thomas Hardy signals that "Justice" had been done and "the President of the Immortals, in Aeschylean phrase, had ended his sport with Tess."

Gradually, and with James Berry's blessing, scaffolds were placed in "execution sheds," outside or adjacent to the jail or prison. Sometimes this was a real shed, garage, or carriage house that had a cellar or pit beneath the floor. More often, it had to be built specially. Berry tried to have the condemned cells located as close to the "shed" as possible. In many places in Great Britain, the prisoner could walk through a sliding door in his cell directly into the "shed." This shortened the time of an execution from minutes to seconds.

Berry also worked hard to bring Scotland up to the standard he was setting all over England. Whenever he made a professional visit, he would make suggestions to the prison governor about how the present system might be improved. He was very much a man of his age. He was all for progress and perfection.

He stuck, however, to his practice of placing his knots under the left ear of his clients and, in 1891, the unfortunate Goodale experience was nearly repeated. Dr. James Barr of Kirkdale Prison, Liverpool, disagreed with the drop that Berry had calculated for John Conway and insisted that Berry lengthen it. Berry protested, but was forced to accept medical opinion. As a result, the head was all but torn from the body. Later, he defended himself: ". . . I am not to blame for anything that has occurred; it's all left to the doctors now, and this comes of not taking my advice." In one account, he added, "They might as well do the whole job themselves. . . ."

What this amounts to is the fact that while there is a scientific dimension to hanging as expressed by a table of weights and drops, there is also the personal experience of the hangman that is required to adjust the drop to take in such things as the age, sex, and physical condition of the condemned. Such things cannot be codified, but depend upon experience, judgement, and other imponderables.

Because Dr. Barr was a local man, the Liverpool press put a lot of the blame upon Berry. The papers said that he had been singing comic songs at the Sessions House Hotel after his arrival in Liverpool, thus suggesting that he was either still drunk or hung over the following morning. He denied the suggestion of levity and drunkenness when he returned to Bradford, and showed the Bradford reporters his bloodstained pinions, quite ruined by Barr's bad judgement. Berry was not restored to his usual good humor for some time.

Meanwhile he continued to keep the appointments in his book without further conflict with the prison authorities or the press. But the damage had been done. Sheriffs began requesting a Bolton hairdresser named James Billington to undertake the work formerly done by Berry. In the press, Billington was given longer write-ups about his performances, while poor Berry saved clippings of his rival's advancement. The Goodale shadow had fallen across his career and there was nothing he could do about it. In fact, it was shortly after this time that he wrote to the Home Secretary:

> Dear Sir,
>
> I herewith tender my resignation as executioner of Great Britain. My reason is on account of Dr Barr interfering with my responsible duty at Kirkdale Gaol, Liverpool, on the last execution there. I shall therefore withdraw my name now as being executioner to England. Trusting this will be accepted by you on behalf of the Sheriffs of England,
>
> I remain, dear sir,
>
> Your obedient servant,
>
> James Berry,
>
> late executioner of England.

Whether this letter is to be taken at face value or not depends a good deal upon one's estimate of Berry's personality. Was he bluffing? Was he telling the Home Secretary that he now had to choose between himself, a faithful servant of eight years' standing, or Billington, the jumped-up Bolton hairdresser? His wording of this resignation at the very least suggests that although he had washed his hands of the interfering English, he still held out for commissions from the Scots and Irish. Further, you can see that Berry had a very high opinion of himself and the office he filled. And it is true that he lifted the dignity of his calling to new heights. But he did give himself airs, which perhaps show up better in his stilted official correspondence than in his memoirs. Berry's desire to become an establishment figure was foredoomed. He never understood officialdom and was even confused about his own position in the scheme of things.

Berry was only thirty-nine when he retired; he'd held the post of executioner for eight years. In addition to getting the official runaround by the Home Office, Berry's own notions about capital punishment were undergoing a change. Little of this creeps into his memoirs, for as long as he remained a Home Office functionary, he held his tongue about his doubts, except for notorious cases like that of Dr. Barr, and, true, there were some episodes where he may have spoken too openly to the press after a job, when he presented himself in the saloon bar of the public house closest to the railway station. Justin Atholl believes that by talking about the hanging he had just performed, Berry exorcised the ghosts of his morning's work. Things talked about in the pub surrounded by convivial male company he didn't have to take back with him to Bradford.

In *My Experiences as an Executioner*, Berry puts forward the view that capital punishment was supported by the scriptures, that it would be irreligious to go against such principles as "An eye for an eye," or "Whoso sheddeth man's blood, by man shall his blood be shed." In this view he was like the majority of his countrymen. But once he had resigned, he appears to have done a complete about-face. Like many another former executioner, he came down strongly against what now was seen as a social evil and went on a lecture tour denouncing not only the practice of hanging as he knew it, but the principle of taking life by the state under even the most humane conditions. Unfortunately, Berry's new ideas collided with those expressed in his memoirs, which were published shortly after his retirement, but were already in the press when he sent in his papers. So it appears that Berry on the public platform supported more enlightened views than Berry in print.

As a token of his change of heart, Berry cleaned out his collection of souvenirs of his years on the gallows: photographs of his clients, "my victims," he'd hung on the walls of the little brick Bradford house. At first glance, these walls covered with pictures resembled many a Victorian parlor, but these were all the faces of the dead, clipped from newspapers and other sources. Other souvenirs were relics of the condemned themselves: locks of hair, snipped by him in the pit where they dangled; gifts, tokens, and keepsakes that had come into his possession either directly or through other agencies. At the close of his career on the scaffold, he sold these off to places like Madame Tussaud's Chamber of Horrors. They robbed him of his sleep and peace of mind, he said, and he felt better as soon as his house was rid of them.

When he was asked by an American entrepreneur if he would consider doing a tour of America describing his experiences as well as promoting his new anti–capital punishment views, he agreed at once. It appears that he was a better platform performer than Marwood. The American tour fell through, but he did get up a routine, had magic-lantern slides prepared showing the process of pinioning and the rest of the hanging ritual, including a photographic slide, now in the collection at Madame Tussaud's, which may show Berry, himself, standing, pinioned, hooded, noosed, and ready to be dropped through the gallows trap. In his talks, he stated that he had always been against capital punishment in principle.

He toured the music halls, competing with the likes of Lillie Langtree and ta-ra-ra-boom-de-ay. He advertised himself as an expert in phrenology as well as neck breaking and, at the end, found the Moody and Sankey route into the revival halls, where he talked about death-cell repentance and confessions made to the hangman. Berry's own personal return to religion and his becoming what we would describe as "born again" appear to have been genuine. Still, when in London, he often visited Madame Tussaud's Chamber of Horrors and never asked Mr. Tussaud to remove his effigy.

He died at the age of sixty-one in October 1913. In obituary notices, his occupation was given, according to Brian Bailey, as "evangelist." He had been away from the scaffold for nearly thirty years.

CHAPTER SIX

Last of the Breed:
The Billingtons, Ellis,
and the Pierrepoints

. . . I do not now believe that any one of the hundreds of executions that I carried out in any way acted as a deterrent against future murder. Capital punishment, in my view, achieved nothing but revenge.

—ALBERT PIERREPOINT

James Billington, whose career paralleled Berry's until Berry resigned, and lasted just into the new century, appears to have been a tireless workman, ambitious to a fault, and without much poetry sticking to his soul. When a daughter of his died in infancy, he told a neighbor, through his tears, "I'd sooner ha'lost five pounds than ha'lost her." Although he had frequented Bolton pubs in his younger days, he was for eight years officially a teetotaller, and proudly wore in his buttonhole a blue ribbon proclaiming this. However, as the reality of his trade in human lives caught up to him, he forswore his blue abstainer's ribbon and became the landlord of a pub, the Derby Arms, in Bolton.

James Billington was not a big man but, according to legend, very strong. He had been a wrestler, a miner, and a mill hand at one time or another, but settled on barbering on Market Street in Farnworth, near Bolton. He was remembered for his powerful singing voice, which, at different periods of his life, was heard in bar-rooms and in the Primitive Methodist Chapel and Sunday School. On the scaffold he wore a dark suit and black skullcap, which was less of a denominational tag in those days, but still perhaps somewhat daunting to the condemned.

Billington hated the reporters who lay in wait for him outside prisons or at railway stations. They all wanted tidbits for their Sunday editions. Some were brave enough to follow him into his shop when he worked as a barber. They sat in his chair while he held a razor to their throats, and they plagued him with questions. The hangman may have been tempted more than once to reduce the number of working journalists.

In an introductory letter to a Nottingham sheriff, Billington boasted that his "system was better than the last," and that

> . . . I shall have no assistance I can do the work myself I don't think it needs two to do the work and as long as they can have a little assistance from the gaol if required. . . .

But he required assistance on the occasion of the last triple hanging at Newgate. The year was 1896 and he was given an assistant from the Home Office list, one William Warbrick. Warbrick was still pinioning the legs of one of his clients when Billington, not seeing that he was still kneeling on the trapdoors, pushed the lever that operated the drop. If Warbrick hadn't grabbed the legs of the man closest to him, he could have sustained serious injury by falling to the bottom of the brick-lined pit. And the criminal whose legs Warbrick caught received a blow to the neck somewhat in excess of the one Billington had calculated for him.

That same year, he executed a former trooper in the Royal Horse Guards, the man who became the central personage in Oscar Wilde's "The Ballad of Reading Gaol." Charles Thomas Wooldridge was made to "dance upon the air," after a drop of six feet seven inches, in the hanging shed described by Wilde in a letter to Robert Ross as looking rather like a photographer's studio on Margate sands because of its skylight.

Brian Bailey, who has done more probing and writing about British executioners than anyone since Horace Bleackley, was the first researcher to dig deeply into the lives and careers of James Billington and his sons, Thomas, John, and William. For the Billingtons formed a sometimes confusing dynasty of dealers in death, confusing both to local sheriffs and to keepers of the Home Office list. The brothers turned up to do jobs their father had been engaged for and they also impersonated one another both as assistants and as chief executioners. Bailey has set the record straight, or at least as straight as it is ever likely to be. In doing so, he has been able to separate fact from fiction, for Billington *fils*, William or "Billie," often embroidered reality, perhaps to escape from it. He was a great yarn-spinner.

James Billington died on Friday, 13 December 1901, at the age of fifty-four. He had sent 147 people to their deaths in a relatively short span of years. His last job was to execute Patrick McKenna, an acquaintance from Bolton. He was almost too ill to take charge, but he played cards through the night with his assistant, Harry Pierrepoint, complaining from time to time, "Ee, Harry, I wish I'd never ha' come." Pierrepoint told his son, Albert, that James Billington was "the best pal a man could have." James was quickly followed to the grave by his older son, Thomas. "Billie" stepped into the shoes of both his father and his older brother.

The Billingtons were bluff, hearty Lancashiremen. Their history on the scaffold is largely unrecorded. None of them was as literate as either William Marwood or James Berry. They left no memoirs, not even ghosted ones.

Few descriptions of what actually happened inside the execution shed after the turn of the century have survived. The lid of security was fastened tightly. We know that George Chapman was carried to the scaffold at Wandsworth Prison in a state of collapse, and that Samuel Holden walked to his death in Birmingham smoking a cigar. These incidents may be taken as a sign of the times. Little escaped the execution shed in the way of news, and when it did, there was hell to pay.

The next part in this history of hangmen is split in two. Both John Ellis and Henry Pierrepoint had assisted the Billingtons; now they went on to careers of their own as they were both promoted on the Home Office list. Although their employers endeavored to keep them busy, it is well to remember that neither was as busy as his predecessors; fewer capital crimes remained on the books and fewer of the people sentenced to death were executed.

John Ellis was born into a comfortable Rochdale family of hairdressers in 1874, the year of William Calcraft's retirement. (It should be noted that the trade of executioner had passed, or so it seems, from the care of St. Crispian, the patron saint of cobblers, to St. Constantine and his mother, St. Helen, the patrons of barbering.) He thought of himself as an ordinary bloke who enjoyed betting the horses and having a pint with his mates at the Rose and Crown. He liked animals, took up poultry breeding, and attended sporting events. He stood five feet nine inches tall and began going bald before middle age. In his dark suit, bowler hat, and soup-strainer mustache, he was indistinguishable from thousands of his contemporaries. In Liverpool one time, standing outside the prison, a stranger approached him, asking, "Has Ellis, the executioner, arrived yet?" One reporter said of him, "He never looked what he was."

Ellis used to say that he took up the trade of executioner on a dare from a friend who didn't think he had the nerve. But there must have been something a little deeper than that to explain his careful application to the Home Office with three references. Three references impressed the Home Office and Jack Ellis's name was added to the list.

John Ellis was a hairdresser and publican when not occupied with "government work." Hated by the rival Pierrepoints, he performed with precision until he retired his name from the Home Office list, and later cut his throat.

Ellis helped "Billie" Billington at Armley Gaol, Leeds, at the double execution of Emily Swann and John Gallagher in 1903. The two had murdered Swann's husband, William, who objected to his boarder carrying on with his wife. When she met her lover on the gallows, she said, "Good morning, John"; he answered, "Good morning, love." They were placed back to back on the trap, the first mention I have come across of this sort of double execution. As Billington slipped the hoods and nooses around their necks and Ellis strapped their legs, the unfortunate lovers spoke again: "Goodbye, John. God bless," to which Gallagher answered, "Goodbye, love." In a moment, they disappeared from sight. This was the last time a man and woman were executed together in the same prison.

Ellis, of course, followed the cases of all of his potential clients closely. He wanted to know whom he was executing. Dr. Hawley Harvey Crippen, for instance, had been the subject of a transatlantic chase. The gentlest of murderers, provoked to the extreme by his overpowering wife, Crippen escaped to Quebec, where he was caught. After Ellis removed Crippen's metal-rimmed glasses, Crippen went to his death calmly, asking to have the photograph of his young lover buried with him.

Because three other men were lying under sentence of death at Pentonville Prison that gray November morning in 1910, and in consideration of their feelings, the traditional tolling of the prison bell to signal the fact that an execution had just taken place was dispensed with at the moment of Crippen's execution. From then on, as had been happening slowly across Britain, beginning in the last decade of the nineteenth century, no bell was sounded, no black flag was raised, but two notices were placed on the prison door attesting to the fact that the criminal had been executed according to the law. These notices read in part:

DECLARATION OF THE SHERIFF
AND OTHERS

We, the undersigned, hereby declare that Judgement of Death was this Day executed on A——— B——— in His Majesty's Prison of ———in our presence.

Dated this ——— day of ———

CERTIFICATE OF SURGEON

I, ———, the Surgeon of His Majesty's Prison of ——— hereby certify that I this day examined the Body of A ——— B———, on whom the Judgement of Death was this day executed in the said Prison; and that on that Examination I found that the said A ——— B ——— was dead.

Dated this ——— day of ———

(Signature)

The same kind of formal language entered into the backstage arrangements for an execution. Nobody wants to carry out an execution without proper authorization. It is important to keep information of your intentions moving back to the Home Office, lest they forget to inquire into the possibilities for a reduction of the sentence too late to be of practical use to the culprit. Everyone along the chain of command leading to the execution shed wanted notice on paper that what they were about to do was authorized by someone higher up. Even James Berry, the executioner,

This rather fanciful depiction of the end of the celebrated Dr. Crippen in 1910 appeared in a French newspaper. Ellis would never have allowed such a niggardly drop, nor were his clients wrapped and tied as shown.

demanded authorization in writing from the sheriff or prison governor. With all of this passing of paper back and forth, a sort of judicial rite of absolution, one would think that the original order from the judge to execute a criminal, to take a human life, would be long and detailed. Not so. Sir William Blackstone notes as an odd fact that the only warrant the sheriff has for a capital execution is the signature of the judge on the calendar, or a list of all prisoners' names, with the judgements against each of the listed names written by hand in the margin.

> As for a capital felony, it is written opposite to the prisoner's name
> "hanged by the neck," formerly in the days of Latin and abbreviation
> "sus. per col." for "suspendatur per collum."

In 1916, when Sir Roger Casement was condemned to death for treason, World War I was raging, and the Irish nationalists had just been pacified after the Easter Rising. Sir Roger had the bad luck to be caught landing in Ireland from a German submarine. A distinguished and respected diplomat, he had brought honor to Britain when he exposed the horrors of slavery and imperialism in the Belgian Congo and in the Upper Amazon. As Brian Bailey says, Casement was "knighted for his selfless service to oppressed peoples in 1911 and, one might argue, hanged for it five years later."

Ellis cared nothing for any of this. Casement was a toff and a bad 'un. The intricacies of Irish politics were not for him, even though he had "put away" a few Irishmen in his time. It was Casement's height, not his politics, that worried Ellis. The condemned man stood six feet four inches tall but was of slight build. Such a light weight called for a long drop, but the proper length would have had Casement's feet hitting the bottom of the brick-lined pit. The drop was shortened by just enough to take in this factor. Casement walked bravely to the scaffold, looked Ellis in the eye, and willingly aided Ellis's assistant as he pinioned his legs together. Afterwards, Ellis noted on paper: "Casement may have been a traitor, but he died like a soldier."

Another of Ellis's clients on the scaffold was Major Herbert Rowse Armstrong, a lawyer in Hay-on-Wye, on the Welsh border, who was convicted of poisoning his wife with arsenic he claimed to have bought to kill dandelions. Armstrong was another toff. He didn't kick up rough like some of the others Ellis had "put away," but died with dignity while continuing to claim his innocence of the crime. In a recent television version of the story, the major went through the drop wearing his spats.

In June 1922, Ellis was engaged to execute Henry Jacoby, a young pantry boy at a London hotel, who had murdered the widow of a former chairman of the London County Council with a hammer when she awoke to discover him burglarizing her room. Edward Shortt, the Home Secretary, chose to ignore the lad's youth—he was only eighteen at the time of his arrest—his rather feeble mentality, and the jury's strong recommendation of mercy. The *Empire News*, a dozen years later, reported Ellis's recollections of the case:

> I saw t'poor lad the day before his death. He was nobbut a child. It was t'
> most harrowing sight I ever saw in my life. And I 'ad to kill him t'next day.

Ellis's family believed that he had been more shaken by this execution than by the pathetic death of Edith Thompson, to the popular mind a more sympathetic subject.

Edith Jessie Thompson may have been guilty of plotting with her young lover, Freddy Bywaters, to murder her pedestrian, sometimes brutal husband, Percy, or she may have been guilty only of a little adultery and daydreaming. There is good reason to believe that she was as surprised as her husband when young Bywaters fatally stabbed him. Bywaters insisted that it was all his fault at the trial, but the Crown used Edith's amorous letters to Bywaters to suggest that through them Bywaters was directed to strike her husband down. On 11 December 1922, Freddy Bywaters and Edith Thompson were both convicted and sentenced to death. Bywaters was just twenty at the time of his trial; Mrs. Thompson was twenty-seven.

Jack Ellis as usual followed the trial in the papers. He was ready when the letter came requesting his services on two days in early January 1923. Later, it was decided to employ two executioners to hang both Bywaters and Mrs. Thompson on the same day. Ellis was asked to choose between two dates in January, the 5th or the 9th. Brian Bailey was struck by this:

> It is chilling to reflect that a woman's life depended on the hangman's convenience. . . . If he had planned to take his whippets out on the Tuesday, Mrs. Thompson might have been "put away" four days earlier. It might have been a mercy for her.

Bailey explains why in his next sentence:

> In the twenty-nine days between her sentence and her execution, Edith Thompson became a mere shadow of a human being.

Aghast at her fate, she fell apart totally, as perhaps only those with lively imaginations can.

There is a persistent rumor that Ellis almost went on strike rather than execute Mrs. Thompson. Certainly, he had received a number of protests through the mail: "Be a man and don't hang a woman. You know you have to die yourself in a few years. Just think." And: "If you go and pull that lever and take a woman's life, Government ain't to answer for it. God'll send the bill to you."

But he wasn't to be intimidated. He flew from Manchester to Croydon, his first trip in an airplane, which cost as much as a Manchester–London return ticket by rail. It was lucky that he decided not to fly home; the plane crashed on the way back, killing three.

A worried Dr. John Morton, who was both the chief medical officer of Holloway and the prison governor, met Ellis and his two assistants. He explained that the prisoner was in a state bordering on complete collapse. Ellis recommended having a chair handy and giving the prisoner a shot of brandy just before nine o'clock, the scheduled time for the execution. Ellis checked and tested the apparatus, drilled his assistants on what they might expect, and tried to get some sleep. Meanwhile, outside, a vigil was being kept by abolitionists and morbid thrill-seekers through the long cold night.

Two professionals are here seen at work ushering Mary Evans into the next world for poisoning her husband. The year was 1799, and Thomas Rowlandson used the face of the same hangman again in later works. Until late in the nineteenth century, the hands of the condemned were fastened in front.

In the morning, Ellis got on with it as well as he could. Mrs. Thompson was able neither to stand nor to walk. Her head was lolling forward, she couldn't grasp what was happening. She had to be carried to the drop and held in position while Ellis did the "necessary." It would appear that the prisoner had been plied with brandy throughout the night rather than being given one strong shot just before the last walk.

No one who was there, who saw the scene in Holloway's execution shed that January morning, was ever able to forget it. Brian Bailey mentions, among others, Mr. Beverley Baxter, M.P., speaking in the House of Commons on 14 April 1948, who said:

> Two of the warders who had taken part in that execution came to my
> office, and their faces were not human. I can assure you, Sir, they were
> like people out of another world. Edith Thompson had disintegrated as a
> human being on her way to the gallows, and yet somehow they had to get
> her there. . . . Those two warders . . . said to me, 'Use your influence;
> never again must a woman be hanged.'

Not only was this execution an event which altered the lives of most of the people who were closely associated with it, it provided fresh and sensational material for the abolitionist movement. This execution was a backward step in the evolution of enlightened thought on the question of capital punishment. Since 1843, no woman had been executed in Britain for a crime committed by a man. It set reform back eighty years.

Ellis did not resign his job after hanging Edith Thompson. Nor did he after hanging Mrs. Susan Newell in Glasgow's Duke Street Prison nine months later. Mrs. Newell was as stalwart as Mrs. Thompson had been a broken reed. She was a child-murderer, and of doubtful sanity. Still, she met the hangman's eyes with a steady look of her own, then walked unflinchingly to the drop, where she argued with Ellis about wearing the traditional white hood.

When he was not running hither and yon across Britain and over to Ireland, Ellis worked both for himself and for his father at the barber's trade. Barbering seems to have attracted a constant stream of morbid gawkers and sensation-seekers as well as put him at the beck and call of anyone who wanted a short back and sides. Later, he became for a time landlord of a pub, the Jolly Butcher in Middleton, where he put both his health and the family fortune in the hazard.

When asked once by a friendly reporter, S. J. Coe, about how one of his clients had behaved, Ellis brushed his huge mustache, banged his pipe against the hob, and told all: "Oh, aw reet," he said, "tha knows." One would have to say that Ellis lacked eloquence. Still he was approached by Thomson's *Weekly News* for his memoirs. They began appearing weekly, with the title "Secrets of My Life Revealed," in April 1924. Under the care of his editors, his eloquence improves:

> Conversations cease suddenly when I am about, and I can feel people
> eyeing me as if I am some exhibit in the chamber of horrors. They will
> avoid shaking hands with me when they are introduced—they shudder at
> the idea of grasping the hand that has pinioned murderers and worked
> the gallows lever. Socially it is a bad business being a hangman.

In March 1924, five months after he had dispatched Susan Newell, Ellis sent in his papers and resigned from the service. After one more execution, in Leeds, he put his pinions and white cap away. He had executed 203 men and women in twenty-three years, serving a term as long as the almost legendary Jack Ketch himself.

It was at this time, a year and a half after Mrs. Thompson's execution, that Ellis first tried to commit suicide. He bungled an attempt to put a bullet in his head after a sleepless night of drinking. When his fractured jaw was still bandaged, he appeared before a magistrate, who said: "I am sorry to see you here, Ellis. I have known you for a long time. If your aim had been as true as some of the drops you have given, it would have been a bad job for you."

He bound Ellis over to keep the peace for a year and to stay away from drink and thoughts of suicide. Ellis may have been bothered by the magistrate's reference to *some* of his drops being true. His history on the scaffold does not contain any of the calamities of James Berry, William Marwood, or William Calcraft. Ellis was a first-rate hangman, even though his rival Thomas Pierrepoint said of him to his nephew, Albert: "Bloody hell, Ellis has tried to commit suicide! He should have done it bloody years ago. It was impossible to work with him."

Ellis did not give up strong drink, although his health continued to worry his family. He appeared once again on the scaffold pinioning and noosing a victim, but this last time was on a public stage in a play about Charlie Peace.

Depressed and in bad health, consoled by drink, undermined by too much of it, oppressed by memories, Ellis again tried to take his life in September 1932. It was nine years since his first attempt. This time he used a cut-throat razor and did a professional job on himself. He was fifty-eight years of age at the time of his death. "Suicide while of unsound mind" was the verdict of the coroner's jury.

From what we know of his record, we would have to agree with the Prison Commissioner who said that Ellis "was one of the coolest and most self-possessed hangmen ever known." But his rivals on the scaffold, like Tom Pierrepoint, already quoted above, and the younger Billington, saw a bumbling tangle of nerves whenever Jack Ellis was on a job. Billington wondered how he had stuck it for so long, "being so nervous and anxious about everything going OK." If Calcraft was a bungler, Marwood an innovator, Berry a master craftsman, Ellis might well be termed a perfectionist.

The last dynasty of British hangmen was ushered in by Henry Pierrepoint. Like most of his fellows, he was born in the Industrial Midlands. The Pierrepoints were of Huguenot stock, who probably escaped religious persecution in France after the revocation of the Edict of Nantes in 1685, and established themselves in the textile trades. Henry, who was usually called

Harry, was born in the Yorkshire village of Clayton, on the west side of Bradford. As one of the older males in a large family, his schooling ended early and he found himself first in a worsteds mill and then in a cartage business. Less demonstrative than his older brother, Tom, Harry was the first of the brothers to apply to the Home Office to have his name added to the list of approved executioners and their assistants.

> Let me tell you how I came to take up this work. It was through reading about the appointment of Mr James Berry as executioner and the carrying out of his first job in London that I got the idea of going in for it myself. I was only a boy then. . . ."That's just the sort of job I should like myself," . . . and from that day forward I had my mind set on becoming an executioner.
>
> No, I hadn't any repugnance to the idea at all, though I saw it would be useless to say anything at home about it. Perhaps the notion of seeing so many different towns had something to do with my desire, for I was very fond of travel.

When Harry first called at the big front door of Strangeways Prison in Manchester to be interviewed, he was too shy to say why he had come. After a misunderstanding—they thought he was applying to become a warder—he was sent down to Newgate for two weeks of training. He first assisted James Billington at Newgate in 1901. When the prison doctor felt his pulse afterwards, he found it steady. According to his son, Albert, the doctor said, "You'll do."

Thereafter, when his name had been added to the list, he assisted all of the Billingtons and acted as principal hangman once or twice. Later, he wrote, "I am very ambitious for work. I love my work on the scaffold." Harry was "Number One" on the list from around 1905 to 1910, when he was ousted by Jack Ellis, who appeared at that time to be more discreet about his office, and probably was in the early days. Harry was second choice after that and learned to hate Ellis: "If I ever meet Ellis, I'll kill him—it doesn't matter if it is in church."

Apart from holding strong feelings about his rival, Harry Pierrepoint was an amiable tradesman. He was used to doing hard work all his life, and enjoyed the company of other chaps like himself in the taproom of the Clogger's Arms in Huddersfield, where he lived for some years. Here he earned a reputation as a master storyteller, a skill which kept him in drink and bad company all of his days. At home he neither drank nor played cards. The center of his life was a piano with a rack full of sentimental ballads and religious carols and hymns. He enjoyed the celebrity that attached itself to him, liked walking to the head of the queue, being on first-name terms with stationmasters, railway conductors, and policemen.

He took his work on the scaffold seriously, however, and encouraged brother Tom, Harry's senior by six years, to send his name in to be put on the list. Before Tom went to London to do his training, Harry had shown him the ropes in the barn, so that he arrived in London already well rehearsed.

Harry, after he retired, twice sold his memoirs to the papers. First, in 1916 to Thomson's *Weekly News*, with a circulation of just over half a million, and later in 1922, in a reworked form, to *Reynolds News*. Like those of Jack Ellis and James Berry before him, these stories for the penny press brought in needed revenue. In these memoirs, he recorded how, as an assistant, he had been given the spare condemned cell next to the French murderer Marcel Faugeron at Newgate, and how he watched him through the spy hole as he counted the strokes of the famous bell of St. Sepulchre's without Newgate, which had been tolling the knell of criminals since the days of Tyburn. Every hour, the prisoner, who didn't speak English, counted off the last hours of his life on his fingers, trying to make human contact with his deathwatch warders.

"The word 'hangman,'" he wrote, or was helped to write by the staff of Thomson's *Weekly News*, the same paper that published Ellis's memoirs,

> almost invariably invokes a shiver from over-sensitive persons. They imagine him a morose, bloodthirsty sort of villain who takes a fellow creature's life in cold blood, and they think of him as haunted by the spectres of his victims.
>
> Well, I have executed over a hundred persons. But I've never seen a ghost yet. And as for the "bloodthirsty" stigma—well, I have a charming wife and a family of young children, and I would refer you to them as to whether I am anything in the way of a brutal villain.

During his first fifteen months as executioner, Harry Pierrepoint hanged fifteen people. Sometimes he acted as the assistant, who fastens a strap about the legs of the prisoner and then gets out of the way as fast as he can, and sometimes he acted as the executioner, who did all the rest. "The second appointment I got after joining the prison service," he recalled in his memoirs, "was as head executioner."

As an innovator, Harry Pierrepoint added little to the craft of instant death. He contributed a special pinioning strap to be used on a one-armed

Hangmen as a breed were tinkerers. They all tried to improve on the craft as they found it. Since some were originally shoemakers, they worked out pinioning straps to keep the hands and feet of their victims out of the way. Here Henry Pierrepoint models his own invention, a pinioning strap for a one-armed man.

client, and had his picture taken wearing it. More useful, he brought his older brother, Tom, into the "family business" and Tom remained on the list for the next forty years.

Tom was always a dependable, careful craftsman. There were never any complaints about his drops or about him talking too much in the pub afterwards. Unlike Harry, Tom left no memoirs behind him. But like his brother, he kept an "execution book" in which he noted the names, height, and weight of each of his clients in the order he encountered them, along with the drops he gave, and the result of the post-mortem findings. These books were to form a legacy for young Albert, when he came along in his turn. His father's experience and that of his Uncle Tom formed a basis upon which he was able to build his own record. Should capital punishment ever be re-established in Britain, the government will begin a search for the "execution books" of the Pierrepoint family. They contain the distillation of more than half a century of experience.

Uncle Tom was a steadier and less talkative fellow than his brother. There lies about him a calm, sometimes puritanical, side that is engaging. "If you can't do it without whisky, don't do it at all." With that go Albert's recollections of the way his uncle slipped a boiled sweet or peppermint into his mouth just before he walked into the condemned cell to take charge of his prisoner. The very idea of a sweet, pleasant sensation in the mouth being used to steady nerves is almost charming. Did Uncle Tom share his sweets? Pass the bag around? It might have had a better effect than the passing of the flask among the official party both beforehand and afterwards.

Tom continued to run a carrier business in addition to his regular appearances as hangman. In time he became a well-known figure, but that was because his was a familiar face at the racetrack, where he worked as a bookie.

On 14 August 1907, Harry and Tom dispatched Rhoda Willis, who was also known as Mrs. Leslie James, in Cardiff. The Pierrepoints were asked to do the job because it was known at the Home Office that John Ellis had expressed a reluctance to execute women, and there were rumors that if he were asked to execute Rhoda Willis, he would go on strike. By calling upon the Pierrepoints, the Home Office cleverly dodged the issue. The Home Office was of all things practical. There was nothing sentimental about it: Rhoda Willis was hanged on her birthday.

When Ellis retired in 1924, Tom Pierrepoint was moved to the top of the list, where he served the Home Office steadily and quietly, in the best tradition of the service, until he was urged to retire in 1943. Although his mobility was retarded by arthritis, at seventy-three he was still raring to go on "topping" his fellow man, but at last, reluctantly, he resigned, leaving the "Number One" job open for "Our Albert." Uncle Tom lived on until 1954, when he died at a ripe old age for a hangman, eighty-five.

Tom's contribution to the craft was a rubber washer, which replaced the leather one invented by William Marwood two or three decades earlier. This circular piece of rubber was cut so that it held the rope with a claw-like grip. It secured the brass ring in place after the hangman made his final adjustment.

Meanwhile, "Our Albert" had been getting along well. He was still a youngster when he learned what his legacy was to be. He was traveling with his father, Harry, one day when he noticed a placard outside a newspaper shop in a station. There was a picture of his father and the headline:

MY TEN YEARS' EXPERIENCES
BY HENRY A. PIERREPOINT
RETIRED EXECUTIONER

Albert was struck first by the decline in his father's health, as shown in the picture. The second shock, he confesses, wasn't altogether a surprise. When his father returned from the station pub to find his son a moment or two later, he introduced him to his friend the stationmaster, saying that Albert would one day step into his shoes as the official executioner.

This Albert Pierrepoint recalled happening before he had gone into long trousers. Harry died at half his older brother's age. The cause of his death has proved impossible to discover. Nobody has been able to find a death certificate.

Albert Pierrepoint, like Mark Twain, exaggerated some things, but in the main, in his autobiography, he told the truth. He is coy about naming names, so one has to do a little digging to identify which of his victims he is talking about at a given moment. He also fails to own up to how many people he executed in his career; while his list wasn't as long as some, it was aided and abetted by World War II, which provided the odd capital court martial, and then batches of spies and war criminals in a rush after 1945. For a while, it was like the old days at Newgate, before the Debtors' Door, when "Our Albert" was invited abroad to dispatch some two hundred war criminals. In Britain alone, he hanged fifteen spies, including William Joyce (Lord Haw-Haw) and John Amory. But while the total numbers might suggest a reversion to an earlier century, Albert never hanged even concentration camp butchers in batches; he worked out a careful schedule, never with more than two on the drop at a time. He worked hard, killing seventeen a day on two occasions and twenty-seven on another. And each of his clients had his or her own drop carefully worked out ahead of time. When two shared a drop, the names were written in chalk under the right rope, so that there would be no mistakes.

These war criminals included notorious doctors, like Rohde, convicted of giving lethal injections to female prisoners in concentration camps, and other Nazis condemned for shooting Allied airmen who had escaped from a prison camp. He even hanged two executioners who plied their trade in extermination camps.

Albert found these concentrated groups of executions a grueling ordeal, leaving him both physically and mentally exhausted, although he says they were not morally repugnant to him. It was his insistence of precision in the details that tired him.

In contrast to Albert's meticulous work, the American executioner Master Sergeant John C. Woods of the U.S. Army, who was given the responsibility of hanging the major groups of war criminals after the Nuremberg trials, in October 1946, made a botch of it. They died, of course, but some took as long as twenty minutes in agony doing it. A true democrat, he gave each of the Nazis the same short five-foot drop. He worked fast, in front of many official witnesses, using three U.S. Army scaffolds in a Nuremberg gymnasium. Each was fitted with a tiny single-leafed trapdoor, which meant that those who did not fall clear of the sides slammed into them on the way through. Herman Goering, as is well known, bit into a poison pellet concealed in a pipe or removed from a scar in his belly—both stories were current at the time—minutes before he was scheduled to mount the steps of the gallows. After Field Marshall Keitel, Ribbentrop, Jodl, Rosenberg, Frick, Streicher, and the others had been executed, it was decided by the authorities in charge of the execution detail to hang Goering as well, even though he was dead. Woods, the hangman, was offered a very large sum of money for the rope that had hanged Ribbentrop, which he was not allowed to accept. After photographs were taken of the cut-down bodies, they were cremated and the ashes dumped into the Ludwigs Kanal. Woods resigned his position as hangman shortly after that, but the scaffolds went on to be used for other

Standing on a ladder leaning against the single-post gallows, the hangman adjusts a short rope around his victim's neck. This settling of accounts with wartime Nazi rulers took place in a Budapest public square in March 1946.

war criminals big and small. When their work in Europe was done, at least one of these collapsible and portable scaffolds ended up in South Africa, where it continued in service long after most of the scaffolds in the world had been demolished.

On Friday, 13 December 1945, Albert executed Josef Kramer, the notorious "Beast of Belsen," and twelve other guards from Belsen concentration camp. The setting for their taking-off was the storybook Pied Piper town of Hameln in Germany. The condemned were under British authority, and confined in the Hameln Gaol, in the smallest cells Albert had ever seen. He worked out a schedule so that the three women in the group would be hanged separately, one at a time, to spare them the waiting, and the ten men in five groups of two. The day before the execution, in order to get the data for his calculations, Albert had each of the prisoners brought out of his or her cell to be weighed and measured. The sinister import of this ritual was not lost upon the former guards and commandant. For many years after this memorable day of death, Albert received an annual Christmas envelope with a five-pound note inside. The first came with a slip of paper upon which was written the word "BELSEN."

Early in 1946, Albert and his wife, Anne, took over the operation of a public house with the curious name of Help The Poor Struggler, at Hollinwood, between Oldham and Manchester. This ended his long association with the grocery trade, which he had been involved in since leaving school at thirteen. He loved the liveliness of the pub because there was a bluff, hearty, good-humored side to Albert Pierrepoint that reveled in the brash good company of friends. The pub was a great local success, as was Anne, who made a popular if unusual hostess, since she didn't drink.

Albert acknowledges that the press helped to make the pub's name, but he insists that he and his regulars discouraged any customers whose interest in him was more morbid than social.

One customer, James Henry Corbitt, a toolmaker with a golden pub-tenor voice, used to still the taproom with his rendition of "Danny Boy." Albert himself used to join him in the singing of the second verse. Corbitt became a regular, and he and Albert used to greet each other with a catch phrase of the time: he'd say "Hallo, Tosh" and Albert would reply, "Hallo, Tish, how are you?" One Saturday night, after leaving the Struggler, Corbitt strangled his girlfriend and wrote "WHORE" on her forehead in indelible pencil. Three months after that, Albert visited Strangeways Prison professionally.

That night one of the death-watch officers had a word with me: "Albert, I've got a queer sort of request to make. He keeps insisting that he knows you. . . . He says you had a nick-name for him. He keeps saying 'I wonder if Albert will let on that he remembers me—it would be easier for me.' . . ."

At twenty seconds to nine next morning I went into the death cell. He seemed under a great strain, but I did not see stark fear in his eyes, only a more childlike worry . . .

"Hallo, Tosh," he said not very confidently.

"Hallo, Tish," I said. "How are you?" I was not effusive, just gave the casual warmth of my nightly greeting from behind the bar.

The man relaxed. Then he breathed in so cheerfully, as if he were greeting a bright morning, that he brought his shoulders forward and his arms high in front of him, and if he had wanted to make trouble I should have needed two men on him. But I gently took his arms in their flow and guided them behind his back, and strapped them in an instant and in his ear, "Come on, Tish old chap."

He went lightly to the scaffold. I would say that he ran. He was on the drop before I turned around, and he lifted the noose with the crown of his head and tried to get his head inside it, so anxious to please, but of course it was wrong. I took off the noose and I put on the cap and did the right things, for the drop fell and the rope stayed still.

After that, Albert felt a pang whenever someone struck up "Danny Boy" in the Struggler. He had felt kinship with a murderer, had sung a duet with him, and had sent him out of this world with as much compassion as he could.

James Henry Corbitt's isn't one of the famous names that comes to mind when Albert Pierrepoint is being discussed. What about the pair from 10 Rillington Place, Timothy Evans and John Reginald Christie? First one and then the other was executed for sensational murders at that Notting Hill Gate address. Of Evans, Pierrepoint in his autobiography only indicates that his hanging furnished statistical data being collected at Pentonville Prison by the Coroner of the Northern District of London. The fact that he had hanged an innocent man became clear only when Christie was condemned for other murders at the same address: a highly unlikely coincidence that two sexually driven stranglers of women should reside at that one address. What does he say about John Reginald Christie, the real killer? What does he say, for that matter, about young Derek Bentley, who was in police custody when his underage accomplice shot and killed a policeman? What does he say about the actual murderer, who

Ruth Ellis, the last woman to hang in Britain, is pictured here with David Blakely, her soon-to-be-murdered lover, in the bar at the "Little Club" in London, which she managed.

escaped the rope because of his youth? And what of the near legendary Ruth Ellis, the last woman hanged in Britain?

Concerning Derek Bentley, he only denies untrue statements that have been made about the execution by others. No, he didn't shake hands with the lad beforehand; no, Bentley did not cry on his way to the drop; no again, Albert did not make notes about the execution, nor did he have to be urged by the prison governor to get on with the job. Albert always seizes the moral high ground from anyone trying to put him on the spot.

> I cannot be provoked into giving the witnessed details which would disprove these tales, but I state unequivocally that they are false.

In talking about Ruth Ellis, Albert takes on the shirty tone again:

> ... When I left Holloway after the execution of Ruth Ellis, the prison was almost besieged by a storming mob. I needed police protection to get me through. I knew that I would have walked out of Strangeways [where a forty-year-old harridan had just been reprieved] a week earlier into an empty street. At Euston Station a crowd of newspapermen were awaiting me. I shielded my face from the cameras as I ran for my train. One young reporter jogged alongside me asking "How did it feel to hang a woman, Mr Pierrepoint?" I did not answer. But I could have asked: "Why weren't you waiting to ask me that question last year, sonny? Wasn't Mrs Christofi a woman too?"

Mrs. Christofi was a Cypriot grandmother who had been dispatched with little press comment after being convicted of murdering her daughter-in-law. Here again Albert's reticence is waved at the reader like a checkered flag. His tone becomes frosty, as though he wasn't a human being, but a force of nature, an act of God. It is wise to remember that he kept a personal "hanging book" in which he recorded the details of weights and

A heavy weight pulls the single-flap trapdoor out of harm's way as doctors check the faltering pulse of Charles Julius Guiteau, who shot President James A. Garfield in 1881. The assassin was given a generous drop somewhat in excess of his own height.

drops and whether or not he had used a calf leather pinion strap that he had had specially made. He used this strap on occasions of more than routine interest for him. There may have been practical reasons for this, but I mention it as tending to prove that Albert was more than an automaton, a functionary totally in the hands of his superiors. He took a human interest in his work. He even played favorites.

When he appeared before the Royal Commission on Capital Punishment, which was started in 1949, he tried to get out of answering a question about how many executions he had actually conducted. He knew that what he said facing a parliamentary committee in camera would eventually become part of a published report. He ducked the question finally, after some negotiating that was off the record, by admitting that he had executed "some hundreds." Elsewhere, to add authority to what he was about to say, he boasted that he had killed more people, except by an act of war, than anyone living. He appears to have been ambivalent about the matter, both proud and ashamed at the same time. When he could, of course, he blamed the Home Office for holding him to the Official Secrets Act. But there is some doubt about this. Official Secrets was made the whipping boy for what was inconvenient to say. The Royal Commission had been set up under the Home Office, after all.

In February 1956, Albert resigned from the list. He wrote out a resignation and sent it to the Prison Commissioners. Shortly after this, the Prison Commissioners asked him to reconsider his decision, which he declined to do.

Pierrepoint approaches the conclusion of his autobiography with the following observations:

> During my twenty-five years as executioner, I believed with all my heart that I was carrying out a public duty. I conducted each execution with great care and a clear conscience. I never allowed myself to get involved with the death penalty controversy.
>
> I now sincerely hope that no man is ever called upon to carry out an execution in my country. . . .
>
> I have seen prison officers faint on the scaffold, strong men weep, and women prison officers sobbing helplessly. I have known prison doctors who could not examine the body after execution because the beat of their own heart was obliterating anything they could distinguish.
>
> I have felt overpowering sorrow for the victims of crime, for little children murdered, for the families of all concerned, for the special worry which policemen's wives always suffer and for the tragic occasions when it is justified. Yet I have had many friends in the police and in the prison service who also feel very strongly against capital punishment.

CHAPTER SEVEN

Off with His Head

"To sit in solemn silence in a dull, dark dock,
In a pestilential prison with a life-long lock,
Awaiting the sensation of a short, sharp shock,
From a cheap and chippy chopper on a big black block!"
—W. S. GILBERT, *THE MIKADO*

"Off with his head—so much for Buckingham."
—SHAKESPEARE, ALTERED BY COLLEY CIBBER

Decapitation is one of the oldest forms of capital punishment, probably suggested more by the shape of the human body than by specific knowledge of the functions of the spine and brain. William the Conqueror brought the practice with him to England from Normandy. He used it sparingly, the first to suffer being Waltheof, Earl of Northumberland, in 1076, ten years after the Battle of Hastings.

From the first, beheading was reserved for offenders of rank. People of higher rank were executed before those of lesser standing. Even the victims of the scaffold followed protocol and precedence. No one was permitted to address the populace wearing his hat. And don't forget to tip the headsman and to forgive him when he asks it of you.

For some reason, or whim, rather, it has always been the belief in western Europe that beheading was more honorable than hanging or strangulation. Asians thought differently. It was considered a singular disgrace in China and Japan to be decapitated.

Well done, whether by ax, sword, or even by machine, beheading was quicker than hanging. But a lot of it was butchery. In Britain, France, and Germany, decapitation became the death of convicted felons and traitors who happened to belong in the top tiers of society. Hanging was reserved for other ranks and riff-raff.

The Greeks and Romans believed that decapitation was the way to go when other exits were closed. Romans, who were good at Latin, called it *decollatio* or *capitis amputatio*. Greeks also used poisons, such as hemlock for Socrates, and rope for disloyal handmaidens. The Roman orator Cicero was beheaded in transit in a litter. He simply leaned his head out and it was struck off when his pursuers caught up to him. Caligula, according to Suetonius, kept a skilled headsman handy and let him try his skills with the short Roman sword on prisoners picked out at random from the prisons.

When Henry VIII wished to be rid of his once-prized queen, Anne Boleyn, in 1536, he sent to Calais, still then an English possession, for a headsman. Some say that he came from St. Omer, but the recent biographer of Henry's famous second queen, E. W. Ives, discounts this. There is another story that Henry sent two English observers to watch Rombaud, the headsman, in action before inviting him to cross the Channel. For his audition piece, Rombaud put two felons to death with the same mighty sweep of his broadsword. Naturally, when both heads tumbled to the scaffold floor together, he was given the commission.

Anne Boleyn had been found guilty of high treason. What was adultery in common folk was high treason in princes. It was Henry's option to have her burned at the stake or beheaded. By having her burned, Henry would be giving credence to rumors of witchcraft which followed his unpopular consort. So, Henry chose to have her beheaded with a sword. Let her kneel with her head raised, not bow her neck to the block where other necks had stretched before. It may have been a last kindness, but Henry's known character stands in the doorway blocking the light of that suggestion.

According to David Hume's *The History of England*, Anne thought that things would go better for her daughter, Elizabeth, if her mother went to the scaffold without complaint, full of "her usual serenity and even with cheerfulness."

> "The executioner," she said to the lieutenant [of the Tower], "is, I hear, very expert; and my neck is very slender:" upon which she grasped it in her hand, and smiled.

Isaac D'Israeli, in his *Curiosities of Literature*, records a curious circumstance that occurred during this execution.

> . . . Anne Bullen, being upon the scaffold, would not consent to have her eyes covered with a bandage . . . [T]he executioner could not bear their tender and mild glances; fearful of missing his aim, he was obliged to invent an expedient to behead the queen. He drew off his shoes, and approached her silently; while he was at her left hand, another person advanced at her right, who made a great noise in walking, so that this circumstance drawing the attention of Anne, she turned her face from the executioner, who was enabled by this artifice to strike the fatal blow without being disarmed by the spirit which shone in the eyes of the lovely Anne Bullen.

Charles I, of England, submits his neck to a very low block on a scaffold outside Inigo Jones's Banqueting Hall in Whitehall. The headsman in this contemporary woodcut is "Young Gregory" Brandon.

Anne was beheaded on Tower Green rather than on Tower Hill, the usual and more public place of execution. Henry's bounty was clearly overflowing. Later on, with Queen Catherine Howard, Henry wasn't so particular; the ordinary block-and-resident headsman of the Tower would do, and by the time of Queen Marie Antoinette in France, familiarity breeding contempt as usual, a machine was good enough for her royal neck as well as for King Louis's.

Just as the ax had more honor in it than the ladder and noose, so was the sword prized above the ax and block. A nobleman in France or Germany would kneel or stand, his arms and hands quite free of pinions of any kind, while the headsman wielded his long, heavy, two-handed sword in the air. In France, they also used the block as well, but with a sword, rather than an ax.

In continental Europe, beheading was often a gift awarded to a culprit as a favor for rank or special pleading, when being broken on the wheel was what the sentence should have been. To be condemned to the wheel was the most dreaded sentence for crime. The victim was either tied to a wheel and beaten to death with an iron bar, or secured to timbers on the ground and repeatedly clubbed with a great cart wheel until death intervened. If ever the punishment of death filled the hearts of criminals with terror, this sentence did above all others, with perhaps the exception of being boiled to death. It was a long and lingering way to die as one limb after another was shattered. The release of death came only when the chest and ribs were broken, sometimes many minutes after the first crushing blows.

Luckily, breaking on the wheel never caught on in Britain, although the stake and a whole torture chamber of other things did. The stake often conveyed a religious message and was used in cases of witchcraft and wizardry as well as for heresy. It was also the punishment meted out for "petty treason," which was what they called the murder of husbands by their wives. They didn't have a name or special penalty for husbands who did away with their spouses. High treason, of course, as opposed to petty, or petit, treason, was a state crime and almost always carried the death penalty. Anything that displeased Henry VIII was high treason. His condemnation of Margaret, Countess of Salisbury, is a classic case of judicial murder. She was the daughter of George, Duke of Clarence—he of the malmsey-butt in *Richard III*. The countess led the headsman a merry chase around the scaffold before he finally brought her down with multiple, savage, inexpert blows. Her crime was in being a leftover from the discredited Yorkist line.

The names of very few headsmen have come down to us. We know that they were kept busy from medieval times through the Tudors and Stuarts, but while they were all more or less proficient in their work, few insinuated their names into history. Cratwell, who was passed over for a foreigner in the case of Anne Boleyn, was himself hanged two years later for stealing. Perhaps his reputation and self-esteem never recovered. Typical of most headsmen of his time, Cratwell probably came out of the criminal classes and descended back into them. Often criminals were respited from

Breaking with a wheel was a variation on the theme of breaking on the wheel. Here the victim is tied down on what looks like steps, or at any rate pieces of wood. The executioner uses a cartwheel to break one limb after another. The final blow is aimed at the ribcage, which quickly brings on unconsciousness and death. The bravest victims began counting the blows.

part or all of their sentences on the condition that they take up the rope and ax themselves. Shakespeare in *Measure for Measure* saves Pompey from his jail-term, but the executioner feels demeaned to have a bawd, or pimp, as an assistant:

> Abhorson: A bawd, sir? Fie upon him! He will discredit our mystery
> [skilled trade].
> Provost: Go to, sir, you weigh equally. A feather will turn the scale.

So, in Shakespeare's time, a pimp and an executioner were of roughly equal social standing. At that time as well, the terms "headsman" and "hangman" were interchangeable. The same villain had to hang as well as decapitate. He also had to be able to brand, nip, flog, burn, rack, gibbet, disembowel, and quarter.

Executioners often were not paid for their services by the sheriff, but given a place to live in, rather the way tenant farmers may claim houses on a large estate. There were perks, of course. Traditionally, the executioner could claim everything the condemned person wore to the scaffold, and he was often presented with a bag of money by his client at the moment of parting just to make sure that his full attention was on his work. Sometimes, the gratuity was divided: half of it delivered by the victim in advance, the rest by a friend of the condemned after the work was accomplished satisfactorily.

Gregory Brandon served as executioner for more than thirty years, and used the term "Esquire" after his name, as did his son, who had the extra distinction of cutting off the head of Charles I. Richard Brandon, usually called "Young Gregory," executed Lord Stafford (May 1641) and Archbishop Laud (10 January 1644–45). Although he swore, when the King was condemned, that he would never raise a hand against him, on 30 January 1649, he was "fetched out of bed by a troup of horse" and marched to the scaffold to do his duty. He received thirty pounds for the job as well as a pomander, a clove-studded orange, from the royal pocket.

The headsman who took off the head of Mary, Queen of Scots, was paid ten pounds. Called Bull, he had to be disguised as a servant when they smuggled him into Fotheringay Castle in 1587. Secretary of State Sir Francis Walsingham wanted no word of Bull's presence to reach the ear of Queen Elizabeth, who, with reluctance, had signed Mary's death warrant. Charles Dickens, who well knew how to tug at the cords of sentiment, describes the Queen's last moments in this way in his *A Child's History of England*:

Blindfolded, Lady Jane Grey (1537–54) gropes for the block on Tower Green. Her husband had lost his head minutes earlier on Tower Hill, which was less private.

. . . When her head and neck were uncovered by the executioners, she said that she was not used to be so undressed by such hands, or before so much company. Finally, one of her women fastened a cloth over her face, and she laid her neck upon the block, and repeated more than once in Latin, "Into thy hands, O Lord, I commend my spirit!" Some say her head was struck off at two blows, some say in three. However that be, when it was held up, streaming with blood, the real hair beneath the false hair she had long worn was seen to be as grey as that of a woman of seventy, though she was at that time only in her forty-sixth year. All her beauty was gone.

But she was beautiful enough to her little dog, who cowered under her dress, frightened, when she went upon the scaffold, and who lay down beside her headless body when all her earthly sorrows were over.

Victorian parents and children alike treasured this picture of the death of the Scottish queen. (Many paintings have tried to catch the poignancy of the moment. Few suggest that the queen was six feet tall.) Indeed, our Victorian ancestors savored last moments of kings and queens. They doted on pictures of ritual slaughter, of tearful partings, of brave walks to the scaffold. Painters provided glimpses of the gory ends of the powerful and famous. Death, violent death, undeserved, heroic, untimely; the Victorians, they loved it!

When one hears the words "Off with his head!" examples of bravery on the scaffold spring to mind: Sir Thomas More's quip to his attendant, "See me safe up [the rickety steps of the scaffold]. For my coming down, I can shift for myself." When the headsman begged forgiveness for the fatal act he was about to perform, More kissed him, saying, "Thou art to do me the greatest benefit that I can receive. Pluck up thy spirit, man, and be not afraid to do thine office. My neck is very short. Take heed therefore that thou strike not awry for saving thine honesty." He then arranged his head on the block after covering his own eyes, and, moving his beard off the block, said, "Pity that thou should be cut," he mused, "that has not committed treason."

In those days, one could be well studied for one's death. In 1601, Sir Walter Raleigh had watched his old rival, the Earl of Essex, mount the scaffold. Two years later, he mounted it himself, prepared to meet his fate, but was spared within sight of the block. His brush with death seems to have stimulated literary activity. Sir Walter was kept waiting in the Tower from 1603 to 1618, long enough to write his *History of the World* before the death he owed was collected. He asked the executioner to show him the ax, and when the headsman hesitated, Raleigh said, "Dost thou think I am afraid of it?" He tried the edge on his thumb before returning it to the headsman. "This is sharp medicine," he said, "but it will cure all diseases." Shortly, the headsman sent him on his way, with his scallop-shell of quiet and his staff of faith, with two blows.

> Of death and judgment, heaven and hell,
> Who oft doth think must needs die well.

While a quick end on the block was the fate of high state prisoners guilty of treason, other traitors were not so lucky. For them the dread sentence of the law read:

> That you and each of you, be taken to the place from whence you came, and from thence be drawn on a hurdle to the place of execution, where you shall be hanged by the neck, not till you are dead; that you be severally taken down, while yet alive, and your bowels be taken out and burnt before your faces—that your heads be then cut off, and your bodies cut in four quarters, to be at the King's disposal. And God Almighty have mercy on your souls.

Until as late as the execution of the Cato Street Conspirators in 1820, shown here, condemned traitors in England were "hanged, drawn, and quartered." Anthony Burgess calls this "the apotheosis of the executioner's art." This old print shows the assistant executioner holding one of the heads and shouting, "Behold the head of a traitor!" to the unseen crowd, according to long-standing practice.

If you had ever wondered exactly what being hanged, drawn, and quartered meant, this is the doom that was handed down. This ghastly sentence was first uttered in the reign of Edward III in the fourteenth century, although a form of it was known as early as 1283, when David, the last native Prince of Wales, was executed at Shrewsbury. Frightful as this form of execution was, it was initiated in brutal times, when a third of the British population was perishing from the Black Death and wars in France and Scotland raged endlessly. The truly shocking thing about it is the fact that it remained the sentence of the law for well over the next five hundred years. It was not until the Cato Street Conspiracy, a plot to assassinate the whole cabinet at dinner, in 1820, that this form of execution was done away with, and that under protest.

In mitigation, it should be said that executioners used to make sure that their victims were more than half-hanged so that they would be insensible to the further indignities planned for them.

In France the practice of drawing and quartering was even more terrible than across the Channel. Although it was reserved almost exclusively

Parricide is not only the murder of a parent, but also the assassination of a sacred personage, such as a king. Here, in 1610, after undergoing terrible tortures, François Ravaillac is torn apart by four horses for stabbing to death France's Henri IV.

for regicides and would-be regicides, its savagery can hardly be paralleled until modern warfare rewrote the book on slaughter. Robert François Damiens, who attempted to murder Louis XV, was treated with boiling pitch and molten lead. Red-hot pincers were applied all over his body by the sweating executioners, who then fastened each of his limbs to a horse and urged the four to pull in four different directions. After pulling for a long time, the more scientifically minded of the observers could see that this was going nowhere, and so informed the executioners, who then made such adjustments in the body of the victim as would enable the horses to do their duty by the state. François Ravaillac, the large, red-headed fanatic, the assassin of Henri IV, had been subjected to much the same treatment in 1610. In this case, one of the horses fainted.

George Selwyn (1717–1791), a friend of Horace Walpole's, attended the execution of Damiens in Paris, and thrust himself so far to the front that he was asked whether he was one of the executioners. He replied that he did not have that honor, he was only an amateur. Selwyn, who was otherwise a man of culture and wit, became known as a collector of these morbid spectacles, and hated ever to miss a hanging. When rebuked for going to see Lord Lovat's head cut off, he replied that he had made up for it by calling at the undertaker's to see it sewn on again. One ailing nobleman who was familiar with Selwyn's morbid preoccupations remarked that if he, the nobleman, survived his present illness, he would be very happy to see Selwyn, and if he didn't, Selwyn would be happy to see him.

In 1773 a Don Cossack, Emelian Pugachev, a one-time soldier, led an unsuccessful insurrection against the rule of Catherine the Great of Russia. Pugachev was brought to Moscow in an iron cage and later drawn and quartered after the French style, with horses pulling him to the cardinal points of the compass. Just as the Eastern Europeans were being influenced by French ideas in cuisine, literature, and government, they also imitated their western neighbor in making an example of a traitor. It must have seemed to them very up-to-date.

In France the gallows never fired the popular imagination as it did in England. The image of the gallows is outflanked by that of the wheel, the sword and, preeminently, the guillotine. The standing gallows of Montfaucon could accommodate sixty clients at a time, and was a permanent structure on at least two levels dating from before Rabelais. Here prisoners were executed and the bodies of the dead left to swing until their bones dropped into the charnel house below. This scene of infinite horror dominated the northeastern outskirts of Paris, and was designed to terrify and disgust lawbreakers and honest citizens alike.

Closer to the center of things, the Place de Grève was another Parisian execution site. The word "grève" means "foreshore," or, as they say in London, "The Strand." Today, the French expression to go on strike, *faire la grève*, goes back to the fact that unemployed workers traditionally met here to grouse with their fellows in medieval times. Located in front of the Hôtel de Ville, the Grève offered a wide-open space for all kinds of public events, including executions. But since this public space was much in demand for other medieval pastimes as well, the scaffold and the dead were removed after each execution. The Place de Grève never became the symbol of macabre horror that Montfaucon had been.

Alexandre Dumas, in a collection of true-crime stories called *Celebrated Crimes*, describes the execution at the Place de Grève of the infamous Marquise de Brinvilliers, whose wicked life might have inspired his own Milady de Winter in *The Three Musketeers*. The year was 1676; so Dumas's account is based upon his research and his own imagination.

> They had no sooner taken their positions than the executioner removed the culprit's hat and cut off her hair behind and at the sides, turning her head around this way and that, sometimes very roughly. . . . When her hair was satisfactorily arranged, he laid bare her neck and shoulders by tearing away the upper part of the shirt he threw over her other clothing when she left the Conciergerie. Finally, he bandaged her eyes, and lifting her chin with his hand, told her to hold her head erect. She obeyed without hesitation, listening all the while to what the doctor [her confessor] was saying in her ear, and repeating from time to time such of his words as seemed particularly appropriate to her situation. . . .

As the marchioness repeated the last word the doctor heard a dull sound like that made by the butcher's cleaver upon the block; at the same instant the voice was silent. The blade had done its work so swiftly that the doctor did not even see a flash as it descended. He ceased to speak himself, with hair erect and a cold sweat upon his forehead; for as the head did not fall, he thought that the executioner had missed his mark, and would be obliged to begin anew. But his fears on that score were short-lived, for the head, a second later, inclined to the left, slipped down upon the shoulder, and rolled to the ground, while the body fell forward upon the block, which was so placed that the spectators could see the bleeding neck. . . .

Dumas devoted 36 of his 105-page account of the crimes of Madame de Brinvilliers to her torture and execution. More than one-third!

Nor were Montfaucon and the Place de Grève the only places where criminals and traitors were executed in Paris. Both in ancient times and in our own, a convenient wall or tree or lamppost has furnished a suitable location for formal and summary executions. Romans beheaded St. Denis and his two fellow martyrs on their way up the slope to Montmartre. The calm and resignation of his victims unnerved the headsman to such a degree that he dispatched them on the way to the place of execution. According to the legend, the martyrs picked up their assorted heads, washed them off in a nearby fountain, and then walked north for four miles until they reached the place that is still known as St. Denis.

For more than forty years, from 1573 to 1617, Master Franz Schmidt was public executioner in Nuremberg. His journal recounts not only his tally of major executions that he performed with sword, iron bar, and rope but also "minor bodily punishments" such as branding, ear lopping, and flogging with rods. Before Master Franz took over, defendants were tried before the court, condemned, and executed, whether they were alive or dead. Corpses were propped up in court and asked to plead! By the year 1526, this farce had been eliminated.

In Germany, the executioner was also the chief torturer. He was known as the "Mate of Death," the *Hoher*, the *Haher*, the *Suspensor*, and later he was called the *Henker, Nachrichter,* and commonly, the *Scharfrichter*. The Nuremberg city records show that it was hard to find suitable candidates. They had to be insensitive enough to stomach the work, but reputable enough to keep the city fathers clear of criticism and embarrassment. A drunken execu-

A headsman in Ratisbon (now Regenburg), Germany, wielded a broadax and wore a mask for this private execution depicted in a 1782 German print. One of the reasons decapitation was a preferred method of death was that it allowed the victim to die without being touched by the executioner. This illustration shows that this was not always the case.

tioner, or one with unsavory habits or friends, was a reflection on his employers. Some executioners were thieves and lawbreakers. Many themselves perished on the scaffold. According to C. Calvert's introduction to Franz Schmidt's journal, Meister Friedrich was burnt alive at Windsheim for coining in 1386; Meister Hans was beheaded by his *Löwe*, or assistant, for treason in 1479; and another headsman was executed for killing his *Löwe* during a quarrel about the rightful division of gratuities after executing five criminals. Two into five won't go. They almost succeeded in killing each other. Such violence reinforces the idea that hangmen back then were nasty, brutish, and often short.

While it is generally true that many lapsed into crime, some executioners brought distinction of a kind to themselves. In 1497, the German executioner Meister Jong, after many years of service to his community, was made a freeman of the City. In England, a headsman who had executed a nobleman could lord it over his fellows. In fact Sir William Segar, the Garter King of Arms, was duped by a herald named Brooke into granting a coat of arms to the executioner Gregory Brandon in 1616. After he officially became a "gentleman," the mob further elevated him—often as he was elevating others—with the further distinction of "Esquire."

In Nuremberg the gallows was a permanent structure beyond the walls of the medieval city. It was erected by all of the tradesmen in town working together, since all benefited from the smooth operation of the justice process.

Master Franz, from his diary, appears to have been a calm technician, with just enough interest in his clients to recount a few details of the crimes for which they suffered. Here are some samples:

Year 1573

1. June 5th. Leonhardt Russ, of Ceyern, a thief, hanged at Statt Steinach. Was my first execution.
2. Wolff Weber, of Guntzendorff, and Barthel Dochendte, of Weisterfelss, both executed at Statt Kronach; Wolff, who was a thief, was hanged; Barthel, who was a murderer and had committed three murders, was executed on the wheel.
3. Gronla Weygla, of Cleucam, a murderer who had committed five murders with his companions, executed on the wheel at Hollfeld.
4. Barthel Meussel, of Mehrenhüel, a murderer, who single handed committed two murders; the first at Bamberg at the mill-weir, when he stabbed a man and took his money, the other at Welckendorff on the mountains, when he cut the throat of a man who was sleeping with him on the straw in a shed, and he took his money—beheaded at Hollfeld and exposed on the wheel. This was my first execution with the sword.

Total: 5 persons.

And so it goes, year by year: a thief hanged; a weaver broken on the wheel; a woman beheaded as a favor. Each year he sums up his totals. For instance, in both 1580 and 1584, Master Franz dispatched twenty culprits. In 1600, he separated fifteen bodies and souls. The last entry in his diary is the following:

300. November 13th. Burnt alive here a miller of Manberna, who however was lately engaged as a carrier of wine, because he and his brother, with the help of others, practiced coining and counterfeiting money and clipping coins fraudulently. . . . This miller, who worked in the town mills here three years ago, fell into the town moat on Whitsunday. It would have been better for him if he had drowned, but it turned out according to the proverb that "What belongs to the gallows cannot drown in water."
This was the last person whom I, Master Franz, executed.

Franz Schmidt's cool prose suggests that even at the end of his career his hand was steady and his eye sharp. Not that he didn't blunder a few times; he frankly records these incidents himself. During his time, he helped to eliminate live burial in a pit and drowning as punishment for women. He used his sword whenever he could. He also used his influence to dampen the local zeal for ferreting out heretics and witches, which other towns were less successful in containing. The denouncing of witches was as popular in Germany in 1600 as it was in Salem, Massachusetts.

⤳

Simon, Lord Lovat, was a Scottish earl who had the distinction of being the last person to lose his head on a block in England. That was on 9 April 1747. The last beheading in the British Isles was nearly three-quarters of a century later. After the Bonnymuir rising in 1820, two men were beheaded at Stirling by a masked headsman, who later turned out to be a young medical student from Glasgow. Judging by this, his only appearance on the scaffold, it is unlikely that he distinguished himself in the final examination in anatomy. The end of beheading does not represent a wave of enlightenment sweeping the ax and block off the stage forever because of public awareness. No, the headsman was still kept busy on the gallows, and the stake was still in use for women convicted of petty treason. In 1769, for example, Suzannah Loth was drawn on a hurdle to Pennington Heath, near Maidstone, strangled, and burned for the poisoning of her husband.

The wielded blade is still used today in such countries as practice a literal interpretation of Islam. Although beheadings are infrequent in Qatar, Yemen, and Saudi Arabia, executions remain public, often in a parking lot or shopping plaza, which has replaced the ancient marketplace. Saeed Al Sayaf told a British journalist in 1989 about his work in Saudi Arabia, where he was the official executioner. This confession was immediately turned into a tabloid headline: I HAVE CHOPPED OFF 600 HEADS

Saeed Al Sayaf used a narrow blade to decapitate this alleged murderer and rapist in a Jeddah car park. Devoutly religious, he selected his blade following the writings of the prophet Mohammed. In executing women, he uses a gun.

According to Brian Lane, who quotes the sixty-year-old headsman's story, Saeed Al Sayaf goes on to say, "When the job is done I get a sense of delight, and thank God for giving me this power."

In France, the fashion for decapitation continued, but it was subjected to the democratization that came into vogue in 1789, as we will see in the next chapter, where we will meet the illustrious Sanson dynasty of executioners and the instrument upon which they played.

CHAPTER EIGHT

The Guillotine and Its Servants

"With this machine I chop your head off in a twinkling, and you do not suffer . . ."

—DR. JOSEPH-IGNACE GUILLOTIN

When I was loaned a mint copy of the *Memoirs of the Sansons* (1881 edition), I knew that at last I could begin to work on a chapter devoted to French executioners. Since the Sanson dynasty represented state executions going back to 1688, I could say that the spine and limbs of my chapter had been written for me by the grandson of the man who guillotined King Louis XVI, Marie Antoinette, and just about everyone who was anyone in France during the infamous Terror of 1793–94. What could be better than the story of this famous family of executioners, as told by the next-to-last of this famous clan of headsmen? I began cutting the pages of this never-before-opened copy with keen anticipation.

Here were the family traditions of succeeding generations of state executioners, known to outsiders by the name of the city where they wielded their broadsword and iron bar. In Paris, one Sanson after another was called "Monsieur de Paris." Here, in the *Memoirs*, was the story of how the first Sanson, a young officer in the French army, fell in love with the beautiful daughter of the headsman of Dieppe and Rouen without knowing her father's trade; how he was duped by a fellow officer, how he was forced to relinquish his rank and station, and at last take up the *métier* of his father-in-law; another story about how he was so overwhelmed by the calm beauty of a noblewoman on the scaffold that he bungled her beheading dreadfully and nearly had to leave town. In the *Memoirs* we hear the executioner's impassioned plea in a courtroom to which he had been dragged because he had dared to share a table and some luncheon conversation in an inn with another titled lady. Defending himself, Henri Sanson's ancestor summons all of the eloquence that one wishes could be placed at one's disposal while passionately fighting a parking ticket in one's dreams:

> . . . my one crime is that I discharge functions that are held to be infamous and disgraceful. Now, I ask you, gentlemen, whether there are infamous and disgraceful functions in the State? . . . I merely act in obedience to

your orders, and if there was aught reprehensible in my avocations it would redound to your discredit, since, by the essence of the laws, the one who orders a crime is more guilty than the person who commits it. . . .

Sanson goes on in this vein for several more pages, saying that if the common executioner is not fit to sit down upon an invitation from a marchioness, then the whole of the judiciary is tainted with the blood of the scaffold, and all judges of low and high degree are stigmatized.

Later in *Memoirs of the Sansons*, the author, Henri Sanson, tells about the great love his grandfather Charles-Henri had for the beautiful young Marie Jeanne Gomart de Vaubernier, who was to become one of his most illustrious victims: the mistress of the old King Louis XV, Madame Du Barry.

As I read on, I noticed a rather novelettish quality developing, with more than a little dramatic irony. There are meetings with King Louis XVI himself. The king, incognito, makes some valuable contributions to the invention of the guillotine. He suggested that all necks, thick ones like his own, for instance, might not be well served by a curved blade and that perhaps an oblique blade might do better.

In all of this, the irony was fairly barking at me. I had to look further to make sure that I wasn't reading hearsay. In *A History of the Guillotine* by Alister Kershaw, I found the following:

> None of the good executing families has achieved so certain a place in history as the Sansons. . . . The trouble is that practically nothing is known about them. Most of those who met them at close quarters had no time to record their impressions; and the volume of memoirs [*Mémoires pour servir à l'histoire de la Révolution française, par Sanson, exécuteur des arrêts criminels pendant la Révolution* (Librairie centrale, Paris, 1829)] ostensibly by Charles-Henri Sanson is in reality by many hands, Balzac's among them, but Sanson's not at all. . . .

All that page-cutting for nothing! Five hundred and three pages of balderdash, of sheep-dip, of utter fiction. But wait a moment! All is not lost. At least it is fiction of some distinction; fiction by one of the greatest fiction-writers of all time: Honoré de Balzac!

I looked farther afield. Rayner Heppenstall, in his *French Crime in the Romantic Age*, mentions Louis-François l'Héritier de l'Ain, a well-known hack of the time, who had collaborated with young Balzac. The older writer is described as an unscrupulous ghost-writer, and it appears that Balzac was taking lessons from him.

Joseph Ignace Guillotin neither invented the machine that bears his name nor perished under its blade. He simply introduced a resolution demanding that the same death penalty be given to all social classes and that this penalty should be carried out by a beheading machine.

Without the ability to look over Balzac's shoulder, one can only imagine a young Rastignac, gap-toothed, ill-clothed, and struggling to make a career for himself in the highly competitive world of publishing. One good thing came out of it, however: in preparing the text, he ran across the name Rastignac among the names of those who perished on the guillotine.

Imagine the temptation from the writer's point of view: in 1829 Balzac, who had only just appeared in print under his own name, and still hadn't added the particle "de" to his signature, had to hustle. In the case of the Sansons, Balzac and l'Héritier de l'Ain simply made things up to suit themselves and popular tastes, but had, of necessity, to throw in what they knew themselves about the Sansons and the traffic to the guillotine. If it isn't history, it is hearsay of a highly diverting order. For while details may be invented, the fiction marches between rigid guidelines of what the book's original readers might be expected to know firsthand.

What do we know for sure about the introduction of the guillotine into use in France in the late eighteenth century? On 9 October 1789, in the National Assembly, Dr. Joseph Ignace Guillotin, a former professor of anatomy in the medical faculty of Paris, gave notice that he was going to put forward certain propositions and, the following day, he did so:

This print from the Feldhaus-Archiv at Wilhelmshaven depicts the martyrdom of St. Matthias. One of several prototypes of the guillotine, such as the Scottish Maiden and the Halifax Gibbet, this instrument never caught on until technology advanced enough to make it practical. Unfortunately, that moment came on the eve of the French Revolution.

I Crimes of the same kind shall be punished by the same kind of punishment, whatever be the rank of the criminal.

II In all cases (whatever be the crime) of capital punishment, it shall be executed by means of a machine [l'effet d'un simple mécanisme]. . . .

The doctor went on to present four additional propositions, making six in all. That day, only the two quoted above were debated. The British politician, writer, and editor John Wilson Croker has written about this in his *History of the Guillotine*:

The first proposition was voted with little or no opposition. On the second a discussion arose, and the Abbé Maury, with a prophetic sagacity, objected to the adoption of decapitation as a general punishment, "because it might tend to deprave the people by *familiarizing them with the sight of blood*. . . ."

But that day, the debate was brought to a hilarious halt when Dr. Guillotin, in answer to some objection, proclaimed enthusiastically: "*Now, with my machine, I strike off your head* [je vous fais sauter la tête] *in a twinkling of an eye, and you never feel it.*"

The Articles were eventually passed, and the building of a machine was contracted. It should be said here that Guillotin's idea of a machine was not entirely new. Such machines had existed before, going back to medieval times. But this one was to be reinvented, utilizing all of the subtlety that modern science could lend to the project. Suffice it to say that the guillotine in its modern form was the invention of Dr. Antoine Louis with contributions from others; Dr. Guillotin did not contribute further. Sanson himself made some practical suggestions about modifications and improvements. At first, dead bodies were "executed" and finally a brutal burglar named Nicolas-Jacques Pelletier was the first live sacrifice to democratic decollation. The crowd witnessing the event dispersed unsatisfied with the new device. It was too modern. Too fast. Where were the pageantry and the spectacle of old?

Hendrik Willem Van Loon, in his 1942 book of biographies, *Van Loon's Lives*, comments upon this situation, which not only cut deeply into the exclusivity of the executing profession, but also reduced the employment situation, since a guillotine could be moved from place to place, from town to town, threatening local operators.

> Believe it or not, but in many towns the introduction of this instrument of mercy led to regular riots. Pickets had not yet been invented, but it is easy to imagine a group of outraged members of the Lyons Local 471, Jack Ketch, Chairman, marching up and down in front of the gallows, bearing placards saying, "The government is unfair to organized hangmen."

Mrs. Rodolph Stawell, in *The Guillotine and Its Servants*, translates a couplet from the French that was chanted in protest against "Saint Guillotine, protectress of patriots":

Give me back my wooden gallows,
Give me back my gallows!

At first the guillotine was called *louison* or *louisette*, after Dr. Antoine Louis, but the name didn't stick. There have always been plenty of nicknames for it: *La Veuve*, the Widow, the National Razor, the Patriotic Shortener, the topper, the slicer, and so on, but it was the name of the doctor of anatomy who first suggested the idea that held the imagination,

An early drawing of the guillotine, showing its working parts, is inaccurate in one detail at least: the blade was attached to a weighted ram that fitted into the grooves at the side of the instrument. The blade alone, even falling from a height, would not produce sufficient force to cut through all the necks presented to it.

much against the doctor's wishes. And so it remains: the guillotine, with a silhouette that has sent shivers down the spine for two centuries.

During the Revolution, the Sanson family walked a thin line. In a state that was doing away with titles and feudal institutions, the Sansons were a dynasty of hereditary executioners. They claimed a genealogical hold on the office of Executioner of High Works. No one elected them. There was never anything democratic about Sanson, in spite of the tricolor badge he wore to be inconspicuous. He had been appointed to his job by the king. As keeper of the National Razor, he was in the aristocratic or feudal business of executing aristocrats in the name of the people. There were times when both active Sansons, father and son, were arrested with their assistants and confined in the Abbaye prison by night, but released during the day to continue the work of the Revolution. Sanson was learning to become a first-rate bureaucrat. In order to survive, he had to. In Lyon, the executioner Jean Ripet and his assistant, Bernard, fell victim to the machine they knew so well. Living through the Terror was like walking a tightrope over Niagara Falls.

Madame Roland, a leading member of the Girondist faction, was condemned to die after most of the others in her group had perished. In the supposed memoir, Sanson says this of her:

> . . . She had very fine black hair, a part of which had to be cut, at which she expressed some concern. My grandfather tried to make her understand, with all kinds of circumlocution, that [otherwise] he would expose her to the most fearful torture. She seemed touched by his arguments, and paraphrasing a celebrated expression of Molière's, she said, smiling, "Strange that humanity should take refuge in such an unlikely person as you!" As her black hair was falling, she rose with much vivacity and exclaimed: "At least leave me enough for you to hold up my head and show it to the people, if they wish to see it!"

Danton, in a similar situation, standing on the scaffold himself, instructed Sanson to show his head to the people too: "It's worth the trouble," he said.

A little over halfway through the Sanson "memoir," its concocters begin a section that purports to be "Charles-Henri Sanson's Diary." Hearsay is now out the window; from now on, they pretend to be giving us a first-hand account. Herewith, a sampling:

> *Frimaire 9.* Five heads fell today: two were those of celebrated men, Barnave, and Dupont du Tertre, who had been minister of justice. . . . Citizen Vervitch and his sister were brought in to be cropped. Barnave and du Tertre were very brave and quiet. The former came up to me, held out his hand, and said:
>
> > "Bind these hands, which were the first to sign the declaration of the rights of man!"
>
> *Frimaire 17.* Madame Du Barry was sentenced to death last night, and

executed this morning. . . . At ten o'clock Citizens Vandenyver—the
father and the two sons—all accomplices of Madame Du Barry, and [two
forgers] were brought in. While the above-named were being "arranged,"
Madame Du Barry came in; her legs could hardly carry her. It was some
twenty years since I had seen her, and I could hardly have known her. . . .
When she saw me she shrieked, covered her eyes with her hands, and
sank down upon her knees, crying: "Do not kill me!" . . . I was more
moved than any one, for this unfortunate woman reminded me of my
young days, of the time when I knew her. . . . When she saw the guillotine
she became quite excited, and struggled with my assistants and tried to
bite them. She was very strong, and three minutes elapsed before they
could carry her up to the platform. She was frightful to look at, and to
the very last second she struggled. . . .

Sanson uses the term "arranged" in speaking about his assistants'
attempts at cutting the prisoners' hair and binding their hands behind
their backs. He calls his assistants "valets." In doing so, he, or rather one of
his ghost-writers, has used the jargon of his trade. These euphemisms and
the other one, attending to their "toilette," are nice touches which must
have given the original readers a *frisson* of reality.

In general, the writers stay away from the operational side of the Terror.
We hear about the victims of the guillotine, their trials and behavior during their last moments, but little about, say, the care and maintenance of
the guillotine itself. Were there improvements made based upon experience? Elsewhere, we learn that the great accumulations of blood in the
Place de la Révolution became a civic health problem, and that steps were
taken to get rid of the smell and stop stray dogs from lapping up some of
the best blood in France. And the blood continued to flow:

A terrible day's work! The guillotine devoured fifty-four victims. My
strength is at an end, and I almost fainted away. . . . I do not boast of
extraordinary squeamishness; I have seen too much blood in my life not
to be callous. If what I feel is not pity, it must be a derangement of the
nerves.

More than 2,500 men, women, and even children perished on the guillotine during the bloody months of the Terror in 1893 and 1894. The machine
stood on the scaffold permanently at this time as every day brought it
more victims. John Wilson Croker says: "These executions were for many
months the amusement of Paris." The guillotine became a familiar device

The parade of tumbrels to the Place de la Révolution brought with it a new kind of observer of public executions. The tricoteuses *were women who calmly knitted as they counted heads and stitches together. These models for Dickens's Madame Defarge were not satisfied until Robespierre himself was bound to the bascule and sent under the knife.*

in design. Its image appeared on plates, cups, and snuffboxes. Children played with toy guillotines. Adult models trimmed cigars or decapitated sparrows, bought for the purpose. Prisoners sentenced to death made fanciful model guillotines. Dickens's picture of Madame Defarge and the other women knitting as they sat watching the butchery was hardly an exaggeration. Men and children watched as well. Stands were erected, chairs rented. Perhaps there were refreshments and programs offered for sale. Eventually the Commune prohibited the building of stands, the waving of walking-sticks in the air, and the throwing of hats as the blade crashed down.

As the Terror grew, and life in France became cheaper, Sanson learned to accommodate more and more victims on the scaffold. He began talking, not of individuals, but of cartloads. The guillotine made it possible, of course. None of the old ways of dealing with enemies of the people could have kept up with the traffic. Without the guillotine, the Terror could not have bitten as deeply into the population as it did. Jail deliveries, mass shootings and drownings may be all very well upon occasion, but they tend to undermine confidence in the continuity of the civil order when they occur too frequently. The people were proud of the speed and efficiency of the guillotine. Not until the energy and determination of the Nazi war machine tackled the Final Solution was death meted out with such ingenuity and efficiency. But, as the Nazis and the French discovered, the smell lingers on down the years.

Most of the victims of the Terror behaved with the greatest of courage during their last ordeal. The cartloads emptied one at a time; the victims stood around beneath the scaffold and politely took leave of their fellows as their names were called. It has been suggested that if there had been less courage, less stoic acceptance, less of the better classes showing to the populous that people with breeding know how to die, then the Terror would have been impossible. If all the victims of the guillotine had behaved the way Madame Du Barry behaved—screaming, struggling, and biting, fighting Sanson and his assistants every inch of the way to the *bascule*—the people would have become disgusted with the spectacle, and public opinion would have turned against the slaughter sooner. There was far, far too much of the far, far better thing. That may be right, but it unfairly places the blame on the victims.

When John Wilson Croker wrote his *History of the Guillotine* in 1853 he stressed the fact that the earliest French historians of the Revolution tried to downplay its violence. For instance, they gloss over the methods used to execute the enemies of the people. He says that, for reasons of patriotism, there is no mention of the guillotine in Thiers's ten-volume account of the events beginning in 1789. Even in Dr. Rees's great 1819 *Encyclopoedia* there is no mention either of the doctor who presented the idea to the National Assembly or of the machine that evolved from his suggestion. In Mignet's *Histoire de la révolution française*, the description of the death of Louis XVI was so ambiguously worded that it could have been describing the death of Charles I of England. The guillotine is nowhere to be found. Croker suggests that there was "a natural reluctance to enter into details so disgraceful to the national character." One is reminded of controversy in our own time about the representations of various aspects of World War II. One thinks at once of the Holocaust deniers. But they are not alone. Even the renowned Smithsonian Institution was not above making changes to an exhibition commemorating the fiftieth anniversary of the dropping of the atomic bombs on Hiroshima and Nagasaki because of the sensibilities of veterans' organizations. The ownership of history is always a thorny question.

After the Terror, the world settled down, first, to a reshaped republic and, gradually, to an empire. Sanson and his son survived the transition and went about their work, which became less arduous and less exciting. The man who had executed the king was sought out by visiting tourists, who wanted to hear how the king had died from the man who was on the scaffold with him. They wanted to know all about the strange machine, so different from the gallows in front of Newgate Prison. Had Marie Antoinette really stepped upon Sanson's foot inadvertently? Had Charlotte Corday's face flushed when it was struck by the novice assistant as he held up her head to the crowd? Is there any consciousness visible in a head that has just fallen into the basket?

Benjamin Appert was a philanthropist and prison reformer living in Paris in the middle of the nineteenth century. His literary dinner parties were the talk of the French capital. Not only did well-known authors appear at his table, but also English milords of a reforming bent, and detectives such as the celebrated Eugène-François Vidocq himself. Henri Sanson was a guest at least once. This time the Englishmen were Sir John Bowring, the diplomat and explorer, and Lord Durham, who was later briefly Governor General of the Canadas. Dumas and Balzac, of course, already knew Vidocq; the latter had virtually kidnapped him into his novels under the name Vautrin. In real life, Vidocq had been a petty criminal who had rehabilitated himself and offered his services to the Sûreté. He was a romantic figure in the rough, but even Sanson thought him crude in

Charlotte Corday asked Sanson to step aside so that she could see the guillotine upon which she was about to die. The headsman had tried to shield her from its sight. When an assistant slapped the cheeks of her severed head, people reported that Corday's face flushed at the insult. The assistant was not asked back.

his manners and insensitive in his speech. This was the younger Sanson, who had acted as his father's assistant during the Revolution. Sanson *fils* was a man of some literary ambition limited by a conservative and conventional cast of mind. There were an even dozen men at Appert's table that evening in 1834. The conversation lingered on the lugubrious subject of the behavior of those condemned to sudden death. In his biography of Vidocq, Philip John Stead describes their talk:

> . . . The conversation turned on executions. M. de Jouy [playwright] remarked that Samson [Stead consistently gets this name wrong] was only the instrument of the law, and Samson hastened to agree.
>
> "I am only the instrument—it is Justice that kills."
>
> Lord Durham, with insular directness, inquired, "How many heads have you cut off to date, Monsieur Samson?"

"About three hundred and sixty, milord."

One of them had been Marie-Antoinette's.

Sir John Bowring wanted to know how Samson felt when he secured the victim to the fatal plank.

"My assistants secure the patient, cut his hair and prepare the baskets to receive his head and body. I am simply present to see that all goes well and swiftly. My work is confined to releasing the cord holding the blade which cuts off the head."

M. de Jouy asked if he thought suffering continued after decapitation.

"Yes, Monsieur. The face is convulsed, the eyes roll, the head is as if it were enraged."

The writers Dumas and Balzac, you will have noticed, said little. They came to listen, not to talk. Balzac cocked his ear in Vidocq's direction, always alert for clues to his Vautrin's character; Dumas listened to Sanson. The author of *The Three Musketeers* had already called upon Sanson *père* at the family home in the rue des Marais du Temple, when Sanson *fils* was absent. He examined the objects on display in a small informal museum dedicated to the past of the family business: two-handed beheading swords and other deadly paraphernalia. Dumas would have collected the whole Sanson dynasty, if he could have; as would Stendhal and Victor Hugo, who were equally interested in crime.

The dinner continued. Sanson and Vidocq agreed on one thing at least: criminals Vidocq had captured always suffered from a dryness in the mouth after they were caught. Sanson added that on the way to the scaffold, he had never seen a condemned criminal spit. Indeed, after the *toilette*, the trimming of collar and hair on the back of the neck, the condemned prisoner's mouth seemed to dry out, as though the very saliva had already abandoned the soon-to-be-severed head.

Continuing this line of morbid inquiry, the young Lord Durham expressed a wish to see the guillotine in action. A date and time were agreed upon, and Lord Durham, with Benjamin Appert, set out to the rue des Marais du Temple to call upon the Executioner of High Works to see "the machine," as Sanson called it. Here again I'll let Philip John Stead pick up the story:

> . . . Lord Durham had told so many people he was coming that half the
> English colony in Paris followed in their carriages. On the way Appert
> had some little difficulty in dissuading Lord Durham from buying a live
> sheep to be decapitated.

Vidocq was waiting with Samson and his son. Lord Durham and his friends . . . handled the working parts of "the machine" and were much gratified by seeing some bales of straw decapitated. . . .

Lord Durham had blazed a trail to the rue des Marais du Temple, one thereafter followed by English tourists in great numbers—just as Thomas Cook had guided tourists to the Place de la Révolution to see the guillotine in action. A criminal, who had been an assistant to Sanson, told Victor Hugo the following story, quoted by Rayner Heppenstall in *French Crime in the Romantic Age*:

. . . [Tourists] were shown into a pretty drawing-room on the ground floor, *furnished throughout in mahogany,* in the middle of the room a good piano, always open, with music on the stand. Presently M. Sanson would appear and beg his callers to be seated. The English commonly wanted to see the guillotine. M. Sanson was always ready to satisfy this wish, doubtless for a small consideration, and conducted the *ladies* and *gentlemen* into the next street (the rue Albouy, I fancy), to the scaffold-maker's. At the back was a closed shed, in which the guillotine stood permanently set up. The foreign visitors gathered round it, and it was made to *work*. Bales of straw were used.

One day, an English family, consisting of father, mother and three fine daughters all fair-haired and all pink-cheeked, presented themselves at Sanson's house. It was to see the guillotine. Sanson took them round to the carpenter's. The instrument was made to work. The blade fell and was hauled up several times, at the request of the girls. One of them, however, the youngest and prettiest, was not satisfied. She made the headsman explain to her, in minute detail, what is known as *the toilet of the condemned.* She was still not content. Finally, she turned shyly to the headsman.

"Monsieur Sanson," she said.

"Mademoiselle?" said he.

"What do you do when the man is on the scaffold? How is he fastened in place?"

The headsman explained this dreadful business to her and said: "We call that *enfourner,* to put him in the oven."

"Well, Monsieur Sanson," said the young lady, "I want you to put me in the oven."

The headsman was startled. He protested. The girl insisted.

"It is a notion I have," she said, "to be able to say that I have been fastened to it."

Sanson turned to the father, to the mother. They said: "Since that is what she wants, you'd better do it."

The headsman had to give way. He made the young miss sit down, tied her legs together with string, her arms with rope behind her back, fastened her to the see-saw and *buckled* her in place with the leather strap. That was as far as he meant to go.

"No, no, that isn't all," she said.

Sanson then tilted the *bascule*, placed the girl's head in the horrible *lunette* and fastened the upper cowl over it. Thereupon she declared herself satisfied.

Later, when he recounted this story, Sanson added: "I could see the moment coming when she would say: *That isn't all. Now let the blade fall.*"

Let me add to this account of mechanical beheading two observations of executions by guillotine by literary Englishmen traveling near Rome: Lord Byron and Charles Dickens.

On the 30 May 1817, Byron wrote to his publisher, John Murray, from Venice. This is what he said:

> . . . The day before I left Rome I saw three robbers guillotined—the cere-mony—including the *masqued* priests—the half-naked executioners—the bandaged criminals—the black Christ & his banner—the scaffold—the soldiery—the slow procession—& the quick rattle and heavy fall of the axe—the splash of blood —& the ghastliness of the exposed heads—is altogether more impressive than the vulgar and ungentlemanly dirty "new drop" & dog-like agony of infliction upon the sufferers of the English sentence. . . . The pain seems little—& yet the effect to the specta-tor—& the preparation to the criminal—is very striking & chilling. . . .

Nearly thirty years later, on Saturday, 8 March 1845, Charles Dickens was traveling in Italy. In Rome, he witnessed another beheading, which must have been a change from visiting the tombs of Italian poets and staring down Alpine gorges. This search for the sublime could excuse the most mor-bid excursions. This is what he wrote and published in *Pictures from Italy*:

> . . . [The victim] immediately kneeled down, below the knife. His neck fitting into a hole, made for the purpose, in a cross plank, was shut down, by another plank above; exactly like the pillory. Immediately below him was a leathern bag. And into it his head rolled instantly.
>
> The executioner was holding it by the hair, and walking with it round the scaffold, showing it to the people, before one quite knew that the knife had fallen heavily, and with a rattling sound. . . .

The Duke of Orléans, an indefatigable Bourbon intriguer, was at last brought to the scaffold. He had tried to save himself by going along with the Revolution, but his birthright caught up to him, as it did to the fictional Charles Darnay.

Seeing his first beheading, Dickens was struck by the apparent total disappearance of the neck of the criminal when he inspected the body afterwards. No wonder the French use the word "decollation" as well as "decapitate" when referring to the process. The head comes off, certainly, but the culprit is also "de-necked."

The last of the Sansons left the scene ignominiously. High living had placed Clément-Henri Sanson in debt. To extricate himself, he put the guillotine in pawn to his creditors. Now the comic muse plays her hand. No sooner was the National Razor in hawk than the authorities called upon Sanson to perform his time-honored function on a certain approaching morning. Sanson's entreaties to his creditors were unavailing. Why should they return the machine, since they knew what he would do with it? It was a noble and life-affirming gesture. At last, Sanson had to admit his folly and the *government* redeemed the guillotine and promptly fired Sanson, the seventh in the dynasty of executioners, after only seven years of service. The nation thereafter retained ownership of the machine. Formerly, the executioners had acted as contractors to the authorities. They supplied the means of death, and the government supplied the criminal. In fact, right to the last, the executioner had to write out a receipt for the prisoner and give it to the top prison official before the prisoner was delivered into his hands. This ceremony often took place while the condemned prisoner was having a last glass of grog or smoking his last cigarette.

Writers as different as Victor Hugo and Albert Camus have reflected on the guillotine. Hugo said that he had, through a medium, contacted the spirit of André Chénier, who told him what happened *after* the fall of the blade. Camus's disaffected young man in *The Stranger* is absorbed by the advent of death. He learns to sleep during daylight hours so that he will hear the first approach of the guards in stocking feet to arouse the condemned man.

> . . . Even though the faintest rustle sent me hurrying to the door and pressing an ear to the rough, cold wood, I listened so intently that I could hear my breathing, quick and hoarse like a dog's panting—even so there was an end; my heart hadn't split, and I knew I had another twenty-four hours respite. . . .

This question of the manner in which the prisoner awaited his death is interesting in that it follows national traditions. In Britain and North

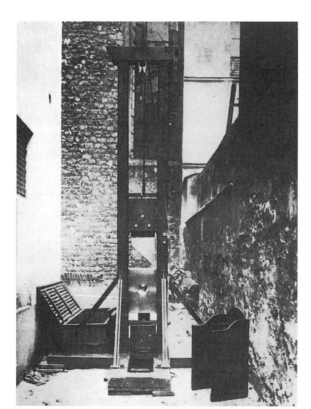

The modern guillotine was once the property of the executioner. When the last of the Sanson dynasty put it in pawn, the government redeemed it and found another headsman. In silhouette, it has changed little from the instrument that made the Reign of Terror possible.

The speed of the guillotine's blade gave rise to speculation about the survival of consciousness after the head dropped into the basket. Experiments were made by scientists, who said they saw the severed head's eyes react to the sound of its own name. Here the heads of Auguste and Abel Pollet, executed in 1909, look puzzled by their new state.

America, the date of a coming execution was known well in advance. There was no attempt to shield the criminal. In France, the prisoner never knew when he was to die until the moment had arrived. He was shaken awake by a senior warder, told that his appeal had failed and that he had to be brave, for the time had come. When he had dressed in the clothes he had worn at his trial—in some cases the prisoner's hat was returned to him with the rest of his clothing—and given as much time as he needed to seek spiritual comfort and write final letters, then, with the option of nicotine and grog, he was led away to the machine.

Although in this chapter I have said a great deal about the Sanson dynasty of headsmen, they were not the only memorable *bourreaux*. There were, in fact, several families, many of them interconnected through the centuries by marriage as well as similar interests. Polite society made it difficult for the children of executioners to find mates outside their own *métier*. An exclusivity was born of necessity. When the Deibler family came to France from Bavaria, they were welcomed into the international brotherhood of executioners because of the traditions they brought with them. A Deibler officiated at one time or another, after the disgrace of the last Sanson, in Rennes, in Algeria, and later in Paris. The *bourreau* worked his way up from post to post until he became Monsieur de Paris, which at that time meant that he was the official Executioner of High Works for all of France.

After the lingering embarrassment of the Revolution, which even two Imperial interludes could not wholly erase, executions in France became less and less public and more clandestine. While they remained for a long while officially public, the place and hour chosen tended to eliminate all but the best-informed and intrepid of sensation-seekers. When Deibler announced that he would resign if forced to execute a woman, French courts began commuting the death sentences involving women. Except for the Vichy years of World War II and immediately afterwards, women were safe from the blade of the guillotine.

The last public execution occurred at dawn in Versailles in 1939. The victim, Eugène Weidmann, was a German-born multiple murderer who killed six people for relatively small rewards. The crowd that came to see him die was large and unruly. Still photographers and a cinematographer recorded the fall of the knife. When it was all over, the authorities began the process of making sure it would never be repeated. The guillotine continued to function in France, although in private, for some years to come. The French held on to the death penalty until pressure from the European Parliament led, first, to a decrease in the use of the guillotine and, finally, to the abandonment of capital punishment altogether in 1981. Thus, the Avenger, the National Razor, the Widow, was finally retired, much to the relief of French lawyers, who had been required to attend the executions of their unlucky clients. Writer Georges Simenon once stated that he had never met a lawyer in France who wasn't opposed to the death penalty. Watching a client perish on the guillotine was a bitter reprimand for sloppy debating.

The guillotine had gone through all the experiences of life; it had been "born," tested, initiated, and had a long career. It had, in 1871, during the Commune, even been "executed." An angry mob threw a guillotine on a bonfire and burnt it in revenge for all the heads it had lopped off over the years. After the Commune, of course, it was rehabilitated and restored to its place for more than a century to come.

CHAPTER NINE

Other Places of Execution

*"... [Ronald Ryan, the last man to be hanged in Australia]
should not have been judicially murdered—a crime for which
every member of the community must accept a share of the
blame...."*

—DR. PHILIP OPAS, QC, ABOUT HIS CLIENT RONALD RYAN

In *Man and Superman*, George Bernard Shaw wrote "... in the arts of life
man invents nothing; but in the arts of death he outdoes Nature herself,
and produces by chemistry and machinery all of the slaughter of plague,
pestilence and famine...." And in all of this murderous invention, nothing
more cruel, more diabolically evil, than crucifixion was ever produced. It
came from the East, where credit for its invention must be shared among
the Phoenicians, Assyrians, Persians, Egyptians, and Carthaginians. Its use
spread further through the known Western world. The Romans used it,
gave it prominence throughout their vast empire. Perhaps a good way to
begin a look at the executioners outside Britain, France, and North
America might start here.

Unfortunately, in the history of crucifixion, no particular executioners
have been recorded. It was not a position that brought much honor or
prestige with it. The often-repeated excuse English hangmen used to justi-
fy their work, that at least they are skillful enough to make the dying easier, doesn't work with crucifiers; the death was *supposed* to be slow and
painful. Kill a fellow quickly on the cross and you've missed the point.

Soldiers were often delegated to do the work, and the victims most
often found hanging from the crosses were slaves, although there is a story
that Malcus, a Carthaginian general, sacrificed his own son on a cross to
win the favor of the god Baal. Crosses were placed near the high roads,
where the dead and dying could be seen by all travelers, who were put into
a properly respectful state of mind towards the resident authorities by
these harrowing examples of what happens to wrongdoers.

Hanging on a cross was a hard death. Victims died of no lethal wounds
or disruption in the supply of air or blood. They died of thirst, starvation,
and exposure. Some victims lasted as long as nine days. Perhaps in order
to speed up matters, victims were traditionally beaten up before they were

Ever "the emblem of suffering and shame," the cross was a familiar sight to travelers visiting the far-flung provinces of Imperial Rome. This woodcut, for reasons of composition, brings the Christ figure closer to the ground than was usual in crucifixions.

affixed to their crosses. Savage whipping and scourging was normal. Sometimes legs were broken, or the victim was pierced by spear or sword. As often, the agony was lengthened by well-meaning friends and relations who brought food or purifying or sedative herbs to the sufferers. The mention of friends holding up hyssop or sponges with myrrh or vinegar on rushes recalls at once images of the Passion.

The Gospels provide four accounts of the crucifixion of Jesus, and all give credible information about the process of this sort of execution. For instance, the crosses upon which the condemned were to suffer were assembled at the place of execution (Golgotha in most of the accounts, and Calvary in Mark); Simon, the Cyrenian, was made to carry the cross member of the cross, which was later nailed in place on the main post and the whole assembly thrust into a prepared socket in the ground. The clothes of the condemned were divided among the executioners: a tradition that lasted down the centuries. The Calvarys and Golgothas of the Roman Empire were well guarded to prevent rescue, or, failing that, the removal of the dead for burial. For some reason, Romans kept the sight of crosses a provincial phenomenon. The many roads leading to Rome were lined with crosses, but not on the outskirts of the capital.

Crosses came in all shapes and sizes. Even a simple upright post used for crucifixion was called a cross. The *crux immissa* had four arms; the *crux commissa*, three; and the *crux decussata* was a St. Andrew's cross. The Greeks used one in the shape of their letter *chi*, another diagonal cross. There were no standard forms in the drill of the executions either. Nails driven through hands and feet were sometimes used to support bodies; as often, ropes. A footrest, called a *suppedanem,* of wood or other material was added to the upright to help the sufferer relieve pressure on the higher points of suspension, but, of course, these would only support the client as long as he retained consciousness. Some Christian martyrs are said to have been crucified upside down. While this seems to add more cruelty, in fact, unconsciousness and death come more quickly to the inverted.

In ancient Rome, according to Cicero and Juvenal, crucifixion was the most common form of execution for those whose rank did not suggest the short Roman sword. It was a punishment that was meted out to slaves who had affairs with free women—often an angry husband's revenge against an ambitious slave. Such executions were often family affairs, settled at home without going before the courts.

Crucifixion was only one of the punishments meted out by the Romans. Vestal virgins who betrayed their vows of chastity were entombed or buried alive. Egyptians did this as well, if *Aïda* is anything to go by. Other capital crimes under the Twelve Tables of the Decemviri (451–450 B.C.) were the following:

> . . . publishing libelous material and insulting songs; furtively cutting or
> causing to be grazed crops raised by ploughing, by an adult; knowingly
> and maliciously burning a house or stack of corn near a house; theft by a
> slave who is taken in the act; cheating, by a Patron, of his client; perjury;
> wilful murder of a freeman; wilful murder of a parent; making distur-
> bances in the City at night. . . .

While we tend to think of crucifixion as an ancient form of punishment, it persisted further into modern times than is generally believed. Constantine outlawed it in the world he oversaw some time after A.D. 315, but when Charles le Bon, Charles the Good, count of Flanders, was assassinated in the church of St. Donat in Bruges in 1127, Bertholde, the murderer, was ordered to be crucified by the French king Louis VI, called Louis the Fat. At the same time, crucifixion was still inflicted on Jews and heretics in France.

While the Crusaders of that time and later did not practice crucifixion, they certainly punished with a vengeance. Crimes committed by non-

Christians weighed more heavily in the book of life and exacted a more serious penalty. For instance, in 1191, King Richard I of England put the entire garrison of Acre to the sword when Saladin was too slow in raising the imposed ransom. In total, 2,700 men were butchered after having been given terms of surrender.

In Japan, a form of crucifixion was used from earliest times until the nineteenth century. There the victim was stretched on a cross and jabbed with a long, thin spear. If the prisoner's friends paid off the executioner well enough, the first thrust would go to the heart; if not, the execution could go on for some time before a vital point was punctured. For aristocratic families in Japan, a traditional form of punishment was hara-kiri, which is, strictly speaking, a form of suicide. But often it was imposed from above, sometimes from the Mikado himself, and had the force and certainty of a normal sentence of death. It required the victim to draw a razor-sharp short sword or knife horizontally across his belly and then to make a second incision and draw the knife up as far as possible. All of this was done as a precise ritual with a handful of officials and friends in attendance. An official known as the *kaishaku* stood beside the dying man and used his samurai sword to behead the sufferer at once if he lost his courage or to end his sufferings once he had disemboweled himself.

Chinese forms of execution in years gone by were ingenious. They cut prisoners in half with a gigantic paper-cutter, they sawed them in half lengthwise after stuffing them upright in a box. They boiled and fried, they buried alive. But beheading was looked on as a disgraceful death. The head, the site of reason and personality, should, by rights, be left intact and unmutilated. This view stands at odds with those of other

Tied by the arms to a cross, a Chinese felon is garroted by an executioner who has passed a stick through a loop of rope around the neck of the prisoner. In Spain, the modern garrote sends a screw into the spinal cord as its jaw tightens around the throat.

countries, where decapitation is seen as an aristocratic and civilized way of quitting this world.

Nonetheless the Chinese, whether they liked decapitation or not, were very good at it. Culprits, sometimes in batches, were dispatched kneeling on the ground by an executioner with a two-handed sword. T. T. Meadows, writing about the Chinese rebellions in the mid-nineteenth century, recorded a rare account of such a multiple execution that he witnessed:

> . . . The following is the manner of decapitation. There is no block, the criminal simply kneels with his face parallel to the earth, thus leaving his neck exposed in a horizontal position. His hands, crossed and bound behind his back, are grasped by the man behind, who, by tilting them up, is enabled in some degree to keep the neck at the proper level. . . . The executioner stands on the criminal's left. The sword ordinarily employed is only about three feet long, inclusive of a six inch handle, and the blade is not broader than an inch and a half at the hilt, narrowing and slightly curving towards the point. It is not thick, and is in fact the short and by no means heavy sabre worn by Chinese military officers when on duty. The executioners, who are taken from the ranks of the army, are indeed *very frequently* required by the officers to "flesh their maiden swords" for them; which is called *kae kow* [opening the edge] and is supposed to imbue the weapon with a certain power of killing. The sabre is firmly held with both hands, the right hand in front, with the thumb projecting over and grasping the hilt. The executioner, with his feet firmly planted some distance apart, holds the sabre for an instant at the right angle to the neck about a foot above it in order to take aim at a joint: then, with a sharp order to the criminal of "Don't move!" he raises it straight before him as high as his head, and brings it rapidly down with the full strength of both arms—giving additional force to the cut by dropping his body perpendicularly to a sitting posture at the moment the sword touches the neck. He never makes a second cut, and the head is seldom left attached even by a portion of the skin, but is severed completely.

Thirty-three criminals were beheaded in a batch as the superintendent of the detail shouted, "*Pan*" (Punish). The middle-sized executioner moved from one kneeling figure to the next until the last head rolled into the dust. It took no more than three minutes.

> Immediately after the first body fell, I observed a man put himself into a sitting posture by the neck, and with a business-like air, commence dipping in the blood a bunch of rush pith.

The collection of blood in the pith was part of a traditional sideline of executioners: potions and medicines were collected, prepared, then sold by executioners as semi-magical unguents outside normal medical services. The blood, hair, even the touch, of an executed criminal possessed, it was believed, powerful magical properties.

If the above description of mass execution in China appears to you as distant, removed in time from the here and now, let me point out that, as recently as May 1995, fifty-one drug traffickers were executed on a single day in the southern Chinese province of Guangdong. They were shot in the back of the head, not beheaded, but the numbers have hardly changed at all in nearly 140 years.

When a culprit is shot in the back of the head, often while organ-transplant collectors are standing by, the victim's family is sent the spent bullet casing afterwards and charged for it. A felon is a member of a family, and in that culture a crime is seen as the failure of the family to cope with its anti-social members.

A form of punishment that has caught the imagination of Westerners is the Eastern Death of a Thousand Cuts. Like something out of the *Arabian Nights*, the punishment of *Ling-chy*, the Torture of the Knife, or the Slicing Process, continues to intrigue. The reality of the Death of a Thousand Cuts is as horrible as its name implies. In its earliest form, a collection of knives was placed in a covered basket. Each weapon was marked by the name of a part of the body: a hand, a leg, an ear. The executioner pulled out from under the cover the first knife his hand touched and he proceeded to cut off the named body part. Then he reached for another blade and obeyed the message written there. He kept on doing this until death intervened. Sometimes relatives or friends of the condemned bribed the executioner to "find" the weapon marked "heart" quickly.

This version of the Death of a Thousand Cuts has been superseded by a more direct approach without the lottery trappings, which only encouraged the executioner's venality. In this version there is no basket and only one knife and, as Scott writes, "the slicings, cuttings, hackings and amputations proceed slowly step by step through the whole ghastly allotted course."

It was some time after the invention of firearms that they were first used to execute military prisoners such as spies, turncoats, hostages, and deserters. In parts of Asia, criminals were actually secured over the muzzle of a cannon before it was discharged, but that was in places where it was not unknown to crush the head of an offender by having an elephant step upon it.

In Sweden, burning at the stake was not abolished until 1841, two years after a woman who had murdered her child was executed in this way. Where in Britain those condemned to the stake were first strangled, in Sweden the woman first had her right hand chopped off, and then her head, before her body was burned in public. In 1734, a Swede could be condemned to the block for sixty-eight crimes ranging from blasphemy, adultery, arson, and bigamy to treason and murder. According to my friend Kildare Dobbs, who recently visited Langholmen prison-museum:

> . . . the last execution [in Sweden] took place in 1910, the murderer Johan
> Alfred Anderson having been beheaded by guillotine, the only occasion
> on which this French artifact was employed. The executioner was Gustav
> Dalman [1848–1920], a former infantry corporal who had beheaded the
> previous five condemned with a broadaxe. . . .

When Hitler restored the death penalty in Germany in the 1930s, it took the form of a headsman dressed in formal evening attire but wearing a mask, and wielding a broadax. When his client was female, she was dressed in immaculate white, as though for her wedding, in an odious and diabolical distortion of the celebration of marriage.

In Russia, capital punishment was often suspended by the czars, perhaps in an attempt to win popularity, but invariably it was restored, at least for state crimes, when it was needed. Meanwhile beatings with the rod and knout, a form of knotted whip, went on. People disappeared or died in custody, but there was no official sanction of this. Many prisoners died under interrogation and were never brought to trial. Indeed, prisoners in many countries apart from Russia were more prone to die of "accidents" where capital punishment had been ended. Justice was certainly seen to be done in those countries where the death penalty remained firm. Elsewhere, the data are muddled.

What marks the justice systems in Russia and eastern Europe are the arbitrary deeds of the powerful. In one such act, Russia nearly sacrificed one of its foremost novelists when Fyodor Mikhailovich Dostoyevsky was still a talented youth. The writer was involved in a plot to assassinate Czar Nicholas I. When the scheme was discovered, the writer was invited to sell his comrades to save his life. He refused. Louis Blake Duff picks up the story in *The County Kerchief*:

Johannes Hus is shown here attached to a stake and with faggots of wood piled about him. If he is lucky, the executioner will strangle him before the fire reaches him; if not, it will be a hard death. It took place in Constance in 1415.

They were all found guilty, of course, but Czar Nicholas I refused to sign the death warrant, but he did wish "to give the young men a good lesson."

That lesson was in the Czar's eyes a comedy. The prisoners were told to prepare for death. They were taken to a public place where a scaffold had been erected. They were made to mount it. One of the conspirators was bound to a post with his eyes bandaged. The soldiers made as if they were about to shoot. At this moment a messenger arrived and announced that the Emperor had changed the death sentence into that of hard labour. Memoirs of the time state . . . that the messenger who was supposed to have come from the Palace was actually already on the spot before the arrival of the conspirators. The condemned knew nothing of these things; they were making ready to die. That, surely, was the most cruel comedy in all history. . . .

Foolishly, the czar thought that the joy of the rescue would banish the terror of looking Death in the eye. Instead, the young men were marked for life by the experience. Harrowed to the core, Dostoyevsky tried to tell it in *The Idiot*, transposing the scene to Lyons, where the scaffold leads to the guillotine:

> . . . And only think it must be like that up to the last quarter of a second, when the head lies on the block and he waits and . . . *knows*, and suddenly hears above him the clang of the iron! If I were lying there, I should listen on purpose and hear. It may last only the tenth part of a second, but one would be sure to hear it. And only fancy, it's still disputed whether, when the head is cut off, it knows for a second after that it has been cut off! What an idea! And what if it knows it for five seconds!

Dostoyevsky's fancy makes it as real as can be; more real than is comfortable.

Nicholas I was in a benevolent mood when he commuted the sentences passed on Dostoyevsky and his young friends. He was not a liberal as history remembers him. But his son, Alexander II, was. Nevertheless he was assassinated by Nihilists, led by one Sofya Perovskaya, a movie producer's idea of perfect casting for a Russian revolutionary leader. Slim and blonde, she was dedicated to the idea that all of Russia's ills could be cured with one or two well-aimed bombs. Sofya masterminded the attack on the czar's sleigh as it drove along the Nevsky Prospect in St. Petersburg on 1 March 1881.

Alexander survived the first blast, but was mortally wounded by the second bomb. The snow was everywhere dotted with blood, but within a month all of the conspirators—an informer included—were brought to the gallows, except for one pregnant young woman. With Sofya Perovskaya leading the way, they were hanged in Semenovsky Square on 3 April 1881. The condemned prisoners were compelled to wear signs reading "Regicide." A hundred thousand people stood by silently as, one by one, the conspirators were hanged.

Much was made in the international press at the time of the trial and execution of the Nihilists. Among those moved to write about it was Émile Zola, who introduces a Russian activist into a group of disgruntled miners trying to organize against brutal mine owners in his 1885 novel *Germinal*. Towards the end of the novel, the Russian, Souvarine, tells the hero, Étienne, about the death of his lover back in Russia after the failure of an anarchist act like the assassination just mentioned. His girlfriend lit the fuse of a bomb and, with others, was caught.

> . . . On the last day in the square I was there. It was raining; they stupidly lost their heads, put out by the falling rain. It took twenty minutes to hang the other four; the cord broke, they could not finish the fourth. Annutchka was standing up waiting. She could not see me, she was looking for me in the crowd. I got on to a post and she saw me, and our eyes

never turned from each other. When she was dead she was still looking at me. I waved my hat; I came away.

Souvarine, a dedicated rationalist, and a warning to all would-be revolutionaries, goes on to say:

> Yes, it is well that she is dead; heroes will be born from her blood, and I no longer have any cowardice at my heart. Ah! Nothing, neither parents, nor wife, nor friend! Nothing to make my hand tremble on the day when I must take others' lives or give up my own.

Étienne remarks, about the walk they are taking, "We have gone far; shall we go back?" For Zola, Souvarine was going too far. As a Frenchman, he feared the sea-green Incorruptible in whatever form it took. Although he claimed to be working for the good of all the downtrodden and exploited, Souvarine will kill scores without a thought for them.

Souvarine's Annutchka could have been one of the condemned in Leonid Andreyev's short novel, *Seven Who Were Hanged*. Her political commitment would have been understood by some of the seven who were transported through a long winter's night by train to the place where the gallows had been set up. Andreyev walks with them at the last as, two by two, six of them walk to the edge of the clearing where all they can see are the movements of lanterns in the dark. The last of the seven walks alone towards the horror. And then:

> With elongated necks, bulging eyes, and blue tongues, like some strange terrible flowers protruding from their mouths, the dead retraced the road by which, living, they had come.

The year before the assassination of Alexander II in St. Petersburg, and halfway around the world, the Australian authorities were congratulating themselves on finally having run the famous bushranger Ned Kelly to earth. Kelly, whose homemade armor was immortalized by the painter Sir Sidney Nolan, had become a legend in his own time. Like Dick Turpin, Robin Hood, or Jesse James, Kelly—through a series of daring robberies—attracted all sorts of stories that tended to enlarge his character among the pioneers in his native Victoria, and in New South Wales as well. In the final shoot-out with the police, his "gang"—not even a handful of men, just three others—was no match for the twelve-pound cannon the police brought with them. The police came armed to fight a legend, not an indifferently armed quartet of horse thieves.

Ned Kelly, Australia's most notorious bushranger, wore homemade armor, and with it walked into legend, with an assist from the painter Sidney Nolan.

Kelly was only twenty-five when he walked to the gallows in Melbourne. Without his armor and reduced to human scale, he seemed to the guards a quiet young fellow. As the hangman adjusted the rope around his neck, Kelly sighed and said, "Such is life."

Kelly's crude armor continues to inspire Australians to this day. It is on display as part of a permanent exhibition showing the early years of the former penal colony. Unfortunately, the armor was concocted from scrap metal some years after Kelly's execution. The real Ned Kelly armor, all one hundred pounds of it, is preserved at police headquarters in Melbourne.

Just as Ned Kelly lives on in the imaginations of modern Australians as a kind of folk hero, so do Mike Howe and Matthew Brady. Howe was a Yorkshireman turned bushranger in Van Diemen's Land, as Tasmania was then called; Brady, an escaped convict turned bushranger. In the end Howe was shot and Brady was hanged in Hobart in 1826. But before that happened, they entertained the colony with their daring exploits. When Lieutenant-Governor Sir George Arthur offered a reward of, first, ten and, later, twenty-five pounds and a conditional pardon to anyone who would assist the authorities in capturing Matthew Brady, Brady nailed the following notice on the door of the Royal Oak Inn at Cross Marsh:

> It has caused Matthew Brady much concern that such a person as Sir George Arthur is still at large. Twenty gallons of rum will be given to any person that can deliver his person to me.

"But," as Robert Hughes says in his helpful book *The Fatal Shore*, "Lieutenant-Governor Arthur was a tirelessly methodical man, and he wore Brady down." He was finally brought to book. The judge was determined to make an example of him, even though he was entertained as a popular hero in his flower-decorated jail cell.

> . . . On May 4, 1826, Brady received his last Communion and mounted the scaffold above a sea of colonial faces, contorted in grief or cheering

him over the drop; only his enemies were silent. The government could not expunge his name from popular memory: A 4,000-foot peak in the Western Tiers, which frowns directly down on Arthur Lake below, is still known as Brady's Lookout, and there's a Brady Lake out past Tungatinah power station on the Lyell Highway—whereas Mike Howe is remembered in less noble geographical detail, a gully near Lawrenny and a marsh east of Table Mountain.

In those days, the gallows seldom stood idle. At the same sessions that condemned Brady, other bushrangers were sentenced to death for bushranging; cattle, horse, and sheep stealing; and murder. Some of these had been "in the bush" with Brady. The last of the group walked to the gallows on 29 April 1926. The condemned men were hanged in batches of two or three at a time and at intervals of a batch every few days until they were all dead.

The government was hard, not only on bushrangers, but on everybody. Order was kept with the lash of the cat-o'-nine-tails. Flogging was the normal punishment for all convicts whose time had not expired. A whole argot grew up around these floggings: names were given to parcels of so many strokes. The punishments were so severe in the convict settlements that offenders sometimes killed a guard or fellow convict just to merit the rope instead.

A look at criminal statistics in Australia, which began its European connection as a dumping-ground for the unwanted criminals of Britain and the political prisoners of Ireland, makes illuminating reading. Early statistics for the colony of New South Wales on every subject, including capital punishment, are patchy up until 1819, when order begins to descend. In the period 1819 to 1824, trials for capital offenses outnumbered those for larcenies and misdemeanors combined by more than three to two. Among the capital crimes on the books were listed many minor violations and infractions that today would carry hardly more than a fine. The conviction rate in those early days was about 32 percent. And of that percentage of men and women put on trial for their lives, 11 percent of them were executed. In 1825, eleven felons were hanged. The following year, the number doubled. Ten years later the situation had changed but little. Deliberate or accidental violence was responsible for 7 percent of the deaths in Botany Bay in the year 1838. Eighty-one people were willfully murdered and two of their murderers were hanged by the authorities. A twenty-seven-year-old man was hanged in Adelaide, South Australia, that year, the first in nine years. To the east, in Sydney, a sixty-five-year-old man was executed in Long Bay Gaol. Both had strangled little girls they had abducted. After 1900 ten or fewer were executed per year, and from 1908 five or fewer.

The first man hanged in Sydney was a seventeen-year-old boy named Thomas Barrett. He is described as being a "most vile character," and seemed from his stammering remarks at the foot of the ladder to have agreed with this assessment. He admitted that he had led a "very wicked life." But in seventeen brief years how very wicked could he have been, when the crime that brought him into the embrace of the hangman was the theft of some butter, pork, and beans in Sydney Cove?

On the prison colony of Norfolk Island, most hated of the dumping-grounds for political prisoners, a mutiny led by Irish prisoners was put down with great severity. Two ringleaders were hanged without trial against the advice of the judge-advocate who was there. This "hands-on" justice was highly applauded, even by King George, and Major Joseph Foveaux, the man in charge, who had ordered the midnight executions by torchlight, was promoted to lieutenant-colonel in 1802.

A year later, two more Irishmen were hanged for "bolting," that is, running off into the bush or onto a boat bound for China. Other offenders got five hundred lashes each, and double chains for the remainder of their sentences. "Absconding" and "bolting" were old traditions in Australia. Attempts were rarely successful, but once in a while the story ended happily. For instance, take the case of Mary Bryant, who was later dubbed by the English press "The Girl from Botany Bay." She, her husband, William, her two children, and seven other convicts sailed in a stolen boat, the governor's own six-oar cutter, north from Sydney to Timor, a distance of 3,250 nautical miles. It took them ten weeks. As an epic voyage against great odds, it can be compared only with the 1789 voyage of the deposed Captain William Bligh in the longboat of the HMS *Bounty*.

Born in Fowey, Cornwall, the daughter of a sailor, Mary Broad had been transported for stealing a cloak. On the voyage out, she married William Bryant, a Cornish fisherman and smuggler. They begged a compass from the master of a Dutch trader, who gave them muskets and charts besides. They arrived in Timor in June 1791, and were sent back to England in a man-of-war. They were treated in Newgate as celebrities and quickly attracted powerful friends, including James Boswell, the friend and biographer of Samuel Johnson. He wrote letters and lobbied until Mary was released. Her friends tarried in Newgate a little longer, but in time all were pardoned.

The good fortune of Mary Bryant—I should mention that it was not all good: both of her children and her husband died on the journey back to London—was based upon the skill she and William used in selecting the crew to abscond with. Thomas Cox was neither as fortunate nor as bright. He bolted from a stockade at Macquarie Harbour in company with Alexander Pearce, a desperate criminal and known cannibal. "Cox," Pearce declared, "was the most delicious food." Pearce had his portrait painted shortly after he expired on the gallows in Hobart. His skull is now part of a collection of similar objects—including shrunken heads—at the Academy of Natural Sciences in Philadelphia, where it may be seen daily.

In 1834 the convicts of Norfolk Island, that hellhole of prison camps, again mutinied. There were skirmishes, shouting of slogans—"Death or Glory!" "Liberty or Death!" "Huzza for Liberty!"—shootings, and death. When the mutiny was put down, it was thought prudent, once again, to make examples of the worst of the offenders. After spending six months rotting in tiny, infested cells, fourteen of the mutineers were told that they would be taken to the gallows. They went to the scaffold in two batches of seven on successive days, full of repentance, religion, and relief. Their religious adviser, the Catholic vicar-general of Australia, later wrote:

> Those who were to live wept bitterly; whilst those doomed to die, without exception, dropped on their knees, and with dry eyes, thanked God that they were to be delivered from such a place. Who can describe their emotions?

Ten years later there was another mutiny in that same hellhole. Mutinies were inevitable because the men were being slowly starved to death. When they did get food, it gave them dysentery. This time the men were hanged in two batches of six on a scaffold overlooking the sea at Kingston beach.

In December 1888, Louisa Andrews Collins was tried for the murder of her husband with arsenic. Called "the Botany Poisoner" in the press, Louisa, who was thirty-nine, was found guilty by the jury and sentenced by Sir Frederick Darley, the Chief Justice of New South Wales, to be hanged. The chief justice spoke truly when he addressed the prisoner in the dock: "I hold out no hope of mercy for you on earth," he said as the prisoner looked at him for some sign. Predictably, pleas for mercy in the press and by petitions from concerned individuals and groups assailed the governor of New South Wales, while formal appeals through legal channels went forward. In *Australians*, a ten-volume look at many aspects of life down under, the authors comment:

> One of the strongest pleas for a reprieve, used especially in petitions addressed to the governor, argued that it was twenty-eight years since a woman had been hanged in New South Wales, and that it would be "abhorrent to every feeling of humanity and a shock to the sentiments of cultured individuals in this 19th century, both here and in other English-speaking communities, that a woman should suffer Death at the hands of a hangman."

The premier, Sir Henry Parkes, defended his Justice Department's handling of the case, while admitting that he was personally opposed to capital punishment. He told the House:

> They knew that when woman yielded to crime she was not stayed by any consideration. (Hear, hear!) The worst of crimes had been committed by women. In the fearful period when France ran riot in blood, those who were the most guilty of the most ferocious delight in blood were women—young women—tender girls. (Hear, hear!). . . .

When it came to women as the weaker vessel, then the state was equally harsh. Three years before Louisa Collins was hanged, four youths were executed for the rape of a sixteen-year-old girl in Moore Park, Sydney. The courts tried eleven boys for the crime, nine were condemned to death. In *Australians*, we read:

> . . . After immense press coverage, public agitation, executive council meetings of unprecedented length, and deputations to the governor, Lord Carrington, who alone could exercise mercy, four were hanged, clumsily, and before a large crowd of officials, in January, 1887. . . .

Apart from the adverb "clumsily," I have been able to discover no further information about this quadruple hanging of teenagers.

Hangmen in Australia seem to have been picked up at random. There were no dynasties, no training programs, no clear appreciation of this important side of the administration of justice, as the following account of an execution in South Australia might indicate. This version comes from *Australians*:

> South Australia's only hanging, the first the colony had seen, was shockingly bungled. The man who was to die, Michael Magee, had been found

guilty of attempting to shoot the sheriff. A crowd of more than five hundred turned out on 2 May to witness his execution, which was to take place under a gum tree beside the River Torrens. As the masked hangman greased the rope, the prisoner prayed fervently and then addressed the crowd, admitting his guilt and acknowledging the justice of his sentence. The cap was drawn over his face, the signal was given; the executioner whipped the horses.

The rest was anti-climax. The cart on which Magee stood moved away very slowly, so that he slid off little by little. His wrists had been badly tied and he had time to free his hands and grab the rope above his head. There he hung, "turning round like a joint of meat before the fire," half-choking but still able to scream, "Oh, God! Oh, Christ! Save me!" The crowd was in tumult. . . . Meanwhile, the hangman had bolted, and had to be brought back by a constable. He finished his work by leaping upon the dying man, forcing him to let go of the rope. All this took thirteen minutes. The appearance of justice was ruined.

While a hanging body on a gum tree was a rare sight in South Australia, it was more common in New South Wales, where in 1838 alone nineteen men went to the gallows. Only the highest courts in the colonies could condemn a person to death, and the death sentence had to be confirmed by the governor and his executive council acting on behalf of Her Majesty Queen Victoria, who had ultimate authority over the lives of her subjects in Australia as elsewhere. "More often than not," write the authors of *Australians*, "councils let the law take its course."

One hundred years earlier, when the army and navy played a larger part in keeping public order, hangmen were recruited either from the ranks or from the convict population. In his novel *The Playmaker*, Thomas Keneally gives a fictional picture of life in the Australian penal colony. The year is 1789, and Lt. Ralph Clark of the Royal Marines is directing George Farquhar's play *The Recruiting Officer*, featuring convicts in all the acting parts. The part of Justice Balance, the bluff father of the leading lady, is to be played by the colony hangman, Ketch Freeman, who was himself sentenced to be hanged before having had this penalty commuted to transportation. In the novel, the fortunes of the actors in the play and the parts they are to enact in the Farquhar comedy have ringing parallels. Just as a theatrical presentation is a dramatic event calculated to seize the imagination, so, as Ketch Freeman could testify, is an execution where six living men are turned into corpses before the same eyes that watched the play. Keneally, who based his novel and its characters upon careful research of the period, found that executions by hanging were so chancy, so likely to go badly, as Michael Magee discovered, that many of the condemned furnished themselves with vials of poison which could be bitten into as they were flung off the ladder or cart.

> Some of the wives and lovers of the condemned called advice and
> endearments before and after the drop, and wept. Nancy Turner . . . kept
> her reserve and closed her eyes as her lover was thrown off the platform.
> Perhaps she would later be comforted by the observations of others that,
> whereas his condemned comrades had brief though terrible struggles,
> and Handy Baker bit through his own tongue, Private Dukes seemed to
> lose his senses at the very instant of the drop.

Alexander Green succeeded Henry Stain as hangman in Sydney, New South Wales, in 1828, when the former executioner died in his sleep. Green was a drunk and had trouble with the women in his life. Robert Howard, the "gentleman hangman" who succeeded the unruly Green, wore a beard to help disguise the fact that he had lost his nose to a horse, a circumstance that added to the poignancy of the hangings in Darlinghurst Gaol's "gallows corner."

The State of Queensland did away with the death penalty in 1921, after many years of not imposing it. In New Zealand, it was abolished in 1942, although there has been, as in 1949, loud clamoring to restore it.

Ronald Ryan, the last man hanged in Australia, was a petty thief doing time in Pentridge. During Ryan's escape from prison with a pal, a warder was shot and killed. While it was never satisfactorily proved that our man pulled the fatal trigger, and after much agitation for clemency, he was led to the gallows in Melbourne on time. His execution, on 3 February 1967, the first in twenty years, was seen as an election maneuver on the part of the premier, Henry Bolte. This hanging is known to have upset the lives of most of the people who had to take a part in it, from the warders and priest to the warden of the prison.

CHAPTER TEN

Hanging in Canada

"She has been condemned to death by hanging. A man may escape this death by becoming the hangman, a woman by marrying the hangman. . . ."

—MARGARET ATWOOD

In Canada, the first person executed for a crime is reputed to have been a young girl. She was hanged at age sixteen for the crime of petty theft. I have been unable to discover her name or the date of her execution. But as early as 1608, a locksmith named Jean Duval was hanged in Quebec. He was a companion of Samuel de Champlain, who had fought off an Indian attack while exploring Cape Cod, where he received an arrow wound. Later he plotted with others to murder Champlain and deliver the new-born colony into the hands of the Spanish or Basques in order to be rich-ly rewarded. Unfortunately for him, and three fellow conspirators, the scheme was uncovered and the ringleaders tricked into going aboard a ship for a drink with Champlain. Duval was hanged, then beheaded, and his head placed on a pike at the highest point of the Habitation he had helped build. The other three were sent back to France "in order that more ample justice should be done to them."

A few years later, also in Quebec, Daniel Vuil was executed for carrying on an illegal traffic in spirits with the Indians. He was shot by harquebus on 7 October 1661. Whether or not he faced a single weapon or a firing squad is unknown. It would have been an early use of the firing squad, if it was.

New France kept better track of her hangmen than did the other Canadian colonies. This is largely because it was so difficult to find people to serve in this capacity. The paperwork that secured them has been preserved.

The unpopularity of the official executioner in New France and else-where is a curious phenomenon. While it might reflect the contempt of the populace for a particularly nasty or brutal incumbent, it is more likely that hangmen were, as a group, bad luck, like black cats and ladders. (Ladders, by the way, are thought to be unlucky because they are mounted by those about to be hanged.) It is also possible that the hangman was the only member of the justice team that could be openly criticized. Thus the place of the hangman in the community represented the true feelings of the people about those in high places and the rule of law generally. According to the *Dictionary of Canadian Biography*:

> At that time Canadian society held in horror the person who exercised this ignoble office and considered all contact of any sort with the hangman and his family degrading. . . .

In Acadia in 1644 a soldier, part of the captured garrison at Fort La Tour, at the mouth of the Saint John River, turned hangman in order to save his own neck. André Bernard was obliged to hang his remaining companions, after Charles de Menou d'Aulnay reneged on his promise to spare all lives if the fort surrendered. The fort had been defended valiantly by Françoise-Marie Jaquelin, through four days of fierce fighting. The angry victor marched the remaining men of the garrison to a gallows hastily constructed inside the breached palisade. André Bernard, the amateur hangman, dispatched the men as well as he was able, while Françoise-Marie was forced to watch the hangings with a rope noosed around her own neck.

A few years later, when Jacques Daigre, the third official hangman in New France, died in Quebec, there was no one to replace him. For the authorities, the timing of Jacques Daigre's death, in March 1680, was unfortunate, for there were several felons lying in prison waiting for their last look at the sun. The timing was happier for Jean Rattier, one of these condemned felons. He was asked whether he wished to continue in prison until an executioner had been chosen who would then usher him into eternity, or would he like to save his neck and take up the job himself. Naturally, he jumped at this second chance.

Born around 1650 in France, Rattier, a farmer in Saint-François-du-Lac, and the father of five, was involved in a quarrel, which concluded in the death of an unnamed girl. Twenty-nine years old, Rattier was held criminally responsible and condemned to be hanged at Trois Rivières. His appeal was rejected in December 1680, and he would have been hanged shortly afterwards had not Daigre died.

The councillors who selected Rattier lived to be glad of their choice. He performed as well as his predecessors, and was young and healthy enough to postpone the inevitable day when again the community would begin searching. Of him, the *Dictionary of Canadian Biography* says:

> . . . the new executioner had great difficulty in finding a dwelling for his family in Quebec. But he had scarcely moved into a house situated outside the town limits of Quebec, for he was not allowed to live within the

town walls, when the inhabitants of Quebec began to take delight in approaching his dwelling to insult his wife and children. The Conseil Souverain was obliged to intervene. As a final blow, it was this same executioner who on 5 July 1695, in the public square of the Lower Town of Quebec, had to put his own wife, who had been found guilty of receiving and concealing [stolen goods, presumably], in the pillory. . . .

This account omits any mention of Rattier's work on the scaffold. But it is safe to say, because of the circumstances of his coming into the trade, that Rattier performed up to the low standards of the day until his death in May 1703.

Rattier was neither the first nor the last hangman to have been treated shabbily by "decent folk." In one case at least, this abuse continued after death. When "Tomahawk," the Halifax hangman, died, his body was taken by a group of young men and dragged by a rope around its neck to the ruins of the old north blockhouse, where, according to Thomas H. Raddall, it was dumped into the latrine, "where his bones could be seen by curious townsfolk for the next seventy years." Like his French-Canadian brothers, "Tomahawk" was a hard-drinking rogue; a loner, he was forced to live away from the haunts of men, in a ramshackle hut near the abandoned blockhouse that was to become his sepulchre.

Rattier was succeeded by Jacques Élie, "a rogue of the worst sort" according to the *Dictionary of Canadian Biography*. In trouble with the law in Port-Royal for stealing, a hanging matter in 1705, he languished in jail because of the usual vacancy. He was offered his neck if he took on the work himself. After suffering the sort of official contempt that required them to live beyond the walls and the sort of abuse and insults from the community that plagued Rattier, the Élies decided to leave Quebec secretly and flee to New England, where the idea of making a fresh start held appeal. They trusted their fortunes and their lives to a Pawnee Indian named Nicholas, who, after promising to guide them safely out of New France, murdered and robbed the whole family while they slept after the first day's journey. This occurred on 23 May 1710.

Élie was succeeded by Rattier's youngest son, Pierre, with whom Élie had been involved in petty crime in a quiet way. A day-laborer, and not to be trusted, Pierre stole tools and building materials from his employers, and in 1710 he and his wife, who had been involved in illegal activities of her own, found themselves in prison. Rattier was offered the neck-saving option and accepted it, becoming the sixth official executioner in New France. He performed on the scaffold and pillory until his death in 1723.

The passing of the younger Rattier left the colony where it usually found itself with regard to an official finisher of the law. There was thought of importing a slave from Martinique to do the work, but this idea bogged down in red tape. The finding of executioners was the responsibility of the Ministry of Marine, in France. Picking the condemned prisoner who was next in line to be topped seems to have been a local shortcut and stopgap, a fiddle to get around the enormous delays that went with being ruled in matters large and small from a great distance away. When the next executioner arrived from France, one Gilles Lenoir, *dit* Le Comte, the fact that he was an inmate of the Hôpital Général of Paris should have served as a clear warning to the authorities in Quebec. Lenoir turned out to be an habitual drunkard, "so violent when he had been drinking and so disorderly in his conduct" that he had to be confined behind bars when he was not actually performing professionally. According to the *Dictionary of Canadian Biography*, he was almost useless as a hangman as well, so he was returned to France in the autumn of 1730, leaving Quebec once more in an awkward situation. An Englishman called Guillaume Langlais replaced Lenoir, but he was so "old and feeble and addicted to wine" that he didn't last long either.

Finally, in 1733, a young, healthy black slave named Mathieu Léveillé was purchased in Martinique for eight hundred pounds. As soon as he arrived at the end of July, he fell ill, not being at all used to the climate in New France, although he first experienced it at its most benign. Over the next ten years, he was confined to the Hôtel Dieu several times because of his health and a developing melancholy, which Intendant Hocquart hoped to displace by buying him a wife in Martinique and bringing her to live with Mathieu in Quebec. This solicitude suggests that Mathieu's skill on the scaffold repaid such attention. A black female slave was bought and transported to Quebec, but all too late. In 1743, Mathieu took to his bed for the last time and perished in the Hôtel Dieu before the banns could be read. The fiancée was baptized in Quebec Angélique-Denise and disposed of in some way that brought between seven and eight hundred pounds to the public treasury. The practice of promoting a likely-looking rascal from among the condemned prisoners persisted.

Take the case of the young drummer boy Jean Corolère, who had been born around 1731, near Quimper, in Brittany. Corolère probably came to New France as a recruit in the colonial regular troops, where he was one of the first drummers in the grenadier and gunner company, formed towards the end of 1750. In 1751, after a bout of drinking, Corolère was thrown in jail for dueling. The courts took their time trying to decide the young drummer's fate. Officially down on dueling, because of an edict by Louis XV, the authorities privately saw little harm in it, as in this case, where both combatants retired to a tavern as soon as a drop of blood had been shed to preserve honor. Meanwhile, Corolère came under the influence of Françoise Laurent, the daughter of the drum major from Montreal Guillaume-Antoine Laurent. The young woman had been condemned to death by hanging after having been found guilty of stealing clothes—and possibly furs, since her wealthy employers, the Pommereaus, were in the seal-hunting business. The sentence had been confirmed on 12 March 1751 and nothing but the lack of a hangman prevented it from being carried out.

Françoise worked upon the lusty young fellow in the cell next to hers. She knew that he could get out of jail by becoming the hangman, and that he could save her from the rope if he asked for her hand in marriage. It was an ingenious scheme, one which Françoise had to play to perfection if she was to save her skin. She had to cause him to fall in love with her, to cure him of any lingering military ambitions, and to belittle the social disadvantages of the sort of life he would be going into. In the end, she managed it. The drummer applied for the job as executioner, and was given the appointment and freed from the remaining time left to serve on his sentence. The following day, 18 August 1751, he urged the councillors "to grant him in marriage the person named Françoise Laurent," in order that they might "settle down solidly" in the colony. The wedding was celebrated the day after, in the chapel of the intendant's palace.

In Margaret Atwood's "Marrying the Hangman," she captures the poignancy of Françoise's predicament and the artful way she worked her way out of it.

> In order to avoid her death, her particular death, with wrung neck and swollen tongue, she must marry the hangman. But there is no hangman, first she must create him, she must persuade this man at the end of the voice, this voice she has never seen and which has never seen her, this darkness, she must persuade him to renounce his face, exchange it for the impersonal mask of death, of official death which has eyes but no mouth, this mask of a dark leper. She must transform his hands so they will be willing to twist the rope around throats that have been singled out as hers was, throats other than hers. She must marry the hangman or no one, but that is not so bad. Who else is there to marry? . . .

The story appears to have ended happily. The last we hear of Jean Corolère and his bride is only eight months after their marriage: after

29 April 1752 they escape history together. Whether they fled the jurisdiction or raised a family amid coils of rope is fodder for speculation.

Corolère was no longer the hangman in 1797. The incumbent was one Ward—history hasn't preserved his first name. To him fell the unfortunate duty of executing David McLane, an American patriot who came to Canada in that year to convince the French that their best interest lay in supporting the young republic to the south. Tried before Chief Justice Osgood in Quebec City, he was condemned to death for high treason. From the dock he heard that he was to be hanged, drawn, and quartered. To the usual sentence was added the following clarification: his head must be cut from his body and the body then quartered and each quarter put on public display in various parts of the city according to the wishes of His Majesty. The fact that McLane was an American cut no ice with the chief justice. The following account of McLane's death is taken from *Hanging in Canada* by Frank W. Anderson:

> . . . It was obvious that neither the hangman nor the attending physician, Dr. Duvert, had any intention of carrying out the full impact of the sentence, for when Ward jerked the ladder away and caused his victim to drop suddenly, he let him hang for 28 minutes until the doctor indicated that no life was left. Only then did he open the body, take out the entrails and burn them in a "rechaud". Following this he cut off the man's head and held the bloody trophy up to the enrapt gaze of the spectators who had pressed hard against the line of soldiers encircling the scaffold. . . .

Nearly one hundred years later, when Louis Riel mounted the gallows in Regina to die as the last man condemned to death in Canada for high treason, the "refinements," as Anderson calls them, had been done away with. In 1833 the sentence had been revised to omit the ghoulish part. Hanging, pure and simple, was good enough for Louis Riel. But while "drawing on a hurdle"—a crude platform with runners, like a sled—was still part of the written text, Riel stepped directly onto the gallows from a window in the Mounted Police barracks where he had been confined. No ride in a sledge or hurdle was necessary. Anderson also has an interesting word to say about "drawing," which has always caused some confusion. It is sometimes assumed that "drawing" has to do with the disemboweling part of the sentence, as in drawing a chicken. In fact it only referred to the ignominious way in which the prisoner was to be brought to the gallows, usually at some distance from the jail.

When the Canadian Criminal Code was modified between 1867 and

A French-Canadian illus-trator, Octave-Henri Julien, drew this idealized group portrait of the lead-ers of the Armed Rising of 1885 for The Illustrated War News. *Louis Riel (center) was no horseman and wore a full beard at the time.*

1869, the sentence was changed again, instructing those responsible that the felon was to be executed "in the prison in which you are confined." As far as the disemboweling part of the old sentence went, the new law provided for bodies to be delivered to a surgeon "to be dissected and anatomized."

The Criminal Code, even the revised one, was strong medicine, imitat-ing as it did inhuman practices in Britain which were even then being amended. In 1795, according to a source Anderson quotes, "no less than 12 thieves were publicly hanged; one of them for stealing a few potatoes." A thirteen-year-old boy was hanged in Montreal in 1803 for stealing a cow.

Canadians of that time had an exalted respect for property. In Upper Canada, in what is Ontario today, there were severe laws about the unlaw-ful removal and destruction of private and public property. It was a capi-tal offense in the nineteenth century to move a boundary marker from one place to another without approval. In the same vein, misdemeanors in church and vandalism of church property were also severely punished. In Lower Canada, or Quebec, the seignorial system gave large landowners the power to punish for various crimes. The number of men and women—not to mention children—who may have lost their lives at the whim of some landlord is unknown. The frugal French, however, probably reckoned that a live farm laborer was a larger asset than a dead petty thief.

During the closing months of the War of 1812, a bloody assize was held at Ancaster, not far from Hamilton, Ontario. The condemned men were for the most part American colonists whose families had come to Upper Canada during or immediately after the Revolutionary War. As United Empire Loyalists, the group that remained true to King George III, they were celebrated. But there was among them a faction whose loyalty stemmed from the promise of free land rather than abiding Tory sympathies. This was the group that took advantage of the presence of American troops in nearby Stoney Creek to loot and otherwise exploit the situation. The authorities called their plundering and pillage high treason and prepared to deal with it with the greatest severity. I have in my possession some notes that passed back and forth between the senior officers in the administration. They deal with issues far wider than those of the actual crimes of the accused. The appearance of the law is uppermost in their minds, and the question of what property in the shape of land and goods that might be recovered from the guilty is never far away.

Attorney General John Beverley Robinson to Robert Roberts Loring, Military Secretary to Lt. General Gordon Drummond, Governor of the Canadas in 1814, March 25th, 1814 from York [Toronto]

...I...beg permission to report to you that out of sixty men against whom I have informations, chiefly for treasonable practices, it will be necessary to prefer Indictments for High treason against thirty, and sufficient evidence may be had to entitle the Crown to convictions.... For the greater part of these, however, and some of them the most notorious, are with the enemy consequently out of the reach of justice/punishment except by the confiscation of their estates.... Eight or nine—against who [*sic*] I have evidence/witness bound by recognizance to appear, whose evidence I am sure is amply sufficient to convict them of High treason unless the Jurors are determined at all costs to acquit them—of these three ought (I mean by the rule of Common Law) to be tried in the District of Niagara, where their offences were committed....

Attorney General John Beverley Robinson, still in his twenties, was in error when he suggested that the accused traitors be tried in the counties where the offenses were committed, as is usual in ordinary cases, but with high treason the trial could take place anywhere convenient to the authorities. And with the American military still active in the neighborhood, Ancaster was the place agreed upon. Of the thirty cases brought by the attorney general, fifteen convictions were handed down by the three judges. Of these, seven were saved from death. The remaining eight were hanged.

They were hanged! But nothing is recorded of the circumstances. Whether they paid the supreme penalty all together or one at a time, or in groups of two or four, we remain in ignorance. This was no hole-in-the-corner crime, but high treason. And yet in spite of the care and attention that the example being made of these eight should not be missed, it was missed. The people stayed away from the execution in Burlington. Only a handful came to witness the deed. There were no cheers, no huzzas for England! No calls of Long Live the King! There is no written, painted, or sketched memento of the event. Not even the judges who sent them to the gallows recorded more than the date, 20 July 1814. Three months after the eight were hanged, the war came to an end.

Other large executions occurred both in eastern Canada and, later, in the west, where eight Cree Indians were hanged in a group at Battleford, North West Territories, in 1885. They had been convicted of killing whites during the North West Rebellion led by Louis Riel. Two hangmen officiated. One of them, Robert Hodson, an ex-student of the English hangman William Calcraft, which is no guarantee of competence, had briefly been held prisoner by some of the very men he came to execute.

A huge gallows had been built in the center of the North West Mounted Police post, and the gates of the fort had been thrown open for the occasion. The condemned men were led to the gallows steps between two rows of soldiers and police. Chanting a traditional Cree song as they were prepared for death, the Indians stood tall and called out a final greeting to one another as the hoods were lowered over their heads. Allowed to swing in the wind for some time, the bodies were cut down and today share a common grave on the North Saskatchewan River.

Earlier, during the rebellion years, around 1838, batches of patriots were turned off in Lower Canada and similar numbers of rebels in Upper Canada. They were called the Patriots and died bravely in groups. Hanging in batches was one way in which the government attempted to re-establish its authority. It helped colonial officials whistle in the dark, knowing that the large, uncommitted middle ground in any dispute could be cowed by a few hangings.

Hanging in batches was always a public event. It made no sense to use excessive force and not let it be seen. But once the Queen's peace had been re-established, once the need for public order had been demonstrated, and the various colonies came together to create a federated state called Canada, then it was time to reduce the number of executions and to sweep the gallows off the town square or marketplace and rebuild it behind jail-house walls.

The hanging of John Lee in 1871 took place in the yard of the prison in Montreal. It was both the first execution in Montreal since Confederation in 1867 and the first in the relative privacy of a jail. This John Lee must not be confused with his namesake in England, who, in 1885, became "The Man They Could Not Hang." *This* Montreal John Lee had robbed and murdered his landlady at Griffintown, Quebec.

There were so many special guests, medical students, doctors, lawyers, reporters, policemen, each carrying an engraved invitation edged in black, according to Frank Anderson, that the hangman felt that he had better hide his face.

> . . . scarcely had the procession stepped into the jail yard than the black
> flag was run to the top of the flagpole and the prison bell began to toll its
> mournful message. . . . When everything was in readiness, the hooded
> hangman jerked the lever and Lee dropped. The crash of the heavy doors
> . . . startled the invited guests, but they quickly recovered their wits and
> surged towards the scaffold. The bottom of the scaffold had been encased
> with boards, hiding the lower part of the body from view, but so great
> was the desire of the professional men to view the last struggles that the
> boards were torn from the sides and alarm was experienced lest a further
> injury occur.

Hangings for domestic crimes in Canada rarely involved more than three on the gallows at a time. When the gallows trap presented more than one prisoner, or when a woman was being executed, interest was keen, and spectators could be counted upon to attempt a repetition of the behavior of the witnesses to John Lee's hanging. On 10 March 1899, Cordelia Viau, a rural church organist, and her paramour, Sam Parslow, were hanged together in Montreal for the murder of the woman's husband. The hangman, John Robert Radclive, foresaw the possibility of rowdiness from the crowd. In spite of his attempts to keep the prison yard free from specta-tors, beyond the official witnesses and press, an unnecessarily large group of two hundred ticket-holders were admitted to the prison yard. Outside the walls, a crowd of two thousand men, women, and children began beating on the gate to be allowed inside. As the attack upon the prison doors became serious, shots were fired over their heads. Below the gallows, the ticket-holders pushed even closer to the scaffold.

> Hardly had the traps dropped than a disgraceful scene took place. The invited guests surged forward and tore down the black curtains which encircled the foot of the gallows. Fearful lest the excited mob remove the bodies from the ropes, prison guards and police moved in and forced the spectators back. It was several minutes before the police could clear the yard, but when this was accomplished the pair were examined by the prison physician and death was pronounced present in the case of Cordelia at seven minutes, and that of Parslow at twelve minutes.
>
> His deadly function performed, Radclive, as was his custom, departed immediately from the platform and hurried into the prison to a room where he had spent the night. There he consumed a full bottle of brandy....

John Robert Radclive was one of the two best-known Canadian executioners. He learned his ropes in the Royal Navy, where he had stitched up pirates in the China Seas. Later, he apprenticed with William Marwood, the Lincolnshire executioner. He appears to have been a humane man in an inhumane trade. Restless, he came out to Canada, where he settled in Toronto with his family, passing along testimonials from his mentor to a few county sheriffs. When not occupied with his "government work," Radclive worked as a steward at the Sunnyside Boating Club under an assumed name.

Like Marwood, Radclive tried to improve his trade, to pass on to his clients the benefit of improvements he introduced. For instance, in addition to using the conventional apparatus of the day, Radclive imported to Canada another way of hanging criminals. As he told the critic and editor Hector Charlesworth:

> "If they're heavy I drops 'em; if they're light I jerks 'em up." I was very slender at the time [wrote Charlesworth] and he added, "Now if I was 'angin' you I would jerk you up," and he indicated the spot on my neck where he would place the knot. . . . "If there 'as to be 'angin's the only merciful thing is to do 'em right . . .!'"

By "jerking 'em up," Radclive was referring to an American system of hanging, which did away with the need for a scaffold and drop. The prisoner stood at ground level, where he was pinioned, hooded, and noosed in the usual way, but when the lever was pulled, it released a heavy weight which fell with great force. The weight was connected by a rope through the gallows frame to the noose. When the weight had dropped far enough to take up the slack in the rope, the prisoner shot up into the air from where he stood, and came to rest, usually after a bounce or two, some seconds after the weight hit the ground. When it worked well, it was as efficient as the old way. The only problem with it was that it happened in full view. There was no trapdoor which swallowed up the body into darkness and masked the moment the falling figure hit the end of the rope. Radclive believed that this system spared the culprit the agonizing climb up the gallows steps. Most people on the point of death, he believed, have no strength left in their knees.

The celebrated murderer Reginald Birchall was dispatched by Radclive with his "jerk 'em up" gallows. Birchall, an Englishman of good family, had lured a well-to-do young greenhorn to his death in an Ontario swamp, with an idea of robbing him. Such was the notoriety of the case that the execution received more than its usual space in the press of the day. The Toronto *Globe* described Radclive as:

> . . . An Englishman of slight build and below medium height, he has a ruddy complexion and is clean-shaven except for a heavy brown mustache. His features are small and regular and he is an intelligent looking man.

Frank Anderson says this of the Birchall execution:

> . . . At shortly after eight, hangman Radclive donned a black Prince Albert coat, which was to become a hallmark, and escorted Birchall to the strange apparatus. His every move was followed by a large number of invited guests. The top of the prison wall was lined with the uninvited, who had scrambled to this vantage point. Among them were many young boys.

It took Birchall eighteen minutes to die. The execution proved to be a bad advertisement for Radclive's innovation. After the 1890s, sheriffs directed him back to more traditional scaffolds, upon which he performed with great efficiency for many years. He arranged to have straps for pinioning ready so that the execution proceeded as quickly as possible. While he used an American-style "hangman's knot," his long drops were calculated with precision. He tied off the slack of the rope with a bit of string so that the noose hung conveniently at the level of the condemned prisoner's head. He did his best to speed up the process.

Trouble for him began when he was recognized at the boating club by an inspector of the North West Mounted Police, who had watched Radclive

John Robert Radclive traveled all the way from Toronto to Fort Macleod in present-day Alberta to hang an Indian named Charcoal who would not stand on the gallows trap-door. He died seated in a chair.

execute an Indian named Charcoal in Fort Macleod, Alberta. He objected in the strongest terms, saying that he would not have his drinks served to him by a common hangman. Radclive was fired at once by the club and after-wards never held a steady job. Like executioners before him, he supple-mented his tiny income by selling the clothes his victims had worn, the death hoods, and ropes, for which he charged a dollar an inch. According to Arthur Ellis, his successor, he sometimes sold three ropes for the same hanging.

Radclive, like the rest of his tribe, could never be absolutely certain of his status. But in 1892, he was made official Canadian hangman by an order-in-council. He was to be paid seven hundred dollars a year by Ottawa and "reasonable travelling expenses by the sheriff or provincial attorney-general." From *The Case of Valentine Shortis,* by Martin Friedland, I learned that Radclive won this bit of security through the efforts of Sir Oliver Mowat, the premier of Ontario. He passed on his recommendation to Sir John Thompson, the federal minister of justice. The attorney general of Ontario was also in Radclive's corner. He recommended that:

> . . . it was highly desirable in order for the due and proper execution of
> capital sentences that some one individual specially experienced and qualified
> should be designated as a permanent office for that purpose . . . holding
> himself available for all capital cases that might occur in any part of Canada.

The hangman Radclive stands just behind Stanislaus Lecroix on a jail-yard scaffold in Hull, Quebec, 21 March 1902. Once he had hooded Lecroix's head, it took only moments to adjust the noose, which is coiled conveniently at shoulder height.

The final execution that Radclive performed in the last days of the old century was that of Hilda Blake, who was scheduled to be hanged in Brandon, Manitoba, on 27 December 1899. You can imagine the pall that threw over the holiday celebrations of the sheriff, police chief, and warders of the jail. Radclive, himself, must have spent Christmas day in a railway car full of newly arrived colonists heading for the prairies and the west somewhere above Lake Superior.

Hilda Blake had pleaded guilty to the murder of her employer, Mrs. Robert Lane. Hilda was one of thousands of orphans sent out to Canada by well-meaning English reformers. Once settled, they were exploited as indentured labor by their sponsors on farms and in factories. Hilda said that she flew into a rage at the difference in treatment she saw between herself and the Lane children, not that many years younger than herself. Frank Anderson, an amateur criminologist, wrote up the execution from contemporary newspaper accounts.

> . . . After pinioning her arms to her waist with two leather straps, Radclive escorted her to the scaffold with extreme gentleness. As she reached the bottom of the steps, she asked him to raise her skirt so that she could put her foot on the bottom step. . . .
>
> Hilda attempted to delay stepping on the fatal trap as long as possible, but was urged gently forward by the hangman. She smiled as Radclive strapped her feet and placed the black hood over her head. As the Lord's Prayer was said, she was seen to sway slightly, but she died with composure.

One of the newspapers recording the execution says that Hilda was the coolest of the official party, with the exception of Radclive, of course. Following the doctor's assurance that death had been instantaneous, Radclive retreated to a cell with a bottle of brandy, where he was left undisturbed until it was time for his train.

More and more, Radclive became undependable. He declined more jobs than he accepted. Jack Holmes, his rival from Regina, began to be asked to officiate instead of Radclive, even though Radclive's work remained both humane and deadly. The spectacle of an executioner getting drunk after the event had to be weighed against having a sober hit-or-miss man like Holmes on the scene.

Radclive's drinking had been noticed by prison officials before March 1899. While he was never a pin-wearing teetotaller, he had been but a modest drinker until an incident at St. Scholastique, Quebec, changed all that. There, while standing on the trap, hooded, noosed, and pinioned, the condemned man suddenly fell dead into Radclive's arms—frightened to death? the victim of a heart attack? who knows? The sheriff insisted that Radclive pull the lever and send the body down through the trap anyway. Radclive reacted strongly to this vicious side of justice that pursued the sentence of death beyond the grave. After St. Scholastique, Radclive consumed a bottle after each of his executions. He would toss about in a cell or small room in the prison until it was time to catch his train. With him in the dark, he claimed, were the ghosts of all those he had hanged, his own private chamber of horrors.

> The remorse which comes over me [Radclive confided] is terrible and my nerves give out until I have not slept days at a time.
>
> I used to say to condemned persons as I beckoned with my hand, "Come with me." Now at night when I lie down, I start up with a roar as victim after victim comes up before me. I can see them on the trap, waiting a second before they face their Maker. They taunt me and they haunt me until I am nearly crazy with an unearthly fear. . . .

In 1912, on the brink of retirement, Radclive was interviewed. He said that he had executed 132 people.

> My family deserted me and changed their names, but I kept right on with the job, because I argued with myself that if I was doing wrong, then the government of the country was doing wrong. I held that I was the Minister of Justice at a hanging and that if I was a murderer then he was also a murderer. . . .

In another interview he said, "I am two hundred times a murderer, but I won't kill another man." And he didn't. Radclive died, at least in part as a consequence of drink, at his home in Toronto in 1912.

⤺

While John Robert Radclive had used his real name in his work on the scaffold, and unsuccessfully tried to hide behind an alias in his job as a steward at the Sunnyside Boating Club, Arthur Bartholomew English reversed this. As a husband and neighbor, Arthur English was an affable fellow who enjoyed his drink, but as Arthur Ellis, he was known and feared from one coast of Canada to the other. Like the name Jack Ketch in Britain, "Arthur Ellis" became synonymous in Canada with "hangman."

Ellis had seen action with the British Army in India, Egypt, and South Africa. When he was mustered out, it was with the rank of captain. Knocking around for something to do, he made the acquaintance of the Billingtons, who eventually led him into the mystery of their trade. One of his uncles was John Ellis, another important English hangman.

After assisting James Billington and his uncle John, Arthur was given a few commissions to execute some prisoners in the Middle East. Later, he crossed the Atlantic and made his home in Montreal, where the sheriffs of Canada were happy to learn that such a well-connected hangman had settled down among them.

In his journeying back and forth across the country, Ellis tried to get sheriffs to bring their gallows indoors. The usual contraption was built in the jail yard open to the weather and to the curious eyes of anyone who could climb a tree or telephone pole. Sometimes neighboring windows looked onto the scaffold. He lobbied for a few permanent scaffolds in each of the provinces, rather than dread the surprises waiting in the next county jail. In Woodstock, Ontario, for instance, the hangman had to make do with a makeshift gallows that had been cobbled together in a woodshed. In 1935, Ellis, not a man noted for his sense of humor, wrote to the Wentworth County sheriff: "The scaffold at Hamilton is in a state of disrepair. It is a dangerous apparatus and should be demolished." Indeed, many felons who had climbed its steps at the old Barton Street Jail had found it so. Ellis wanted to see a higher standard right across the country that would allow him to work quickly, efficiently, and privately. When Ellis hanged John Krafchenko in 1914, the spectacle was hidden from the curious only when Ellis insisted that planks be nailed together to obstruct the view. When he traveled to Fort Macleod, Alberta, on the occasion of the execution of two Russians, no attempt to obscure the drama had been made and it was too late to make other arrangements after Ellis arrived.

At the end of his career in Canada, which went from 1913 to 1935, Ellis spoke to A. M. Klein, the lawyer and poet.

Arthur Ellis, Canada's best-known hangman, was actually Arthur Bartholomew English, born in England in 1864. Like Radclive before him, he brought military training with him to the job.

He wore a felt hat, horn-rimmed glasses,—the better to see you with, my dear,—a hard collar, and a dark suit sporting a white handkerchief in his lapel pocket.... He stood there, a firm solid parcel of a man, somewhat graying at the temples, somewhat wrinkled, and somewhat florid, but vigorous, broadshouldered, and apparently untouched by his gruesome labours....

Klein quizzed Ellis about the behavior of the condemned on the scaffold. Did he ever encounter violence in a condemned man about to be executed?

"Seldom," he smiled. "Indeed only once. Usually they are quite docile and prayerful, resigned, the guts knocked out of them, dragging themselves to the gallows, or walking with an air of assumed bravado. But once I had a tough customer, a husky fellow, who swore he would break me in two when I came. When I came, he started something.... But I wasn't lightweight champion in the army for nothing."

Asked whether he ever feared revenge, Ellis replied:

"I fear nobody. I do my duty. I publish my picture and my name in the papers. I walk the streets daily. Every morning sees me at the Montreal post office [where sheriffs write him, care of his box]. I fulfill the orders of justice and only a lunatic would hold me personally responsible for that; and from attacks by lunatics nobody is immune. The secrecy that I maintain concerning my identity and residence is for the purpose of protecting my family from cranks and nuisances."

Ellis told Klein that he took a portable gallows with him on the train to rural districts. It was put together, he said proudly, with nuts and bolts, not nails, and was painted red. He impressed Klein as a virtuoso discussing his Stradivarius. Part of the woodwork went all the way back to the scaffold upon which the Patriots of 1837 were hanged. To each execution, Ellis brought his rope, well stretched and noosed, hand and leg straps, as well as the county kerchief, or black hood. To that he might have added a bit of chalk—for toeing the mark—and a piece of string for tying the rope well out of the way. He also presented himself dressed appropriately for the job.

Ellis once interrupted a performance of an opera at the Orpheum Theatre in Montreal by brandishing a .38-caliber revolver and shouting angrily. He was taken to the Chennonville Police Station, where he was charged with being drunk and disorderly in a public place and being in possession of a loaded firearm.

Thomasino Sarao was Arthur Ellis's undoing. She was to him what Robert Goodale was to James Berry. Both were decapitated by being dropped too far. The subsequent careers of both executioners were affected by these incidents. Ellis told Klein his side of the story:

> "The length of the drop"—Ellis adopted a school-master's manner—"is determined by the weight of the condemned person. The jail authorities give me a slip of paper indicating the weight of the unfortunate prisoner, and I make my calculations accordingly. Here," he took a much fingered piece of paper from his breast pocket, "is the slip pertaining to Madame Sarao." It indicated an average avoirdupois [145 pounds]. "Naturally I allowed for a greater drop. But in fact she weighed one hundred and eighty pounds [187, according to Frank Anderson]. The law of gravity tore her head off. And mind you the authorities at Bordeaux jail are not at fault—they had no scales, and so they merely guessed her weight. A million-dollar institution without a twenty-dollar pair of scales. . . ."

Nor was this a unique occurrence. He had taken the head off Dan Prociev in Manitoba in 1926 as well. Called upon less and less, Ellis slipped deeper into the bottle, and became a difficult person to help, although there were several who tried. When he died in 1938, he still clung to his belief in capital punishment, although he tended to favor switching to the electric chair as it was faster, surer, and less dangerous for those whose duty it was to carry out the sentence.

> I know murderers and murderesses as nobody else does [he told Klein], and tell you that the death penalty is highly necessary,—no, not to provide me with a livelihood—but as a deterrent against crime. . . .

The last hanging in Canada was a double execution in Toronto's Don Jail, which took place almost a quarter-century after the death of Arthur Ellis. When Ronald Turpin and Arthur Lucas dropped through the trap in the early dawn of 11 December 1962, a corner had been turned. Whoever the hangman was on that occasion, dressed in a plain business suit and wearing no mask, he closed the book on four hundred years of continuous death on the scaffold, without any sign that society was a whit more safe and secure than it would have been without the rope, the noose, and the gallows. And was this last hanging a credit to the trade? It was not. Brigadier Cyril Everitt, a Salvation Army chaplain, was there and saw everything:

> The hangman botched it [Everitt said], bungled it, there's no other way to describe it. It was a gruesome mess.

CHAPTER ELEVEN

The American Way of Death

". . . The hangman's knot that is generally favored in the United States is rather less efficient [than the British noose with its metal ring], if only because rope slides across rope less facilely than across metal. But when the knot is made by competent hands it works very well, and is not cruel. . . ."

—H. L. MENCKEN

America had a history of cruel and merciless death long before its shores were seen by European sailors. The human sacrifices of the Mayans, Incas, Aztecs, and others stood at the center of the religious rituals of these native Americans, and the executioners were themselves high priests, high-ranking members of the society. The wielding of the sacrificial obsidian blade instilled fear in the thousands who watched the sacred drama. There may have been executioners who eliminated malefactors as well as these high-placed figures, but nowhere in the European or Asian traditions did the executioner rank as high as he did in these cultures, where victims were sacrificed on stone altars to win the favor of the gods.

The European invaders brought their traditional means of meting out punishment with them in their galleons. To put fear in the hearts of the natives, they introduced the whip, the pillory, the rack, the branding iron, and the hot poker; the gallows, the ax, the block, and the stake.

The first murders by Europeans in the New World, according to Carl Sifakis's *Encyclopedia of American Crime*, were committed by Vikings, who had arrived from Greenland and attempted to set up a colony. The Norse sagas tell us that Leif Ericsson and his brother Thorfinn Karlsefni, who arrived around A.D. 1000, murdered eight of the first nine Indians who came to see them.

The next American murderer could justly claim to be of the most distinguished company. He came over on the *Mayflower*. But even before he landed with the rest at Plymouth Rock, Massachusetts, in 1620, John Billington had given Captain Miles Standish a bellyful with his brawling and bad language. This product of the London slums was punished several times by Standish during the voyage. In the Plymouth colony he started feuds and fights with his neighbors, eventually ambushing one of them, John

Newcomen, who had gone into the bush to hunt. The colony quickly tried Billington and sentenced him to be hanged. The year was 1630; the colony was only ten years old. In that period, the colony had been augmented by the arrival of other ships, but it is not at all unlikely that the hangman who ended Billington's earthly days also came over on the *Mayflower*.

In 1638, Arthur Peach, a white settler in New England, and three confederates were hanged for the murder of an Indian whom they had robbed as he returned from trading with the Massachusetts Bay Colony. The question asked, in and around the community, was "should any Englishman suffer the death penalty for the murder of a native American?" Governor William Bradford was quick to see the moral question, but it was probably the need to keep the peace with the surrounding Indians that settled the sentence for him. Should the murder not be quickly and dispassionately avenged, "it would raise a war" it was feared. So, Peach, described at the time as a "lustie and desperate yonge man," and his partners in crime marched to the gallows, where their deaths were witnessed by Indian chiefs specially invited to see English justice triumph in the American colony. The spectacle of seeing the trio turned off "gave them & all the countrie good satisfaction."

In 1626 an unidentified Indian was on his way with a load of newly trapped furs to the trading post in New Amsterdam. He was accompanied by his nephew. He made the mistake of showing off his wares to three woodchoppers at Fresh Water Pond. They murdered the Indian and took his goods, while the nephew ran off to his village. Fifteen years later an Indian laden with furs, bound towards the trading post, fell in with a wheelwright and woodchopper named Claes Smits, who proposed to trade for the Indian's goods. The bargaining turned rough. When the Indian saw that one of the things offered in trade was an ax, the Indian slew Smits with it. The situation reminded him of a time when his uncle had been killed in similar circumstances. He was the nephew who had escaped the three woodchoppers. Once again, the Indian made his way back to his people. Now, of course, the Dutch colony was enraged. One of their own had been slain and they demanded that the Indians surrender the culprit to the law. But, the Indians argued, if a murder hadn't been committed in 1726, then no murder had occurred in 1741 either. Sauce for the goose is sauce for the gander. The immediate result of this was a full-scale Indian war in which many innocent people on both sides were slaughtered. New Yorkers still date the first New York homicide as 1741, not 1726.

The Old Dominion of Virginia earned a bloody reputation during its earliest years for the severity with which it dealt with its Indians and slaves. There was much ear- and hand-lopping, as well as the nailing of ears to the pillory as a warning to others. When the bonded servant Thomas Hellier, a white man, took an ax to his master, a wealthy farmer named Cutbread Williamson, he was hunted down and hanged. His body was chained to a large tree overlooking the James River, where slaves and bonded servants might see it. For many years, until the last of his bones dropped into the river, the body of Thomas Hellier served as a mute warning on the part of landowners to all fomenters of unrest.

Mary Dyer did not look like a fomenter of unrest or like any other kind of threat to the good Puritans of the Massachusetts Bay Colony. But appearances are misleading. The Dyers settled in Boston, where they lived in peace with their neighbors for some time. When Mary returned to England, she was converted to Quakerism, and returned to Boston with the zeal of a convert gleaming in her eyes. She was imprisoned in Boston for spreading the doctrine of the Friends and later banished for the same reason. In 1657 she was also banished from New Haven. Lawmakers at that time in the Massachusetts Bay Colony passed a law that made return from banishment a crime punishable by death. Just the same, Mary Dyer returned to the colony to minister to other persecuted Quakers in their prison cells. She was arrested, tried, and convicted under the "return of banished persons act," and saved from the gallows only by the persistence of her son. In May 1660, she returned once more to Massachusetts, this time, it would appear, either seeking martyrdom or trying to test the nerve of the colony's legislators. Would the good people of Boston really hang a woman merely for returning to her home? She guessed that they were bluffing. She guessed wrong. She was again arrested, tried, and condemned. This time it was not just a woman that was on trial but a principle: Is Boston to be ruled by law or by whim? On 1 June 1660, they took Mary Dyer to Boston Common, where a gallows had been erected, and there they hanged her until she was dead. She is, as Carl Sifakis reminds us, considered today as a Quaker martyr, and may have been the only person executed in America to test the validity of a law.

Mary Dyer had picked the wrong place and the wrong time to test the law. A very few years later and only a few miles north of Boston, near Salem, a group of excited repressed girls were so frightened by their stern parents and minister when caught playing at being bewitched that to escape punishment they blamed some harmless old women as the cause of their strange behavior. Their Puritan elders smelled "familiar spirits" and suspected the old women were witches in direct contact with the Devil himself. Adult pressure on the children seemed to offer no way of escaping punishment for their pranks, unless they stuck to their accusations. But once in the hands of the authorities, a kind of inflexible logic took over, which had a score of innocent people legally murdered on the nomination of these frightened youngsters. A leading spirit in the persecution was the famed Puritan preacher Cotton Mather (1663–1728), an erudite but foolish man, author of more than two hundred books.

But the ground was ripe for a witch-hunt. There were no acceptable outlets for envy or anger in the repressed Puritan settlements. Witch mania pulled out all the stops for them. The people of Essex County were a litigious lot, arguing all the time over boundary markers and strayed cattle. The habit of blaming others for one's own bad luck or mismanagement was endemic. Mrs. Putnum, of Salem, for instance, wondered why Rebecca Nurse enjoyed her children and grandchildren while she, a good churchgoing woman, had buried all but one of her eight children. In that climate it was only natural to see satanic influences at work, and Rebecca Nurse became an early victim of the madness.

In Salem, only those who denied having truck or trade with the Devil were condemned to death. Those who "confessed" were spared. This was a peculiar reading of the Bible. Everyone knew the words of the Book of Exodus: "Thou shalt not suffer a witch to live." Yet it was only those accused but who denied the allegation who were drawn to Gallows Hill.

Indeed witch fever was possessing a large piece of Europe at this time, resulting in the executions of many times more people, and lasting well into the eighteenth century. In England, special ministers were licensed to hunt down witches and test them with special dagger-like probes before turning them over to the law. Sixteen hundred "witches" were burned in Spain during the reign of Philip V, from 1700 to 1746. "In 1724 and 1725 fires were lighted in the Place de Grève for offences which at Versailles passed for schoolboys' tricks," according to Jules Michelet in his *Satanism and Witchcraft*.

The tide began to change in Salem when pastor George Burroughs was brought to Gallows Hill in a cart with seven women as fellow sufferers. This is Marion L. Starkey's account of what happened, drawn from her lively book *The Devil in Massachusetts*. Burroughs was allowed to speak from the ladder and did so so simply and so well that "unthinking people" wept to hear him. At the end, slowly, gravely, faultlessly, he repeated the Lord's Prayer.

When he had done a murmuring went through the crowd. Was not this the supreme test? According to all the books, all the goodwives and all the ministers, no servant of Satan is capable of doing what Burroughs had just done. One of the girls shrilled out that she had seen the black man at his shoulder giving him his cues, but this was no explanation at all. The devil can't do it either.

The murmuring grew as Burroughs mounted the ladder, and with it came a surging forward, almost as if there were some in the crowd who proposed to snatch him away from the sheriff. Then a young man dressed all in black swung upon his horse, stood high in his stirrups and addressed the crowd.

It was Cotton Mather, an old hand at hangings and not without valor. Solemnly he reminded them of Lawson's warning that the devil is never more subtly himself than when he most appears like an angel of light. Burroughs was not at all what he appeared to be; he was not even an ordained minister.

This last remark was an irrelevant quibble which was true in fact but totally beside the point as Burroughs was standing on the ladder with the noose blowing back and forth in front of him.

. . . Nevertheless Mather's words served their purpose; the mutterings diminished and the sheriff was allowed to finish his work. . . .

Heavy fruit dangled from the branches of the big oak tree. They came in batches of five or seven after the initiation by old Bridget Bishop, who died without company. The bodies were buried on the hill, all except that of Rebecca Nurse, who, according to her family tradition, was exhumed from her shallow grave and taken to the family burying ground, where today a granite pillar stands to mark the place.

The strangest and easily the cruelest death that came out of the witch-craft trials in Essex County was that of the elderly farmer Giles Corey. After eighty years in the settlement, most of them spent in hard work on his farm, he was still hale and healthy when the madness of 1692 started. He was subject to superstitions, as were most people in his day, and mentioned that he had observed his wife, his third, reading books. That was enough to bring her to the attention of the witch-hunters. His efforts to stop the insane persecution landed him in front of the judges. Giles was a

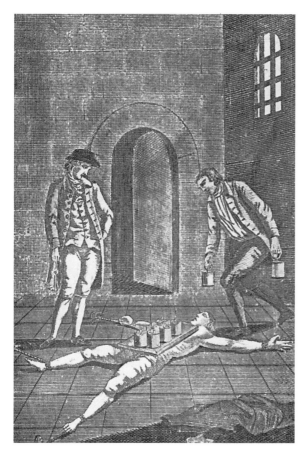

Pressing to death, or peine forte et dure, was not, strictly speaking, a form of execution. When the accused refused to plead "guilty" or "not guilty," they were stretched on a floor and weights were added to their chests until they agree to plea or they died. Both sexes suffered this fate, and even those who were congenitally mute suffered all the same. Pressing was not abolished in Britain until 1772.

crafty sort; he knew that his property might be confiscated by the state if he was condemned as a wizard. To avoid this and to ensure that his sons would inherit his land, he refused to plead. When asked whether he was guilty or not guilty, he stood mute. Under English law, he could be thrice asked to plead. After standing mute, he could not then be tried, but he could be, and was, subjected to the old punishment of *peine forte et dure*, which is usually translated as "pressing to death." The accused person was made to lie on a flat floor on his back. His limbs were extended and secured to rings in the floor or to posts. A board was placed on top of the body and heaps of weights were added. The victim was fed and given water on alternate days until death intervened. Sometimes, as in the case of Major Strangeways in 1658, a sharp stone was placed under the back of the accused, to intensify the torture. When the law was used against Giles Corey, he behaved with dignity. His last words were: "Put on more weight." This is the only recorded incident of pressing to death in America.

Meanwhile in Salem, with the jails crammed with well over one hundred accused and "proven" witches, with twenty of the condemned taken to Gallows Hill and executed, the spell was finally broken. No longer was "spectral evidence" enough to convict. The antics of the "possessed" girls were discounted at last. The trials continued to condemn, but Governor Phips reprieved all who were sentenced to death.

By September 1692, it was all over. There were empty houses, abandoned farms, wandering starving horses and cows, broken fences with no one to mend them. Opinion turned against the girls. Prosecutors and judges admitted that they had been mistaken. A declaration was signed by the jurors stating that they had been "under the power of a strong and general delusion."

But memories are short. By the time the state began to try to make financial amends to the victims, some of the leading forces in the Salem madness came forward with their hands out to claim a share in the damages.

Notorious pirates and highwaymen added to the ordinary hazards of life in the eastern states in the eighteenth century. When caught, they were tried and executed in a civilized manner. But on the frontier, where law and order were in short supply, the vigilantes' rope was often the best rough justice available. At their worst, vigilantes were no better than a mob keeping all rivals in check. The best that can be said for them is that they represented a crude desire to become more civilized, that they welcomed the coming of normal law enforcement and courts of justice.

When the Revolution wrested control of justice from the British, the results were better than were feared, although there were some ugly moments. For example, when the newly constituted court of Massachusetts tried its first capital case, the Tory sympathies of the chief defendant, Bathsheba Spooner, weighted the quality of mercy against her. She was almost certainly guilty, but might have been respited by a less partisan jury because of being with child. Her case is treated in greater detail in a later chapter.

In the nineteenth century, the free spectacle of an execution became rarer, not because of some abolitionist zeal, but because of the pecuniary opportunities hangings afforded. Take the case of Alfred Hicks, a much-feared underworld character of Manhattan. When he came to the gallows, it was for piracy on the high seas, not the sort of crime that Hicks usually included in his repertory. According to one account, he joined the crew of an oyster-boat headed to Deep Creek, Virginia, and murdered all three on board before they reached port.

More than ten thousand people came in rowboats, skiffs, and steamers to see Albert E. Hicks hanged on Bedloe's Island in 1860. His body was jerked up from the floor as a heavy weight was dropped. The execution excursion proved profitable to a number of entrepreneurs, including P. T. Barnum. Like the Lincoln assassination conspirators, Sacco and Vanzetti, and the Rosenbergs, this was an execution under federal, not state, authority.

Since piracy is a federal crime in America, Hicksie, as he was called, became a federal prisoner, who could not, they thought, be executed in the city of New York. It was decided to transport him by ship to Bedloe's Island, in the outer harbor. From the beginning, it was designed to be a "sheriff's ball"—a paying attraction. For instance, since access to the island was limited to those with boats, people wanting to see would have to charter boats, skiffs, yachts, and steamships. People who paid a price would be admitted to the island. Another exchange of money admitted the ticket-holder to the *Red Jacket*, the very ship that would carry the condemned prisoner and the official party to the place of execution. Scalpers worked hand in glove with the federal marshal, Captain Isaiah Rynders, who controlled who got to stand on the scaffold, who stood in the first row in front, and who got a piece of the rope afterwards. When all of his commissions were paid, Rynders cleared more than a thousand dollars from the execution.

A motley flotilla bearing ten thousand souls was anchored in sight of the gallows. Two hundred marines formed three sides of a hollow square surrounding it. A Mr. Isaacs placed the rope around the prisoner's neck and covered his face. Then the hangman cut the rope that controlled the falling weight from the privacy of a small booth beside the scaffold. The weight shot down to the ground hoisting Hicks after it. It took eleven minutes for him to die. After hanging for the usual length of time, the body was placed in a coffin and returned to Manhattan for burial. The official party, along with the paying guests, came back on the *Red Jacket*. Refreshed with drinks and sandwiches, the whole party approached the city in an exuberant and morally uplifted state of mind. After that, Bedloe's Island slipped back into obscurity again until, a quarter-century later, it became the location of the Statue of Liberty.

In America, executioners were recruited when and where they were required. Few had the depth of experience of British hangmen. They championed a standard drop of four or five feet, and the famous cowboy noose, with its rattlesnake coils. Hanging in America was more often than not a hard way to go.

Ingenuity was there, of course. It was an American who invented the "jerk 'em up" scaffold, a gallows with neither drop nor trapdoor, such as the one upon which Alfred Hicks perished. A heavy weight was attached to a noosed rope, which was passed over a horizontal beam. The rope jerked the prisoner up and sideways, often to a quick death. The problem was that the whole of the drama could be seen. The body didn't disappear from sight.

There were also attempts to muffle or disguise the fact of an execution by covering the body of the condemned with a white robe. Once the hood hid the face from view, the condemned man had been transformed into a nearly inanimate bundle, which would not be altered much once the drop fell. Only an exposed elongated stretch of neck remained to remind spectators that the life of a human being had just been stifled.

There are few names of hangmen that American historians can shout in answer to the British gallery of Calcraft, Marwood, Berry, Pierrepoint, and Jack Ketch. The American hangman, whether by his design or society's, stood out of the light. He made use of stratagems such as having a private area or booth in which to release the trap. Mechanisms worked by running water or steel balls made "springing the trap" unnecessary. The victim did it himself when he stepped on the drop. In some places to protect the hangman's identity, three men cut three strings, only one of which actually worked the trapdoors. Nobody knew which of them had done the deed.

American tradition favored the condemned prisoner. He who was about to die was a celebrity and was treated as such. He was offered, for example, the traditional Last Meal, the best available on the prison menu. In the western gold camps and mining towns, in places where law and order had only recently taken the place of the vigilantes, the condemned man was often offered more on his last night than a hearty meal. The madame of the local brothel was consulted and a suitable candidate was slipped into the jail for a few hours. It is unclear who paid for this last indulgence.

When "Black Jack" Ketchum climbed the stairs to the gallows' platform in Santa Fe, New Mexico, in 1911, he was on good terms with his executioners. Jack and his brother were train robbers, the only serious rivals to Butch Cassidy and his gang. But, by 1901, time was running out for the six-gun, the cattle-rustler, and the posse.

When his time came, Ketchum was prepared to make a brave end, as the New York *Times* correspondent reported. Black Jack, far from having to be dragged, "leaped" up the gallows' steps and assisted the hangman in adjusting the noose around his neck, while trading banter with his executioners. "I'll be in Hell before you start breakfast," he said cheerfully. A moment later, when the black hood had been placed over his head, Ketchum yelled, "Let 'er go!"

At the moment that the drop fell, and Black Jack plunged through the floor, his head was torn from his body, showering blood in all directions. Ketchum's hangman was an amateur. Although this unexpected twist in the story was ghoulish enough for most tastes, some writers went on to improve it. Instead of "Let 'er go!" they had Black Jack saying, with a dying man's prescience, "Let 'er rip!"

The most famous American hangman of the old west must be George Maledon, a small, left-handed, ex–Union soldier, with deep-set eyes and long, unruly beard, who from 1875 to 1895 acted as executioner exclusively for "Hanging" Judge Isaac C. Parker of Fort Smith in what was still Indian Territory, but which became Arkansas. After the Civil War he took various jobs as a lawman, his highest position having been deputy U.S. marshal. To earn extra money, he offered his services as hangman, getting as much as one hundred dollars per client, minus the pittance it took to bury the body afterwards.

With Judge Parker on the bench, and the west being its usual unruly self, Maledon was kept busy. Never were judge and executioner so closely associated. "Parker," the wags said, "pronounced sentence, and Maledon 'suspended sentence.'" During their twenty-one-year association, George Maledon executed eighty-eight men. He took his work seriously and built

An inexperienced hangman adjusts the noose around the throat of Black Jack Ketchum in April 1901. The hanging of this outlaw, who was as famous as Butch Cassidy, caused a sensation when a long drop wrenched off the hooded head of the second-most wanted man in the Southwest.

a special scaffold that could hang up to a dozen men at a time. He bought special ropes in St. Louis made from Kentucky hemp, soft but strong, and had them stretched with sandbags to take the bounce out of them and greased up the knots with linseed oil so that they would slip easily. While not a witty sort of person, Maledon did say that "I never hanged a man who came back to have the job done over. There are no ghosts hanging around the old gibbet."

Maledon never did hang twelve men at a time. His largest crowd on the gallows on one occasion was six. The eastern newspapers called this the "Dance of Death." Such write-ups got back to Judge Parker, who later tried to keep the total number in a batch to four. Four dealt with his backlog in the filthy holding tank of condemned men, but didn't attract too much attention in New York, Philadelphia, or Washington.

When Maledon's daughter, Anne, was murdered by her sweetheart, it appeared to the townspeople of Fort Smith that Maledon would reap personal and public justice when he gave Frank Carver a "long twitch" on the end of one of his oiled ropes. But it was not to be. Carver's sentence was commuted on appeal, to the disgust of Maledon, Judge Parker, and the whole town, which had geared up to celebrate the hanging.

Maledon survived Judge Parker and kept on with his job until he retired. For a while, like James Berry, the English hangman, he took to the lecture platform with his ropes and hanging hoods and pinions and newspaper clippings, but was not a great success at it.

Another hangman, proud of his position as "Monsieur New York" (*c.* 1822), the official state executioner, kept his identity a secret, but boasted of his prowess on the scaffold, a boast borne out by the fact that all of his professional engagements were successful: that is to say, painless and quick for his clients, and not embarrassing to the authorities. Across the Hudson River in the state of New Jersey, the official hangman showed none of Monsieur New York's attributes, and hated to have the New Yorker's efficiency thrown up to him. A rivalry grew up between them. On one occasion, Monsieur New York was treated to a ticket to see the Irish murderess Bridget O'Brien launched into eternity from the prison gallows in New Brunswick, New Jersey. When he saw the gallows, and the preparations that had been made with the rope and noose, he shook his head sadly. "Boys, that Jerseyman will make a mess of the job."

After the unfortunate Bridget made her appearance on the drop, and the hangman fumbled with the noose, sensing disaster Monsieur New York leaped up. "What are you trying to do, you damned fool?" "Then," according to one written account of what followed, "unable to restrain himself, the scientific strangler pushed his way through the crowd and saw to it that Bridget was sent out of this vale of tears in as laudable style as conditions would permit and the hand of an artist could assure."

There has never been a case in Britain where a future prime minister has acted on the scaffold, yet in the state of New York, the future president, Grover Cleveland, as sheriff of Erie County, refused to delegate to another the responsibility of executing a criminal. He did the job himself. The criminal, a murderer named Patrick Morrissey, walked to the scaffold wearing a black robe which reached from his neck to his shoes. The fatal rope was already in place around his neck as he came into the prison yard. It is not known whether the sheriff did this or not. But it is not unusual in the United States for the executioner's function to be split up. If the hand that places the knot around the victim's neck is not the same as the hand that pulls the lever, then the guilt is never precisely assigned to one individual. Sheriff Cleveland did not see the prisoner on the scaffold. He operated the drop mechanism from below. It was Under-sheriff Smith who read the warrant to the prisoner and generally officiated on the platform.

When Ben Hecht worked for the Chicago *Daily News*, a veteran reporter at twenty, he went to Wheaton, Illinois, to cover the hanging of Henry Spencer, scheduled for 14 August 1914. Spencer had murdered a lonely spinster named Allison Rexroat with a hammer. In prison, he had found an evangelical form of religion, which sustained him as time moved on towards his execution. Hecht was amazed at the transformation in Spencer, but his cynical colleague, Wallace Smith, was convinced that it was a false front, nothing but a fraud. "Henry's a rat and he'll die like a rat." Religion, he thought, had merely given him the necessary "hop" to get through his last few hours.

The night before the hanging, Hecht and his fellow journalists killed time and several bottles in the stockade that had been built at the edge of town to hide the gallows and the spectacle from those who had not obtained tickets.

> I drank and looked admiringly at the stockade. It was almost a Colosseum. Its fence rose fifteen feet in the air. Fifty rows of empty picnic benches faced the gallows. And this, too, was an astonishing structure. It was twice as high as any gallows I had ever seen. The gallows' platform was some thirty feet above the ground. A dangerous-looking, unbroken flight of small steps let up to it.
>
> "Graft," said the Wheaton *Journal* reporter. "This whole hanging is shot through with graft and corruption. Here's a story for you fellas. I can't print it because my editor's a pal of the sheriff. . . . But you fellas can spill it. The sheriff's running for re-election next month. That's why this stockade is five times as big as it ought to be. He's given out tickets to every political worker in the county. . . . Not only that, but the whole stockade is a swindle. The sheriff's brother-in-law owns the Wheaton Lumber Mill. He got the construction job and put in three times more lumber for everything than required. He soaked the county plenty. . . . The stairs, the fence, the gallows—everything is graft."

The reporters, to pass the time, and to make the repentant murderer's death more "interesting," placed bets upon which step Spencer would trip on, on his way to the top. They were certain he would falter and they all contributed ten dollars to the pot, which was in the hands of three reporters forced to be judges. The reporters experimented, running and walking to the scaffold's platform, and taking blocks of five steps each. Hecht's steps were the final five.

The next morning, the sun rose over the stockade as it began filling up. Not long "after standing-room" had been admitted, the sheriff, his aides, and the prisoner, with a spiritual adviser on either hand, arrived. Hecht, in his autobiography, *A Child of the Century*, continues:

> . . . Henry had reached the gallows' steps and was starting up. Wallace [Smith, the author's cynical colleague], next to me, his ten dollars at stake, was staring intently at Henry's feet.
>
> Henry Spencer started up the steep, towering steps as if taking part in an athletic event. He went up swiftly, with the agility and eagerness of a man in a track meet. He reached the gallows' platform without missing a step or tripping once.
>
> "Nobody wins," I said to Wallace.
>
> "I should have figured on the hop," said Wallace. "A man full of hop can do anything."

Meanwhile, the sheriff, who had never hanged anyone before and was showing his nervousness, slipped the noose around Henry's neck and adjusted the knot, with trembling fingers, behind the prisoner's ear. The sheriff's aides pinioned Spencer's arms to his sides and hung around him a white shroud-like robe which obscured his neck and fell to the gallows trapdoor, hiding the condemned man's feet.

But I am getting ahead of myself. Henry is still standing there in his white robe. He is asked by the sheriff if he has any last words. Henry's face beams as he begins: "This is the happiest moment of my life. . . ." He speaks of the contentment in his soul. He looks up at the sky. He goes on for some time, while his two spiritual aides smile encouragement. Henry repeats a psalm. Many in the stockade are bareheaded and weeping. When Henry is finished, the sheriff clears his throat and asks if he is finished talking. Henry Spencer then takes his eyes away from the sky and begins to call for more time. He denies having killed Allison Rexroat. "I never touched her. I never harmed a hair on her head," he says, "so help me God!" He calls everyone bastards and is about to say more when the sheriff pulls the lever.

> And with this mighty lie on his lips, Henry Spencer went through the suddenly opened gallows' drop. It banged down. The white-robed body fell through space and was arrested in mid-air. The figure started spinning, its head bent to the side, its mouth open and tongue sticking out. The

sheriff had forgotten to put the white hood over the head, and the noose knot had been inexpertly placed. The neck had not broken, and we watched Spencer spin on the humming rope, his chest heave, his face blacken as he choked to death for twelve minutes.

Wallace nudged me . . .

"I told you," he said, "he gave up his chance of Heaven for another minute of life."

But my heart was heavy. . . .

Confused afterwards, Hecht explained his problem to Sherman Reilly Duffy, an older colleague, who said, "You'll find out that's the easiest thing people can do, change into swine." He then quoted Dostoyevsky at the cub reporter: "Man survives where swine perish, and laughs where gods go mad."

Elsewhere, Ben Hecht recounts the case of a preacher who strayed from the straight and narrow into murder. A well-spoken, calm man, he stood on the gallows' trap with dignity. When he was asked if he had any last words, he replied, surprisingly under the circumstances, "Not at this time." Whether he was planning a press conference in the next world is not known.

In his memoirs, *Travels by Night*, Douglas Fetherling meets an old-fashioned, hard-drinking, alimony-paying reporter who remembered what hanging days were like in West Virginia:

> . . . when convicts were hanged in the high concrete room in the penitentiary at Moundsville . . . it was the warden's custom to place bottles of good bourbon along the gallery desk so the reporters and legal witnesses could get some refreshment before the gruesome ceremony. Most would require more than a little such preparation. . . .

The executions that followed the Nuremberg War Crimes Trials in 1946 required a stiff drink beforehand as well. The technique employed by John C. Woods, the American Army master sergeant in charge, was both slow and unscientific. In the Pacific, Lieutenant Charles Rexroad, the son of an itinerant minister, and himself something of a preacher, supervised the hanging or death by firing squad of fifty-three war criminals in the Philippines and Japan before the U.S. Navy brought him to Guam for more of the same. In his time he executed more war criminals than even Master Sergeant Woods did in Europe.

When Albert Pierrepoint, the greatest English hangman of his day and almost the last, was asked to officiate in Britain at U.S. Army camps, to carry out the sentence of a court martial, he was impressed by the inhumanity of it all. At a time when wartime Britons were nearly starving for want of certain foods, the Americans always laid on a great feast to accompany an execution. Whereas Pierrepoint got an execution over as quickly as possible, a time measured in seconds, the Americans kept the poor condemned man standing on the trap while his charge sheet was read out to him and his sentence explained, and he was asked for any last words. He could be standing with his feet tied together and the rope around his neck for six minutes and more. No wonder people standing around fainted. No wonder they kept handy a tall backboard with straps attached to it to brace up the sagging body of the condemned if the starch went out of him. And no wonder there was always a bottle. Pierrepoint, of course, didn't touch a drop.

No, in the old ways of hanging, formal hangings, not lynchings, Americans will always be compared unfavorably with the British. Hanging belongs to the past, which is Britain's forte; America and the New World required something more characteristically modern than the rope. They needed the "Death House" and the electric chair, the lethal chamber, and the needle, which we will examine next.

CHAPTER TWELVE

The Death House and Its Place in the American Dream

". . . in a matter of seconds, the prisoner is strapped into the chair by the guards. . . . Then a mask of leather is placed over the face and a skull-cap fitted to the head by the executioner. This skull-cap contains one of the electrodes, the other electrode is attached to the right leg. . . ."

—GEORGE RYLEY SCOTT

". . . The good thing about this thing is that they carry you out—you don't have to walk. . . ."

—LAST WORDS OF CLAUDE UDWINE

Thanks to Benjamin Franklin, the world sees electricity as an American phenomenon, a source of vast power associated with the New World, symbolizing progress in a clean, unpolluted environment. What image could represent this better than the greatest single source of that power, Niagara Falls?

The electric chair was introduced in 1890 through the concurrence of a number of factors. In 1885, Governor Hill of New York State formed a legislative commission to examine the whole question of hanging as a means of capital punishment and to look into alternative methods for exterminating the condemned. "After viewing a number of hangings," Carl Sifakis says, "including that of a woman who slowly strangled to death, the members decided that the noose had to go."

At this time Thomas Alva Edison, and his rival, the inventor George Westinghouse, were locked in a heated commercial war over how electricity would be transmitted to the American home. Edison championed his Direct Current (DC), Westinghouse, Alternating Current (AC). Edison charged that Alternating Current was dangerous to be near. He caused a colleague to go through the state of New York demonstrating the deadly nature of AC on stray cats and dogs and on an orangutan, which not only died, but caught fire. Members of the governor's commission on the death penalty heard about Edison's debunking experiments with Westinghouse's

Alternating Current. If it could kill an orangutan, it might be used to kill primates nominally higher on the evolutionary ladder. Governor Hill had his way. On 4 June 1888, he signed into law a bill substituting electricity for hanging in New York. The death sentence was altered to read: "The sentence of the court is that a current of electricity be passed through your body until you are dead—and may God have mercy on your soul."

The first man to die in the electric chair was William Kemmler, alias John Hart, on 6 August 1890 at Auburn Prison, New York. The execution was sheer butchery. The condemned man, who submitted to all sorts of minor adjustments to the brand-new chair before the current was turned on, was tortured and burned in the long, drawn-out process of killing him. Earlier he had jokingly hoped that they wouldn't experiment too much on him, but he could have had no idea of what he was to suffer and what the witnesses had to watch. The executioner had forgotten to wet with brine the sponges that surrounded the electrodes. As a result, parts of Kemmler were cooked, even burnt. Some witnesses fainted; one ran out of the room retching. Westinghouse himself said afterwards, "It could have been done better with an ax." While true, this comment by Westinghouse was a cheap shot; Kemmler would have had an easier death if Westinghouse had allowed the state to use his most advanced equipment.

The earliest of the "hot seats" differed from the familiar form in several ways. The electrode that is now attached to the right leg of the victim was then applied to the base of his spine. In early versions, a footrest was included. The condemned prisoners were quick to include the electric chair in the argot of prison life. From the beginning, "the chair" was kept in a room of its own. The prisoners' walk to the "hot seat" from a holding cell, "the dance hall" in "death house" parlance, through the "green door," which may not be green, into the execution chamber is called "the last mile," although it is never more than a few yards. When the executioner "turns on the juice," the condemned is "fried" or "burned"; he "rides the lightning" over the wall.

At Sing Sing, a few rows of pews face the death chair. These are for the required witnesses, often journalists. There has always been a long waiting list. Nowadays, in Florida's death chamber, where "Old Sparky" reigns supreme, a glass partition, with the ready censor of a venetian blind on the chamber side, separates the witnesses, who come and go through their own special entrance. This arrangement saves the witnesses from some of the unpleasant non-visual aspects of an execution: the smell of perspiration, urine, and feces.

The electric chair has many nicknames: "the chair," "the hot seat," and "Old Sparky," where the condemned "fry," "burn," or "ride the lightning" out of this world and into the next. The original chair had a footrest. The electrode that is now fastened to one leg was originally attached to the base of the spine.

In spite of much agitation within the United States and overseas, after the Kemmler fiasco, electrocution continued. A chair was built for Sing Sing Prison on the Hudson River. (That's where the term "up the river" for going to prison comes from.) Four men died, one after another, on a July morning in 1891 in the first electrocution at Sing Sing. The *Police Gazette* recorded the event with a center-page spread. But, in spite of the initial reluctance of the last victim to come out of his cell, the quadruple execution went without a hitch. This was partly because the warden of Sing Sing had invited the warden of Auburn to supervise the event. It gave him a chance to improve on his earlier performance.

The distinction of being the first woman to die in the electric chair belongs to Martha Place, who walked into the death chamber on the arm of the warden and said, as she was being strapped into the chair, "God save me!" The French, who were intrigued by the event, illustrated the execution in their newspapers, showing the murderess sitting in a fanciful chair with her feet secured to a matching footstool, while a female official holding a pocket watch in her hand takes her leave of the prisoner.

The electric chair was next adopted in Ohio, but it wasn't actually tried until nine years later, when it was used to hurtle two criminals into the hereafter. The Columbus *Enquirer* covered the event:

SEARED

INTO THEIR VERY SOULS

PENT-UP LIGHTNING KILLS A MURDEROUS PAIR

BLASTED AS THEY SAT IN DEATH'S ARM-CHAIR

THE ELECTRIC CURRENT AVENGES TWO SLAIN WOMEN

OHIO'S MAIDEN ELECTROCUTION PROVES A

DECIDED SUCCESS

. . . The new method of inflicting the death penalty was well tested tonight and found to be all that it was promised. Within less than the passing of a moment, two men, in perfect health when they took their seats in that fatal chair, had gone to the great beyond.

Formerly it required much more time to take the life of a first-degree murderer. Twenty-seven minutes was the period some of them struggled, and others suffered more than half that time. . . .

Warden E.G. Coffin who threw the switch is impressed with the simplicity and the certainty of the new method and pronounces it the greatest innovation in the criminal history of the state.

After New York and Ohio, other states quickly followed. In 1950 twenty-one states, including North Dakota, could legally use the electric chair, although, in 1950, North Dakota did not possess one.

In some southern states, the chair was portable. It could be moved from prison to prison in a van, which contained its own generator. It provided death on wheels and included the services of the executioner, who saw to the installation of the chair where it was needed: in a room in a prison, or often in the very courtroom where the condemned criminal first heard the sentence of death pronounced. When a journalist once complained within the hearing of U.S. Senator Theodore G. Bilbo that a courtroom electrocution was not much improvement on a lynching, the latter replied with the authority of a connoisseur, "Ah, this is pretty tame compared to a lynching."

Still, an electrocution can be harrowing enough for the stoutest heart. The prisoner may fight with his guards all the way from the holding cell to the chair. Terror of death in the chair can reduce a murderer to sub-human behavior, more like a reluctant, frightened cat being spread-eagled on a vet's examining table than like a sentient human being; with bowel and bladder sphincters open, and screaming for another minute of life, the prisoner's agony can be horrible.

In 1899, Mattie Place was the first woman to sit in the electric chair. She walked calmly to her death on the arm of the warden. This imagined picture of the event was created for a French-language newspaper.

At the same time, despite their fears of "burning" in the chair, some condemned retain their sense of themselves, some have deeply touched the sensibilities of those whose duty it was to put them to death. One murderess, only moments from oblivion, warned the attendant priest to stand farther away from her so that he wasn't accidentally electrocuted with her.

Contrary to English custom, stimulants are never given to the condemned in the United States. It is generally accepted that the occupant of the chair should be expelled from this world to the next with a clear head. The health and well-being of the condemned have a high priority in the prison. Each is given a haircut on the fatal day, each is issued with a new suit, only the trousers of which will be worn by him before his death. The jacket is for the funeral. In America the state has never shown an interest in the remains of an executed criminal. Bodies are returned to the families that request them. In Britain, the bodies of the hanged were always buried within the prison.

The Last Meal has always been an American tradition. It is always something the press likes to report. Some criminals eat a hearty Last Meal, others pass theirs on to another prisoner whose time has not yet come.

Robert G. Elliott, the executioner who was closely associated with the Sing Sing Death House in the 1920s and 1930s, lived in upstate New York, where the one-time electrician was known to be a dedicated gardener. The quiet-spoken son of an Irish immigrant, Elliott became the official executioner in six Eastern states. He was called "the gentle executioner," perhaps, as Denis Brian suggests in his book *Murderers Die*, because he didn't seem to enjoy the job. After he executed the convicted anarchists Sacco and Vanzetti, he received hundreds of threatening letters. Once his house was bombed, and the state assisted him in paying for the necessary repairs. In his career as executioner, he put to death three hundred and eighty-two men and five women. Elliott recalled in his memoir, *Agent of Death*, that he made it a rule never to establish eye contact with the condemned. He forgot his own good advice once. For a slender moment two men, the executioner and his victim, looked into each other's eyes and established briefly an exchange of . . . Of what? Compassion, farewell, forgiveness, a sense of the human condition?

The first woman that Elliott executed was the celebrated Ruth Snyder in January 1928. Ruth was the suburban wife of a magazine editor. She had taken up with Judd Gray, a salesman for the Bien Jolie Corset Company. Snyder assisted Gray in hitting Albert, her husband, repeatedly with a window-sash weight, chloroforming, and finally strangling him. After an absurd attempt to make the murder appear to have been the work of burglars, the two were tricked into confessing by being told that the other had already blabbed. In court "Lover Boy" and "Mamma" blamed each other. The newspapers called Ruth the "Granite Woman," possibly because she had insured Albert's life for $48,000, with a double-indemnity clause in case of accidental death which made it $96,000. Until the very hour of her death, Ruth continued writing to the insurance company to pay up.

After Ruth entered the Death House, she found religion, and went to her death quoting some of Christ's own last words as her own: "Father, forgive them; for they know not what they do."

Gene Fowler, a friend of Ben Hecht's and a product of the same hard-drinking school of journalism, wrote the following description of Ruth Snyder's execution in the old *New York American*:

> They led Ruth Brown Snyder from her steel cage tonight. Then the powerful guards thrust her irrevocably into the obscene, sprawling oak arms of the ugly electric chair. . . . The body that once throbbed with the joy of her sordid bacchanals turned brick red as the current struck. . . . That was

only thirty minutes ago. The memory of the crazed woman in her last agony as she struggled against the unholy embrace of the chair is yet too harrowing. . . . She wore blue bloomers. . . .

But Fowler and the other twenty-three men sitting in front of the "hot seat" were not the only witnesses to the death of Ruth Snyder. All of New York saw her die. The front page of the New York *Daily News* the next day featured only one word: DEAD! Below it, taking up the rest of the page, was a blurry but riveting photograph of the woman, caught forever by the camera's lens, held in the lethal grip of the electric chair. It was a *Daily News* EXTRA!

The photograph, perhaps the most famous picture in the history of tabloid journalism, was taken by a news photographer named Thomas Howard. He had been hired away from the Chicago *Tribune* by the *Daily*

A camera strapped to the photographer's leg captured this graphic image of Ruth Snyder caught in the lethal embrace of the electric chair in January 1928. The picture filled the front page of the New York Daily News *the following day.*

News, the way a hitman is imported to make a particular hit and then get out of town. It was very easy to arrange since the same company owned both papers. John Faber, in his *Great Moments in News Photography*, gives the dirt on how the photograph came to be made. Three men engineered it: *Daily News* city editor, Harvey Duell; picture-assignment editor, Ted Dalton; and his assistant, George Schmidt. They brought in their hit man, put him up at a hotel, and got him to experiment with a miniature camera strapped to his left leg. How do you aim a camera without looking through a view-finder? Tom Howard worked it out. He knew that he would have only the one exposure and worked out the focus with the help of blueprints of the death chamber itself. A lot was riding on the photographer's ability to get this history-making shot. It was not only the first picture of a woman in the chair, but the first photograph of anyone in the act of being electrocuted. In order to get the picture, Howard had to run a shutter-release wire up his pant-leg to a bulb in his pocket. When Robert G. Elliott pulled the copper handle that sent the first shock into Ruth Snyder, Howard lifted his trouser-leg, pressed the bulb, and caught a slightly blurry image of the dying woman twelve feet in front of him and a little to his left. Faber's account of the fatal moment is a little ambiguous, leaving it unclear whether one or two exposures were made on the same glass plate. Did the blurriness, which added shock value to the image, come from the moving of the body in the chair or from being a double exposure? Whatever happened, a car was ready to whisk Tom Howard back from Ossining, New York, to Manhattan and a darkroom, where the negative was processed, touched up, and printed. When the *News* EXTRA hit the streets, 1,193,000 paper-buying New Yorkers were shocked out of their wits. Tom Howard's scoop photo went into the history books along with Ruth Snyder.

When Robert Elliott died in 1949, the mail of Sing Sing's warden, Lewis E. Lawes, was full of applicants to fill the vacancy. One in five of the letters were from women. Denis Brian found out about some of them.

> Two widows vied with each other for the job. One who described herself as having plenty of nerve and the ability to repair her own radio felt confident she could quickly learn the "little trick" of electrocution. If the warden turned her down she asked him to find her a "nice honest husband." She didn't want him to choose one from the prison population, though.
>
> Her rival had worked as a nurse but would like to be an executioner because it was odd and different. She said she was in perfect health,

didn't have any bad habits, and "I am not hard-hearted, neither am I chicken-hearted."

One applicant [male, this time] modestly requested a one-shot execution, needing the one hundred and fifty dollar fee to send his son to college, and another man was seeking cash for a dowry to marry off his daughter.

The idea of a female executioner, the literal *femme fatale*, was not unique to New York State. Across the Atlantic in Dublin, a hangwoman was an established part of the scene in the mid-nineteenth century. Called "Lady Betty," she was a rather heavy-featured woman with a reputation for being harder on her own kind than on the men who came her way. She carried out floggings as well as hangings with skill enough to satisfy everyone involved. Her name was used by mothers to frighten children into good behavior much the way the bogeyman's name is invoked: "Be good or Lady Betty will get you!"

Sing Sing's warden had requests from people who, for a fee, or for good-hearted, generous reasons, wished to take the place of the condemned prisoner and walk the last mile to the chair instead. Naturally, the warden had no legal power to even consider such a proposal. A death sentence, like a passport, is legally untransferable.

The gas chamber is another form of execution unique to the United States—that is, if we keep German wartime extermination camps out of it.

Up until 1921, condemned criminals in Nevada had to decide themselves whether they wanted to be executed on the gallows or by a firing squad. Both methods tended to be chancy and messy. Under the influence of Dr. Allen McLean Hamilton, a Nevada toxicologist, a search was started to find a new, humane method that was neither messy nor chancy. Hamilton favored gas, and in that year the legislature ruled that gas would henceforward be the legal means of capital punishment.

On 8 February 1924, the first victim of lethal gas stepped into the new death chamber, which so far had killed only two stray cats, the day before. The man was Gee Jon, who had brutally killed another Chinese in a tong war. The lethal chamber was fairly primitive by modern standards, but at the time it was the cutting edge of modern technology harnessed for a lethal purpose. The gas in this first Nevada chamber was introduced through a hand pump. Once the gas was in the chamber, there was no way of telling whether the prisoner was dead or not. They left him steeping in the fumes for some time, and then another half-hour while fans cleared the gas from the chamber.

Gee Jon died quickly and easily, it was announced. Lethal gas was a success. By the year 1960 eight other states had switched to lethal gas and had had death chambers replace their gallows and electric chairs. The chief advantage of the lethal chamber appears to have been the lack of mess: there was no blood as in a shooting or decapitation; there was no sudden evacuations because of terminal trauma as you get in both hanging and electrocution. Tidiness won out along with speed and the name of science. But there still remained the psychologically painful preparations. Just as the victim of the chair must have his hair shaved to create a place for the electrodes, the victims of lethal gas have stethoscopes taped over their hearts some time before the walk to the lethal chamber, and in some states, the victim is stripped to his shorts before he enters the chamber so that no wisps of gas will remain caught in the folds of his clothing, which might be dangerous to the guards removing the body.

The modern lethal chamber looks like a submarine or spaceship more than a room. It is built of metal, has bulkhead-like connections, and is round or polygonal. Gasketed windows for the witnesses and officials surround the structure. The door is an air-lock, controlled by a wheel, which fits tightly against a rubber sealer. Inside, two metal chairs are anchored to the floor. There are straps for arms, legs, hips, and chest. Somewhere there is a tube that will be attached to the stethoscope the prisoner is wearing. The attending physician listens on his side of the glass through the familiar stethoscope ear-pieces. Nowadays it is connected to a vital-signs monitor, which shows a straight line at the time of death.

Death enters the modern lethal chamber as follows. Under the chairs are shallow pans, into which sulfuric acid is introduced through tubes. Already fixed beneath the chairs, wrapped in cheesecloth and attached to levers leading outside, are cyanide pellets the size of eggs. On a signal from the warden, the executioner works the lever, the "eggs" drop into the acid, and the fumes begin to rise. Caryl Chessman, one of the most celebrated criminals ever to walk into the lethal chamber at San Quentin Prison in California, described what he believed happened next in his book, *Death By Ordeal*:

> . . . You inhale the deadly fumes. You become giddy. You strain against the straps as the blackness closes in. You exhale, inhale again. Your head aches. There's a pain in your chest. But the ache, the pain is nothing. You're hardly aware of it. You're slipping into unconsciousness. You're dying. Your head jerks back. Only for an awful instant do you float free. The veil is drawn swiftly. Consciousness is forever gone. . . .

This is how Chessman imagined it would be. In the event, he arranged to signal a reporter if he found that the ordeal was more painful than he had estimated. Through the glass he gave the signal.

For eleven years Caryl Chessman fought the courts to save his life, rather the way Gary Gilmore fought to have himself executed. Chessman never claimed to be an angel, but he said that he was not guilty of the crime for which he had been condemned. From Cell 2455, Death Row, Chessman wrote several autobiographical books which explained to the world what it felt like to be in his shoes. He told it how it was to be poor and victimized by the state. Chessman was found guilty of being the "Red-Light Bandit," a small-time robber and sometime-rapist, who shone a red light in the eyes of necking couples parked in various lovers' lanes. Whether Chessman was in fact the "Red-Light Bandit" was never proved beyond any doubt. His death sentence came from a rather unusual use of California's "Little Lindbergh" law. The original Lindbergh law cleared the way for federal police agencies to enter a kidnapping case on the assumption that the victim has been taken over a state line. The "Little Lindbergh" law in California made the death penalty mandatory in cases of kidnapping "with bodily harm." Chessman's claim was that he was not the man they were looking for, and, if he was, he had not kidnapped anyone, and no one had been killed. The state maintained that, since the offenses were committed in a car, the kidnapping law could be applied. Thousands of people wrote to defend Chessman's right to life, including some of the best-known names from around the world: Pablo Casals, François Mauriac, Eleanor Roosevelt, André Maurois, Aldous Huxley, Norman Mailer, Arthur Koestler, Billy Graham, the Queen of Belgium, Christopher Isherwood, Karl Menninger, Ray Bradbury, Norman Corwin, and Robert Frost. To these were added many millions of unknown names from Britain, North America, Brazil, and Switzerland. But in the end the only name that counted was that of California's governor, Edmund G. Brown, who refused, in spite of his own expressed feelings about capital punishment, to interfere.

Caryl Chessman's case made the question of capital punishment a matter of debate across America in the 1950s. After a media blitz that rivaled that surrounding the Sacco and Vanzetti case, he was finally executed. But the way to an unofficial abolition of the death penalty for a hiatus of ten years had been well advanced.

While Chessman managed to delay his execution for a dozen years, and long waits in the Death House became common, the case of Carl Austin

Caryl Chessman's death in the San Quentin gas chamber in 1960, after twelve years of legal battles, brought America to a temporary halt in carrying out capital sentences. Chessman's books, and the movies based on them, added to the abolitionist cause. This picture shows him in a 1957 court appearance.

Hall and Bonnie Brown Heady went forward with uncommon swiftness. Six-year-old Bobby Greenlease was kidnapped from his private school in Kansas City in September 1953. The child was murdered even before the ransom demand was delivered. A ransom of $600,000 was paid by the boy's wealthy father to the kidnappers, who went on a spending and drinking binge which led to their capture, trial, and joint execution in the lethal gas chamber in December of the same year. Swift justice is promised in Habeas Corpus and British Common Law, but, in fact, it rarely moves so quickly.

When the time came for Hall and Heady, they went into the death chamber together. Bonnie was concerned that her lover not be strapped into his chair too tightly. "You got plenty of room, honey?" she asked as her own straps were being adjusted.

"Yes, Mamma," he replied.

The deaths of the Greenlease kidnappers left one mystery unsolved. The ransom money had been divided between two metal suitcases. The brief binge the kidnappers went on couldn't have cost more than a few thousand dollars at most. The St. Louis Police, from the Eleventh Precinct, admitted that they had recovered $295,140. That leaves to this day a missing $300,000. The FBI thinks that the local police know more than they are saying, but no charges were ever brought, not even by the bereaved father of the kidnap victim.

You will have noticed in both of the last two cases that there has not been one word said about the executioner. Who, in fact, is the executioner in a lethal-gas-chamber death? Is it the guard who wraps the cyanide pellets and hangs them below the chair? Is it the doctor who informs the warden when life is extinct? Is it the man who fills the pan with acid, the one who shuts the steel door to seal the chamber, or the person who drops the pellets into the acid? The dropping of the pellets certainly is the point of no return. Nothing can be done once this has happened. Twice, while researching this section, I ran across stories of stays of execution being granted just after the pellets dropped. Caryl Chessman himself was one of these. But too late is too late. There has never been, outside the movies, an attempt made to free a convict from the death chamber once the cyanide has hit the acid. Nor has there been a *failed* gassing as there have been failed hangings and electrocutions. The death isn't as clean nor as easy as its first promoters promised, but it isn't any more cruel or unusual than the other choices available. Carl Sifakis's comments might be useful here:

> . . . Essentially, the victim strangles to death without the courtesy of a rope. He is forced to do it himself as he battles for oxygen that is no longer there. . . . The condemned person is often told that as soon as he smells an odor resembling rotten eggs, he should count to 10 and then take several deep breaths. This, he is told, will cause him to pass out quickly and die without pain. It doesn't happen that way. Man's instinct, the body's instinct, is to live. The victim will gasp and wheeze, struggling for air. His mouth opens and shuts like a beached fish. Often, he screams or sobs. Choking, he thrashes about. He pulls on his bonds. Occasionally, it is said, a victim will break an arm free, usually in the process severing the skin, so that his blood may spurt over the windows through which the witnesses are watching.
>
> The asphyxiation process is slow. The thrashing victim's face turns purple, his eyes bulge. He starts to drool. A swollen tongue hangs out. But death still has not occurred. . . .

It usually takes about eight or nine minutes to die like that. The slowest on record was eleven minutes in North Carolina.

A celebrated victim of the gas chamber at San Quentin was the controversial blonde good-time girl Barbara Graham. She was convicted of being the third member of a gang of small-time crooks who robbed and strangled an elderly, crippled housewife, Mrs. Mabel Monahan. Barbara claimed to have left the gang before the day of the robbery and murder. Her accomplices said she was there. The prison psychologist argued that

Barbara Graham's crimes were crimes of weakness: prostitution, drunkenness, drugs, excess, theft, but not violence. Violence, he thought, was quite outside her scope, although Barbara admitted to Ed Montgomery, the reporter who had followed her case, in a last letter written as dawn was breaking over San Quentin on the day she died, that she had hated people all of her life.

> . . . But what I want to tell you, the thing that hurts most, is that so much of my life was spent hating people. I can't remember any time as a child when I wasn't alone and afraid and filled with hate. But now, when this thing is happening, so awful that never in all my fears and hatreds did I ever imagine anything like this, I've stopped hating. I only think of the many people who had no reason to care, but they did care. This is the thing I'm taking with me. It's a big thing, and I want you to always remember that you were part of it.
>
> Good-bye,
> Barbara

Barbara Graham didn't have an easy death that June day in 1955. Twice on the way to the chamber the telephone rang and told them to delay the execution. It was never a full stay of execution, just a delay in getting it over with. She started out on the arms of two priests, feeling stronger than she had been. There was no need to use the wheelchair that had been provided. Barbara wore lipstick and earrings. "Her dark brown hair, no longer bleached blonde, looked soft and shiny," said Denis Brian, whose book *Murderers Die* pays special attention to Barbara Graham. At the first delay, Barbara, who had steeled herself for her walk to the chamber, fainted. When the execution was interrupted a second time, she said, "I can't take it. Why didn't they let me go at ten? I was ready to go." Before she set out the third time, she put on a black sleep-mask borrowed from the matron. "I don't want to look at those people," she said. When she was instructed by one of the guards who strapped her into the chair to count ten after hearing the pellets drop and then take a deep breath, Barbara asked, "How the hell would you know?"

California, which has executed only three people in the last thirty years, has recently junked its lethal gas chamber and adopted, as of February 1996, the lethal needle. William Bonin, the Freeway Killer, was its first victim.

In 1972 the Supreme Court of the United States ruled that the death sentence represented cruel and unusual punishment, and thus violated the Eighth Amendment to the Constitution. It also could find no sign that it acted as a deterrent to the commission of new crimes. From 1967 to 1972, public pressure stayed the hand of the executioner. From 1972 until 1976, no one was put to death, because it was illegal. Thus for ten years, until the Supreme Court noticed that public opinion had shifted away from this abolitionist position, no one was executed in the United States. But a majority was demanding a return to the death penalty, and the Supreme Court was listening. The ruling was successfully challenged and a less liberal court reversed itself.

But this was not a return to the America prior to *Furman* vs *Georgia*. No longer was the death penalty exclusively a state issue. The federal courts now played a role, as David C. Baldus and others have said:

> . . . the United States Supreme Court accepted the proposition, until then
> a novel one, that the manner in which the states convicted and condemned
> capital offenders was a proper subject for judicial supervision. . . .

With the stage set for the return of the executioner, it was only a question of which state would be the first to begin again. Then, in Utah State Prison on 17 January 1977, Gary Gilmore forced the state of Utah to execute him. The thirty-six-year-old multiple-murderer, by not appealing his death sentence, ended the hiatus. Sitting in an old office chair, he faced a firing squad of five riflemen. Capital punishment was back with a vengeance.

But this was not the familiar military firing party: a straight line of riflemen and an officer with a raised sabre. In Utah the riflemen, who apply for the job, are hidden behind a screen, so that neither the prisoner nor any of the spectators can see their faces. By having them fire from cover, as at a turkey shoot, their desire for anonymity is reconciled with the equal urge to be in at the kill. In Utah, prisoners may choose between the rope and a volley of bullets. No one has ever chosen the rope. Joe Hill, the radical reformer of the folk-song, picked the firing squad as well in 1915.

It is a tradition that one of the riflemen in a firing squad shoots a blank round. The tradition is military in origin. Since the soldiers in a firing party are not professional executioners, it seemed fair to give each member of the squad a shred of doubt about whether or not he had fired a live round or a blank. The tradition is somewhat stretched when applied to marksmen who volunteer to shoot at convicted criminals. Riflemen claim that they can tell from the jolt whether their shot was a blank or not.

Since Gary Gilmore faced death in Utah, and Florida dusted off "Old Sparky," its venerable electric chair, to use on John Spenkelink in Starke Prison, outside Raiford, in May 1979, executions have been a normal part of American life. Especially in Texas and Florida. Three hundred and twenty-two people have been executed since 1976, a third of them in Texas. Reporter Timothy Appleby of the Toronto *Globe and Mail* calls this new America "the vengeful society." A "get tough" attitude to crime is reflected in both federal and state initiatives. The fact that the crime rate is decreasing confirms to anti-abolitionists that the policy is working. Vengeance works. The horror, even when the prisoner kicks up rough, as Spenkelink did, doesn't seem to register any more.

For anyone whose memory needs refreshing, John Spenkelink, the thirty-year-old convict, staged a battle royal when guards tried to drag him to the death chamber. In the chamber itself, venetian blinds over a partition window suddenly cut off the view of the chair, bewildering the assembled witnesses. When it finally was opened again, Spenkelink was firmly strapped into the chair with a gag in his mouth. When the executioner gave him an initial jolt of electricity, his hair caught fire around the head electrode. (The executioner tries to keep the current under six amps so that the prisoner isn't cooked while he is being killed.) It took three jolts and five minutes to finish him, although it is said that it only takes 1/240th of a second to render the victim unconscious. The witnesses aren't that lucky.

There have been hundreds of harrowing scenes in the death chamber, few with a happy ending. There was one, however, involving Florida's "Old Sparky." The year was 1926 and the man in the chair was Jim Williams, an unspectacular villain, who had steeled his nerves to ride the lightning out of this world. In this case there was no executioner standing at the switch and an argument broke out between Warden John S. Blitch and Sheriff R. J. Hancock. Each thought that it was the other's duty to pull the switch. According to Carl Sifakis:

> . . . The argument went on for twenty minutes until poor Williams collapsed. He was carried back to his cell while the dispute went into the courts. Eventually, a ruling was made that the sheriff had to do the job, but by then the Board of Pardons decided Williams had done enough penance and commuted his death sentence to life imprisonment.

In December 1982, the state of Texas executed a black man named Charlie Brooks for the murder of a secondhand-car salesman of Fort Worth. There was nothing particularly sensational about the crime, but Brooks made legal history. He was the first person to be executed in Texas in eighteen years, and he was also the first human being executed by means of a lethal injection. Both Texas and neighboring Oklahoma had adopted this method in 1977, but hadn't had occasion to try it until Charlie Brooks's sentence had to be carried out. Once it was known that Brooks was to become, like William Kemmler and Gee Jon, another American first, the media paid attention. The sentence was unfair, it was argued, because Brooks's partner in the shooting had plea-bargained himself off death row on a technicality. It was patently unfair that one killer should be executed and the other given a forty-year prison term.

Before the coming of the fatal day for Charlie Brooks, the American Medical Association did what it could to separate itself from the quasi-medical nature of this kind of execution. In a statement of its position, the AMA said:

> The use of a lethal injection as a means of terminating the life of a convict is not the practice of medicine. A physician who accepts the task of performing an execution on behalf of the State obviously does not enhance the image of the medical profession. . . .This is not an appropriate role for a physician.

None of this helped Brooks lying under sentence of death. He was stretched out on a hospital trolley and rolled into the execution chamber. This is how Brian Lane describes the rest in his book, *The Encyclopedia of Cruel and Unusual Punishments*:

> . . . Just after midnight the condemned man's arm was bound to a padded board and his veins examined by the doctor [in spite of the AMA ruling] to ensure that they were large enough to take the injection catheter. (This is a particular problem in subjects who have been habitual drug users, where veins may be weak and scarred, requiring surgery to expose a deeper vein.) The needle was inserted into his vein and attached to a rubber tube which went across the floor and through a hole in the wall to the execution chamber. . . .
>
> At 12:07 a.m. a dose of the barbiturate drug sodium thiopental was added to the intravenous drip which had already been started to keep the vein open. Brooks was observed to clench his fist, raise his head and appear to yawn or gasp for breath before falling into unconsciousness. The second ingredient of the deadly cocktail was added—pancuronium bromide, a muscle relaxant used in sufficient quantity to paralyse the lungs; and then the third—potassium chloride to induce cardiac arrest. At 12:16 Charlie Brooks was pronounced dead.

It would appear on the surface that this was, at last, the long-sought escape from the capital-punishment dilemma. But it hasn't turned out like that. In many of the cases in which it has been used, there have been problems. In one case in 1985 not fewer than twenty-three attempts were made on the criminal to find a suitable vein. It took them forty minutes to find one. Meanwhile the victim was strapped to the trolley, waiting, and not without some physical and much psychological pain.

When notorious serial killer John Wayne Gacy, the murderer of thirty-three young men and boys, went to his death in 1994, it took at least eighteen minutes for the drugs to kill him. In Illinois, where Gacy was executed, the state used a "death machine," which was the invention of Fred Leuchter, who styles himself an "execution expert." According to Chicago lawyer Stuart Altschuler:

> It turns out that Mr. Leuchter has no scientific credentials, was prosecuted by Massachusetts for posing as an engineer without a licence, and is a Holocaust revisionist to boot. . . . Embarrassed by these disclosures, Illinois cancelled its "consulting contract" with Mr. Leuchter in 1990 but continues to use his machine.

Stuart Altschuler was representing some of the condemned convicts on death row when this execution machine was introduced. The machine works on the same principles as the one described above: it renders the victim unconscious, stops his breathing, and then his heart, with three drugs added one at a time through a catheter in the victim's arm. Altschuler tried to challenge the lethal-injection method in the courts as being illegal and subject to the kind of accident that prolonged Gacy's execution to nearly twenty minutes. (In Texas, the 1988 death of Raymond Landry took twenty-four minutes after the tube leading into his arm leaked. In another case the poisons shot out around the chamber because the pressure was too great for the victim's body.) The arguments were rejected, although exactly what the accidents were that prolonged both the first execution and Gacy's were never revealed. An inquiry is said to be under way to discover this information.

The authorities in Illinois repeatedly state that Gacy felt no pain. In saying this they are taking a big chance, since more and more of the people who put them in office are looking for something else entirely: they don't want less pain, but *more*. The criminal should feel as much pain as his victim, they say, without thinking how is it possible for one man to bear the pain of thirty-three separate victims. Revenge and retribution are the ends of capital punishment today. The fine rhetoric and the fancy names have been abandoned. We are back to Old Testament sentiments like "an eye for an eye." This sentiment would seem to be at odds with the ongoing hunt for a method of terminating the lives of criminals by methods that may be seen as progressively more and more humane. While in the 1890s the electric chair was seen as the way of the future and the gift of the New World to the Old, which was never taken up, today the "hot seat" is hardly less barbaric than the gallows or the stake. In fact, in some states, it is illegal to do to animals what is routinely done to murderers without penalty. *ABC News* reporter Cynthia McFadden reported that chinchilla ranchers are under prosecution for electrocuting their animals. According to the American Veterinary Medical Association, animal euthanasia by electricity must be preceded by rendering the beasts unconscious first. Anything less than that is thought to be inhumane.

While the needle is currently the state of the art, it goes back at least to the New York Death Commission that eventually brought in the electric chair. Nicholas Jenkins in a *New Yorker* commentary suggests the fecklessness of our efforts and the muddle-headedness of the people involved when he observes that the pretend medical staff at an execution by lethal injection still swab the prisoner's forearm with a disinfectant prior to trying the next most likely vein. Have they forgotten that the prisoner has no medical future? That he will not catch cold or die of cancer or of a perforated ulcer. He needs the disinfectant like a moose needs a hat rack, as Jack Benny used to say.

The killing of anyone, criminal or otherwise, is a brutal act. Its brutality is sometimes augmented by pretending that one can be civilized about it. Making it appear like an operation or medical procedure is a transparent veil. There's no health in it. Maybe the military people have always had the right idea. They are our professional killers, after all. The best rough justice is all one can hope for where blood and more blood are being called for.

The Supreme Court is required to supervise convictions and condemnations in capital cases. It has failed to effect the fairness it was thought that it would bring to the process. The South has remained "the death belt"; Hispanics and blacks are disproportionately represented in the Death House. At every step of the legal process, the deck is stacked against these minorities. For example, 40 percent of Death Row inmates today are black, while blacks represent only 12 percent of the population.

Hemingway noted in *The Sun Also Rises* that the beautiful Lady Brett

Ashley had a knack of turning men into swine. They called her Circe, after the temptress of Ulysses. It seems that the struggle to find a perfect method of ridding the world of its murderers, rapists, kidnappers, and traitors tends to turn the seekers into swine too. One can't shovel manure without getting stained. You can't deal in death without losing an important element of life. The state that takes life has less respect for it than one that does not.

CHAPTER THIRTEEN

Death and the Maiden

*"And this yere in Feurelle the xxth day [1523] was the ladye
Alys Hungerford lede from the Tower vn-to Holborne, and there
put in-to a carte at the churchyerde with one of hare seruanttes,
and so carred vn-to Tyborne, and there bothe hongyd, and she
burryd at Grayfreeres in the nether end of the myddes of the
churche on the northe syde."*

—CHRONICLES OF GREY FRIARS

There never was a time when convicted women were free from the touch
of the hangman. Women thieves and murderers, traitors and forgers, pickpockets and coiners suffered alongside their brothers from the beginnings
of British history until the ban on state killing protected both sexes equally. But while women were certainly handed over to the hangman, who used
both blade and noose as required, the law also reserved certain punishments for women. Indeed, certain crimes, because of their nature, involved
only women. In Britain, the chief of these was husband-killing, for which
they invented the term "petty treason." But lesser crimes, such as murdering newborn infants, prostitution, and concealing pregnancy, were also
punished differently. "Scolds" were treated to the "ducking-stool" when the
court deemed that their tongues had run away with them. While the vil-
lagers got great enjoyment from the spectacle of a woman tied to a chair
being dunked like a human doughnut into the millpond several times, it
often proved fatal to the unhappy scold who couldn't catch her breath.
Women settling matters between themselves, as men did without raising
official eyebrows, were deemed harridans who had offended against the
public peace, and were sentenced to a ducking to "cool their immoderate
heat."

Any woman whose moral conduct was not above suspicion might be in
for a ducking. Things have always gone badly for the "woman taken in adultery." A similar fate awaited the "ale wife" who sold bad beer. The double
standard of man's inhumanity to woman is operating here. But as terrible
as the ducking stool might have been, it seems kindness itself when compared with certain Continental punishments. In some places she was suffo-
cated in mud. In others she was sewn into a sack in company with an ape,

a poisonous snake, a dog, and a cockerel, and flung into a pool to drown.

The punishments described above began in early Saxon times and had, by and large, disappeared by the time of the learned Judge Jeffreys near the end of the seventeenth century. Mark this Daniel's adjuration to the jailer in sentencing a woman to be whipped:

> I charge you to pay particular attention to this lady. Scourge her soundly, man; scourge her till the blood runs down. It is Christmas—a cold time for madam to strip. See that you warm her shoulders thoroughly.

During the reign of Henry III, the fair Ivetta de Balsham was sentenced to be hanged for harboring thieves. According to Bernard O'Donnell, whom I must thank for this story:

> The occasion apparently demanded but slight ceremony and the rope having been pulled taut around her shapely neck, she was left to die to the best of her ability.

How O'Donnell knew that her neck was shapely, we'll have to leave to the next assizes, when journalists of all kinds will answer for crimes of exaggeration and enhancement. In the meantime, this story has a happy ending. When the hangman returned to the gallows the next morning to remove her body, he was astounded to find the young woman still alive at the end of his rope. It must have been twelve hours or more, and her breath was still in her. The hangman, who is perhaps the first hangman we know of who acted on his own initiative, promptly cut the rope and tried to bring the woman back to consciousness. When she was quite herself again, he reported to the authorities what had transpired, and was told that the woman would receive a free pardon. How odd, as Bernard O'Donnell notes, that in a barbarous age, 1264 to be exact, when people were being hacked and stretched and boiled and burned for things that are not even misdemeanors today, being hanged overnight was enough to satisfy the law whether the wench was dead or not. In more recent, more generous, more rational times, the letter of the law: "To be hanged by the neck *until dead*" was almost always insisted upon. Accidents with the rope or drop hardly ever saved the condemned. They only kindled a momentary hope, at once extinguished by the literal drudges of the law.

The gallows in Ivetta's day was a low-tech contraption. It had no moving parts. It was simply a frame fixed in the landscape, not unlike the swings in children's playgrounds today. The hangman brought what he needed to the gallows and made his preparations while his victims looked on.

A celebrated case from the mid-eighteenth century involved a pretty

Oxford woman named Mary Blandy, who poisoned her father. He stood against her marriage to a young fortune-hunter, who escaped to the Continent just in time. Mary wasn't so lucky. At her trial, she claimed to be ignorant of the lethal properties of the powders her lover gave her to mix with her father's meals. The jury didn't believe her: she was sentenced to be hanged.

Anxious to glimpse the gallows, Mary got dressed early on the morning of her execution, and peered out a high window overlooking Castle Green to see that a pole had been laid across the arms of two trees.

> . . . She went out of the Castle about nine o'clock . . . dress'd in a black crape sack, with her arms and hands ty'd with black paduasoy ribbons, and her whole dress extremely neat; her countenance was solemn, and her behaviour well suited to her deplorable circumstances. . . . As she ascended the ladder, after she had got up five steps, she said, "Gentlemen, do not hang me high, for the sake of decency"; then being desired to step up a little higher, she did two steps, and then turning herself about, she trembled, and said, "I am afraid I shall fall." After this, the halter was put about her neck, and she pulled down her handkerchief over her face, without shedding one tear all the time. In this manner she prayed a little while upon the ladder, then gave the signal, by holding out a little book which she had in her hands. . . . After hanging above half an hour the Sheriff gave orders for her to be cut down. Thus far the utmost decorum was observed, but for want of some proper person to take care of her body, this melancholy scene became still more shocking to human nature. There was neither coffin to put her body in, nor hearse to carry it away; nor was it taken back into the Castle, which was only a few yards, but upon being cut down was carried through the crowd upon the shoulders of one of the Sheriff's men in the most beastly manner, with her legs exposed very indecently for several hundred yards, and then deposited in the Sheriff's man's house, 'till about half an hour past five o'clock, when the body was put in a hearse, and carried to Henley, where it was interred. . . .

The above is a contemporary account of the execution, in 1752, and is appended to the full text of her trial published in 1914. When Louis Blake Duff wrote his account of her death in 1949, he adds that "serene and fearless she walked like a queen to the foot of the ladder." He has her dressed in a black gown and her hands and arms tied with "strong black silk ribbons." He also adds:

> While the rope was being put around her neck it touched her face, and she gave a deep sigh. Then with her own fingers she moved it to one side.

The victim of an unhappy love affair, Mary Blandy was turned off a ladder resting against a beam supported by two trees. Her plea not to be hanged "too high" was apparently heeded by the hangman.

Where did this poignant detail spring from? Are there other accounts that mention it? But how like a writer to be moved by what he is writing and to go back to the well for more.

Of Mary's request that she not be hanged high, Justin Atholl speculates:

> To put it bluntly she feared that if she was raised more than a foot or two from the scaffold the indelicate amongst the crowd would be able to see under her skirt.

There is extant an engraving of a painting of Mary Blandy holding a rose and, apparently, not at all concerned about her décolletage. Below is a panel showing the execution scene itself: the two trees, the ladder wrapped in black cloth leaning against the deadly looking pole (almost literally "the fatal tree"), a concourse of curious citizens of Oxford on the Castle Green, and, of course, the black-clad body of Mary, herself, hanging with her feet a foot or so from the ground, as she had wished. Except for the discovery that there had been no provisions made to receive the corpse, all had gone according to Hoyle. One is tempted to infer that it was the commanding personality of Mary herself that had blinded those in charge of the event to the necessity of coffin and hearse.

Another possibility is the fact that an act had recently been passed whereby persons condemned should be executed the next day after sentencing and their bodies "be given over to the Surgeons' Company at their Hall with a view to dissection, and also, at the discretion of the judge, be hanged in chains." Perhaps the sheriff didn't know how to implement this new provision of the law. In the nineteenth century, condemned women in England used to "beg their bodies" from the judges who had just sentenced them to death. They hoped to escape that part of the sentence about being anatomized and exposed. When Elizabeth Fenning was hanged in London in 1815, her distraught father had to pay fourteen shillings and sixpence before he could bypass the anatomizers and take Elizabeth's body home for burial. Later, the bodies of executed prisoners were never released to their families, but buried within the walls of the jails where they were last confined. In fact, some of the condemned walked over their already opened graves—covered with boards—on their last short walk to the drop.

Sir William Blackstone, who was in Oxford at the time of Mary Blandy's death, may have stood on the Castle Green on that fatal morning working out his opinion on the treatment of women for crimes where men were hanged, drawn, and quartered. What he eventually wrote years later in his *Commentaries* was this:

> . . . decency due to the sex [that is to say: women] forbids the exposing and public mangling of their bodies and their sentence is, to be drawn to the gallows and there to be burnt alive. . . .

To be fair, the men convicted of such crimes as treason had no deathbed of roses: they were drawn to the gallows on a sledge, hanged, cut down while still alive; had their bowels, or at least a token piece, taken; and then they were beheaded before being cut into four pieces, which could be displayed on gates to the city or bridges, wherever the deadly majesty of the law designated. In practice, too, women condemned to the stake were strangled first by the executioner and were dead— or at least unconscious—by the time the flames reached them. That was the merciful theory, anyway. In 1733 Elizabeth Wright, a counterfeiter or coiner, was taken with those condemned with her to the place of execution:

> [She] begged hard to be hanged with them. She was afterwards fastened to the stake set up on purpose and burned to ashes, but was dead before the flames touched her, the executioner having first thrown down the stool on which she stood from under her feet, and given her several blows on the breast.

Elizabeth Wright's comparatively easy death was made possible by the hangman, who had devised a way in which the woman could be quietly hanged, while the onlookers were waiting for the fire to be lighted. In 1726, a few years before Elizabeth Wright went to the stake, Catherine Hayes was not so lucky. She was literally burned to death, the executioner having lost

Catherine Hayes was burned at the stake in 1725 for helping in the death and dismemberment of her husband. Husband-murder was called "petty treason" and carried the stiffest of penalties. It remained in force until 1793. As shown here, the flames have reached the executioner's hands, preventing him from strangling Hayes before the fire claims her.

his grip on the rope with which he had planned to strangle her. The *Newgate Calendar* picks up the story:

> . . . the spectators beheld her pushing the faggots from her, while she rent the air with her cries and lamentations. Other faggots were instantly thrown on her; but she survived amidst the flames for a considerable time, and her body was not perfectly reduced to ashes in less than three hours.

After that one might well close this book and never open it again. But there is worse. In old age, Thomas Hardy recalled hearing a Dorset traditional tale that when Mary Channing was burnt at Maumbury Rings in 1702, milk spouted from her breasts into the flames, she being with child. Hardy told this story, and others like it, with "a sort of gaiety and a sort of *gaillardise*."

The treatment of men and women differently on the scaffold has a long and grisly history. The notion of equality was always present, especially in English law, but there runs through it the recurring feeling that hanging was somehow unsuitable for women. This idea is found in other places as well. The Nuremberg hangman Franz Schmidt, who hanged and hacked and drowned and broke on the wheel some thousands of both sexes, reveals in his diary (1573–1617) that he often beheaded a woman "as a favor," because hanging left a bad odor among the survivors even in the lowest society.

With the development of the "New Drop" at Newgate in London, the question of modesty raised by Mary Blandy no longer applied. The condemned dropped through a trapdoor, which in its earliest form hid the feet of the prisoners, and prevented thrashing legs from adding to the piquancy of the moment for some of the witnesses.

There has always been a reluctance on the part of hangmen to execute women. Whatever their crimes were, women, the givers of life, have affected those whose duty it has been to put them to death. James Berry, the Bradford hangman, whose second execution was that of a woman, said: "I hope I never have another woman to hang." Fond hope! Between 1884 and 1890, he executed five. "I never liked to hang a woman. It always made me shiver like a leaf," he said in his retirement. But Berry could harden himself when circumstances demanded it. Once he had to hang a woman he had met socially at the Manchester Police Ball. On looking through the judas window in the door of her cell, he recognized the woman he had spent most of the evening with. He recalled walking home with her afterwards. The thirty-one-year-old widow, Elizabeth Berry, had been convicted of poisoning her eleven-year-old daughter. Although no kin of her executioner, they were probably introduced to each other because of the similarity of names. When he saw her in the condemned cell in Liverpool the night before her execution, they talked about that earlier meeting. The hangman reported this in his memoir, a clipped and cliché-ridden version of what really passed between them:

> "I did not then realize [at the ball] I should have to officiate at the execution of a friend."
>
> "No, I suppose you didn't," he says Mrs Berry replied.
>
> "I am sorry to have to do it," said Berry, "but if you are brave I can promise I shall not allow you to suffer."

This scene cries out for a novelist or playwright. Berry's skill at writing dialogue was not his strong point.

Elizabeth Berry had been under more than usual strain even for someone in the condemned cell. For some days she had heard the noise of carpentry as the scaffold upon which she was to die was being constructed. She told Berry that she was terrified of the physical pain that she must face. The hangman again and again reassured her: "I won't keep you alive a moment longer than necessary." In his biography of Berry, Justin Atholl tells that his victim's preoccupation with the agonies of hanging and not its humiliation led the hangman to the conclusion that she was "the greatest coward he had met." Still, all his skills could not provide her with an easy prelude to her death. Since she had been moved out of earshot of the carpenters, she had a long walk, over snow-covered ground, to the gallows.

> She walked alone until she saw the scaffold, when she groaned and the ever alert Berry walking just behind her thought she was going to collapse. He stepped forward to support her, but the touch of the hangman's hand seems to have made her take a grip of herself. "Don't touch me, Mr Berry, and I will go bravely," she said, and it was two warders and not the executioner who supported her.
>
> On the scaffold she exclaimed, "God forbid!" again and again and fainted. She was lifted on to the trap and held while Berry pinioned her legs and adjusted the noose. But she appears to have recovered, for she exclaimed "May God forgive me" as Berry pulled the white cap down. Berry recorded that he was greatly relieved when on descending to the pit by a ladder with two doctors he found that she had died "a merciful death".

In spite of Berry's "just the facts, Ma'am" approach to this story and the pains he goes to to cover any trace of sentiment, he does tell us that when he went down into the pit to remove the body from the rope, he cut off a lock of Elizabeth Berry's "beautiful chestnut hair" as a memento of their last meeting and added it to his growing collection of grisly keepsakes. In showing them off, he remarked in a rather competitive spirit, "I never executed a woman without suffering as severe mental and bodily pains as my victim." In later years Berry believed that this lock of hair had an "evil influence" upon him and he was happier when he got rid of it.

When Harry and Tom Pierrepoint approached Rhoda Willis, alias Leslie James, in her cell at Cardiff on 14 August 1907, they found her on her knees in prayer. Patrick Wilson describes her in his book *Murderess* as thirty-nine and heavy-jawed. She left quite a different impression on Harry Pierrepoint. This is his account of what happened:

> I said "Be brave," and helped her gently to her feet. These words seemed to comfort her a little, and as quickly as possible we fastened her arms behind her back, and walked out into the corridor, the chaplain in his white surplice leading the way. It was only a few steps to the yard. As she stepped out into the open, what a glorious sight there was, no picture could be painted better. The sun shone brilliantly on her auburn hair, just for a moment, a prettier sight no one could wish to see. . . .

Elsewhere Harry Pierrepoint is quoted as saying:

> . . . I was attracted and fascinated by the blaze of her yellow hair, and as
> she left her cell and walked in the procession to the scaffold the sunlight
> caused her hair to gleam like molten gold. For the first time in my career
> as a public executioner I felt ashamed. I had hanged women before, but
> never one so beautiful or so appealing to a man who, after all, had senti-
> mental leanings. But it had to be, and the procession moved to the scaf-
> fold, where a beautiful fiend met the death she certainly merited.

Apart from the difference in hair color, the impact of that meeting in
Cardiff remained intact with Harry Pierrepoint until the day he died.
Harry and Tom Pierrepoint were not, according to Justin Atholl, the first
executioners called upon to execute the beautiful Rhoda Willis. The story
he tells is that John Ellis, when first approached by the Home Office,
refused to have any part in the business. There was talk of a "hangman's
strike." Ellen Hayes, for many years Inspector of Prisons, said in her remi-
niscences that, when Ellis refused to officiate, the authorities received many
offers from people (including one from a woman) offering to carry out the
sentence for them. Here is Justin Atholl again:

> The idea of a "hangman's strike" over having to execute a woman would
> not be unique. In France, where perhaps notions of gallantry linger
> longer, it was reported in 1938 that Henri Deibler, the official execution-
> er, had informed the Ministry of Justice that he would retire rather than
> execute a woman. He had, it was said, always refused to execute a woman
> on the grounds that misfortune invariably overtook the executioner of a
> woman. . . .

In 1949 Albert Pierrepoint, Harry's son, was asked to appear before a
royal commission looking into the death penalty.

> Q. Would you say there was anything either particularly difficult or par-
> ticularly unpleasant in the execution of a woman?
> A. No. I think a woman is braver than a man, and I have seen more exe-
> cutions than anybody living.
> Q. Have you ever known of a case where it was too much for the woman
> at the last?
> A. I have never known it. I have never seen a man braver than a woman.

Albert, the last in this three-man dynasty, was as partial to the ladies as
his father. In 1945, in Hameln, where he was taken to execute thirteen war

criminals, he seemed to be quite taken by Irma Grese, whose notorious reign at Belsen he was familiar with. When she was brought out to be weighed and measured the day before her execution, Pierrepoint recorded, "She walked out of her cell and came towards us laughing. She seemed as bonny a girl as one could ever wish to meet." Albert knew that this blonde, twenty-one-year-old habitually lashed prisoners to death with her riding whip, sometimes thirty in a day. Still, they shared a joke about her being coyly reluctant to give her age, as her height was being noted on the clipboard carried by Albert's assistant. "Schnell!" she said as she stepped on the scales. "Let's get this over with."

The following morning on the gallows, the first of the thirteen to die that day, she repeated "Schnell" in her languid voice just before the trap crashed down.

As far as I can gather, there is no particular difficulty presented in hanging women. The only change in the routine is that women have their legs tied so that the skirts are secured. What the fashion for shorter skirts from time to time has meant is not known. Pierrepoint refers to the changed position of the leg strap in his memoir. He says that this is done "for the sake of decency." Mary Blandy was finally getting through.

The only serious difficulty in hanging women is the fact that there is a great lack of statistical data. When a successful hanging depends upon tables of weights, drops, and the precise measurement of the lethal impact needed, there isn't much to go on. Ruth Ellis, who in 1955 became the last woman to be hanged in Great Britain, was only the sixteenth woman executed since the beginning of the century.

Across the sea in America, where indigenous law had its origins in English law to a great degree, men and women appeared as equals in the prisoners' dock. Where women were legally abused by being treated differently in property law and civil law generally, they were accorded the right to be tried before judge and jury as the equals of men. Consequently America has legally executed many women. In fact, the first recorded case of capital punishment in the New World was the hanging of a girl of sixteen convicted of petty theft by Samuel de Champlain at his Habitation in New France. Many followed her.

Never as good at the job as the English, American executioners have been an up-and-down lot. No one in his right mind in the United States would have been able to say, as Berry did when he stitched up Charlie Peace: "'e passed hoff like a summer's day." But some went better than oth-

Albert Pierrepoint called Irma Grese "as bonny a girl as you could ever wish to meet," when he weighed her and took her height prior to hanging her the following morning in Hameln, Germany, as part of a batch of war criminals. She was responsible for some of the most brutal concentration-camp deaths.

ers. In 1859, for instance, in St. Paul, Minnesota, the law ended its sport with Ann Bilansky. Married to an older man of means, Ann thought she could have her husband's fortune and young John Walker, if things worked out. They didn't. A more incompetent case of arsenic poisoning has rarely been filed. Witnesses appeared who were able to swear to who bought the poison and who had then administered it. In spite of a reluctance to sentence a woman to death in the state of Minnesota, the judge did just that. Ann remained confident that her appeals would be heard, but they were all of them denied. In the words of Jay Robert Nash:

> . . . on Friday, March 23, 1860, Ann Bilansky was marched to the gallows, a
> company of smartly uniformed Pioneer Guards solemnly in step with her.
>   Several thousand St. Paul residents had turned out for the spectacle.
> Ann mounted the scaffold stairs without faltering. She glanced at the

black coffin awaiting her at the front of the gallows, then knelt upon the trapdoor, displaying in prayers the fervor of the religion she had found while awaiting execution.

For a moment the crowd thought that it was not going to get its money's worth. If Ann submitted meekly to the noose, the day would be over and the long wait hardly justified. Seeming to understand this, Ann stood up, arms akimbo, and berated the crowd, telling them that she looked to divine, not human justice: "May you all profit by my death. Your courts of justice are not courts of justice, but I will get justice in Heaven! . . . I die prepared to meet my God!" Jay Robert Nash continues:

> A deputy walked up behind Ann Bilansky and slipped the noose over her head, whispering: "That's quite enough, don't you think?"
>
> Ann turned an angry face to him, spitting indignantly: "How can you stain your hands by putting that rope around my neck—the instrument of my death?"
>
> "I assure you," replied the deputy in a polite tone, "that it is only my duty which compels me to do so."

With that he secured the woman's hands and tied her skirts to her body before covering her head with a black cap. She swayed under the beam for a moment. "Be sure that my face is well covered," she said from behind the dark cloth. The deputy obliged.

> This last vanity uttered, Ann Bilansky, poisoner, gave out her last words: "Lord Jesus Christ receive my soul!"
>
> The trapdoor snapped open at her last word and she dropped four feet, her body convulsing only once before being stilled by death. Ann Bilansky's last-second reprieve, which she had so confidently expected, never arrived. The state of Minnesota had dared to hang a woman—its first executed and its last. The crowd must have sensed the historic moment, for hundreds broke through the cordon of troops and, ever-mindful of souvenirs, tore the hangman's rope to pieces.

In this story, the hangman appears to have been a deputy. It may have been a case, as already mentioned, where the hangman operated the trap mechanism alone. The deputy worked on the scaffold, while the hangman stood apart. On a signal, he chopped the rope, pulled the bolt, or pushed the handle. He could go home to his bed that night having had no hand in putting the noose in position around Ann Bilansky's guilty neck.

One of the most pathetic cases of an injustice on record is the case of Eliza Fenning, who was convicted and condemned to death on evidence that, to quote Bernard O'Donnell in *Should Women Hang?*, "would not have hanged a cat." There is no better case for putting aside the rope than this case of a girl hanged on what was to have been her wedding day. Eliza was cook to a druggist's family. Her conviction was based upon the jury's belief that she had put arsenic into dumplings she had served to the family. Her mistress died, the druggist became slightly ill, and Eliza was arrested as the most likely culprit, even though the arsenic in her employer's store went missing before Eliza was hired. Further, the druggist told several people that there was insanity in his family and that he thought that he should be put away before any harm came to his wife. He confessed to a friend that he at times had an overpowering obsession to murder his shrew of a wife.

None of this was heard by the jury. Nor when he heard it was the Lord Chancellor moved to dismiss the charges against Eliza. If Eliza was right, he reasoned, then the law of England was wrong, which was absurd. There were no courts of appeal in 1815. The law could not be shown to be fallible. So, while the country continued rejoicing at the defeat of Napoleon at Waterloo, Eliza Fenning prepared to meet Langley, the hangman. Of Eliza, Horace Bleackley says:

> Comely and graceful, with a small but shapely figure, she was the most attractive perhaps of all the poor young women who have suffered as she did. When summoned to her doom, her courage in the Press yard was undaunted. Evidently on this occasion Langley was admitted into the prison, and while he was binding her elbows to her sides and fastening her hands together in front—acting instead of the Yeoman of the Halter—she did not show the slightest trace of fear. Even when he wound the halter around her waist according to the custom she remained firm and unwavering, without a quiver on her lips or a tear in her eye.

The crowd, which was by definition callous, crude, and bloodthirsty, on this occasion appeared to be sympathetic to the young woman mounting the gallows. Hushed were the usual cat-calls and jeers. The unusually large throng seemed full of grief on her account. Eliza stood firmly, calmly, and patiently on the trap, beneath the fatal beam, speaking with the Reverend Horace Cotton, the ordinary, and her own priest beside her. Meanwhile the hangman tried to adjust a small white nightcap over her cap, but it wouldn't go on. Here is Bleackley again:

Failing in his purpose, Langley bound a muslin handkerchief over her face, and since this was not sufficient cover, he substituted a dirty pocket handkerchief. For the first time she began to rebel.

"Pray do not let him put it on, Mr Cotton," she implored in disgust. "Pray let him take it off; pray do, Mr Cotton."

"My dear," stammered the perplexed Cotton, "it must be on—he must put it on."

And so, since they could think of no expedient, it had to remain.

There have been cases where the condemned prisoner has requested that the hangman not cover his face with the traditional cap or hood. In some cases this is bravado, rather like turning aside the proffered blindfold as the condemned stares across the courtyard at the firing squad. But, in the case of a prisoner about to be hanged, it is for the sake of the living witnesses that the face of the prisoner is covered. In Eliza's case, there was no bravado; a clean cloth would have suited her. From Langley's side, it was an act of charity as he saw it. It was *his* dirty handkerchief after all, not the Old Bailey's, not the court's.

> . . . Having placed the rope around the girl's neck, he ascended a pair of steps, and, throwing the end of the rope over the beam, he fastened it with several knots. Next the other two criminals who were to suffer with the girl were brought out and were tied up in turn likewise. . . . Meanwhile, poor Eliza Fenning continued to pray with her priest, brave and tranquil to the end. . . .

Lest my dependence on Horace Bleackley's account suggest that his view of Eliza Fenning's last moments was untypical of the telling of this story, let Bernard O'Donnell close this sad history from his own book:

> . . . when a magistrate, who had tried, with many others, to save her, saw her he exclaimed, "Tell me in the name of God that you are innocent."
>
> Elizabeth, calm and undismayed replied with a smile, "In the name of God, then, I am innocent." These were the last words she spoke and within a few minutes the gibbet had claimed her and an errant breeze billowed the frock which enclosed her dead body.

I have given rather a lot of space to the final scene in Eliza Fenning's short life for a good reason. The reader must have noticed that the descriptions of the execution by both the quoted writers are almost loving. Far from being "a tumble and a kick," as more than one wag has described a hanging, the last moments of Eliza Fenning are lingered over as though the whole story of her death cannot be grasped in a simple statement of fact. The truth is that, by detailing every particular of her execution, another level of meaning is being added.

This other element is perhaps more than mere morbid curiosity. If it were simply that, why not tell about the slaughter of thousands on a battle-field? No, there is something in the accounts of these events that is more than an appeal to callous, prurient interest. There is something of the mystery of life and death itself that forms part of the fascination: the moment when a living creature stops being one. On the battlefield that moment can never be predicted with any certainty, but within the framework of an execution there is no doubt. An execution is like a play in a theater; all of the actors have their parts to play and the timing of all the acts is known beforehand. The audience focuses on the main actors of the tragedy, who either give a satisfactory performance or a bad one. The supporting cast is there to encourage the principals to give of their best. The leads, because of the audience, go through their paces as well as they are able.

There is another element that I would like to lead up to through an incident in the life of the young Thomas Hardy. In 1856, the future author of *Tess of the d'Urbervilles* and *Return of the Native* was apprenticed to an architect in Dorset. Apart from letters and a little journalism, he had not yet started writing. Shortly after he started his apprenticeship, he attended a public hanging in Dorchester which soundly and indelibly stirred his young imagination and imprinted upon it images which remained with him until his death. The hanging was that of a woman, Elizabeth Martha Brown, who had been condemned for the murder of her husband, a carter, or "tranter," to use the local name. It was a case of jealousy. He, twenty years younger than his wife, had been making love to another woman. She hit him with a hatchet when he came home one night in a drunken rage, threatening her with a horsewhip. Had she not clung to a silly story about him being kicked by his horse, she might have received a lighter sentence. The story of the crime was well known in the district and a large crowd had assembled outside the jail to witness the final scene. Hardy was early and secured a place close to the gallows, which were erected high over the gateway of Dorchester Gaol. Robert Gittings, Hardy's biographer, describes that August morning in 1856:

> . . . a large crowd turned out in the early morning drizzle. . . . Her hand-
> some appearance, younger than her years, and her lovely hair, added to the

morbid curiosity. So did her utterly calm behaviour, though her own vicar
... chose to regard this as callousness. After shaking hands with the prison
officials, she walked firmly to the scaffold, and seemed to show no fear. . . .

When Martha Brown had been, to use the phrase then in almost weekly use, "launched into eternity," the sixteen-year-old writer-to-be experienced a complex series of emotions with a strong sexual component. He
was so moved by the experience that in his eighties he was able to write:

> I remember what a fine figure she showed against the sky as she hung in
> the misty rain, and how the tight black silk gown set off her shape as she
> wheeled half round and back. . . .

Robert Gittings, in his *Young Thomas Hardy,* believes that this clearly
highly dramatic and sexually charged incident was made more poignant
when Calcraft had tied the prisoner's dress close to her body. "For one
ardent watcher at least, the hangman's would-be humanitarian action created
an additional excitement." Hardy himself realized that his recollections of
this scene and the veiled delight he took in them were disreputable even in
a man of letters, a survivor of the Victorian age. Whenever he wrote about
this, he gives himself the excuse of his tender years. In one account he calls
it a jaunt, in another he claims that he had to be in Dorchester for other
reasons. But for a repressed post-Victorian octogenarian, these small confessions must have given great pleasure and relief.

Hardy told stories about other executions as well. Was this after-dinner
talk over cigars in the smoking room with the women excluded? Was this
the conventional sort of conversation *entres hommes?* Was this Hardy
behaving as he had perhaps seen real gentlemen behaving in smoky privacy,
the port decanter nearby? Certainly in other upper-middle-class houses
and in stately homes, it was the moment to bring out the collection of
pornography, to show off hanging hoods and pieces of hanging ropes with
tags indicating which illustrious criminals of the past had perished on
them. This was the dark side of English gentility, an underground that
needed a social surveyor with the talents of a Henry Mayhew to explore.
Hardy had a need to conform to his adopted class, but however guarded
he was about his humble origins, he couldn't resist testing his obsessions
on the sensibilities of his visitors. Whatever it was, the rustle of the condemned woman's black gown whispered in the ear of that old man.

Thomas Hardy's private morbidity should not surprise us, considering
the repressions of his time. We are lucky that he was able to channel it into

works of art that are still being read well over a hundred years after the events which lent some of their emotional power to their creation. In fact, Hardy was able to find energy for his fiction in death of all kinds, male or female, natural or unnatural, sudden or lingering. In truth, as I have suggested, the sound of silk rubbing on silk was enough to inspire a chapter or two.

All readers know the fate of Hardy's Tess. But, although Hardy's sensibility was fired by the sights of violent deaths that he had witnessed, he was cunning enough to leave the execution scene out of *Tess of the d'Urbervilles*. Hemingway was not the first great artist to see that a work is strengthened by what it leaves out.

According to ancient practice, designed to protect the clergy, and called "benefit of clergy," anyone who could demonstrate that he could read could look for a reprieve from the cart ride through Holborn to the Deadly Never-Green tree at Tyburn. This was, except for literate nuns, an exclusively male preserve. Although Mary Blandy could both read and write, she was unable to avail herself of "benefit of clergy." At the same time, the life of many an illiterate male was saved by his ability to recite his "neck verse," the memorized first verse of Psalm LI:

> Have mercy upon me, O God, according to thy loving-kindness; accord-
> ing unto the multitude of thy tender mercies blot out my transgressions.

I mention this life-saving device for men because, although few women could claim it, no man could "plead his belly." Women open to the capital charge often provided themselves conveniently with child when their cases were tried. Being pregnant mitigated their sentences, calling for transportation instead of the scaffold. At the very least, no one would execute a pregnant woman until after the baby had been born. The months of her confinement, in both senses, gave the condemned woman time for other legal maneuvering, and often the reprieve was never rescinded, the public being outraged at the sight of a woman on her way to the gallows with a babe at her breast. The following, quoted in Donald Rumbelow's excellent *The Triple Tree*, was written in 1698:

> The Women or Wenches that are condemn'd to Death, never fail to plead
> they are with Child, (if they are old enough) in order to stop Execution
> till they are delivered. Upon this they are order'd to be visited by
> Matrons: if the Matrons do not find them Quick, they are sure to swing
> next execution-Day; but very often they declare that they are with child,

and often too the poor Criminals are so indeed; for tho' they came never so good Virgins into the Prison, they are a Sett of Wags there that take Care of these Matters. No doubt they are diligent to inform them the very Moment they come in, that if they are not with Child already, they must go to work immediately to be so; that in case they have the Misfortune to be condemn'd, they may get Time, and so perhaps save their Lives. Who would not hearken to such wholesome Advice?

In a Massachusetts torn apart by revolution, Bathsheba Spooner (1746–1778) had the doubly bad luck of being involved in a murder and on the unpopular royalist side in the War of Independence. Her father had been Chief Justice of Massachusetts under the British. Called the Tory Murderess at her trial, she and her male confederates were condemned to death in 1778. Although she was certainly guilty of murdering her elderly husband, her sentence might have been more merciful if she had been a good republican. Bathsheba pleaded her belly.

Since both English law and custom forbade the execution of a pregnant woman, a stay of execution was granted by the Massachusetts Council in order to allow Bathsheba to be examined by a panel consisting of "two men midwives and twelve descreet lawful matrons" who were to proceed "by the breast and by the belly" to test the validity of Bathsheba's claim. When the panel unanimously found that she was not with child, her spiritual adviser claimed that the panel had been swayed by political sympathies. He put together a panel of his own —"three men midwives and three lawful matrons"—who decided, four to two, that she was indeed pregnant. This second panel had no legal status, and preparations went ahead for the hanging. In a last effort to save herself, she wrote to the Council, requesting

> that my body be examined after I am executed by a committee of competent physicians, who will, perforce, belatedly substantiate my claims. . . . The midwives who have examined me have taken into greater account my father's Royalist leanings than they have the stirrings in my body which should have stirred their consciences. The truth is that they want my father's daughter dead and with her my father's grandchild.

The four were hanged on 2 July 1778, in the square at Worcester, after a violent thunderstorm caused a further delay in the proceedings. After the four were dead, the three men were nailed into their coffins, while Bathsheba's body was examined for the last time by surgeons. A "perfectly developed male foetus, aged between five and six months," was taken from her body. I'll leave the last word to Carl Sifakis, to whom I am indebted for this succinct version of the story:

> . . . one definite result of the affair was that certain male midwives and discreet lawful matrons needed a lengthy period of remorse before they could once more walk the streets of Worcester without downcast eyes.

This chapter, dedicated to Death and the Maiden, would be incomplete without some mention of the fashions worn to the place of execution. To be honest, men on the point of death, throughout the long process from Newgate to Tyburn in the eighteenth century, exhibited more interest in clothes than their female companions. Justin Atholl suggests reason for this:

> The most notorious women to hang were murderers and they were, consequently, hanged within two or three days of being sentenced, with little time to secure fashionable dress if they were so minded. The most notorious male criminals of the period were usually highwaymen whose "order for execution" might not come through for weeks after trial and who had, consequently, plenty of time to prepare themselves sartorially as well as spiritually.

Elizabeth Fenning was hanged at the Old Bailey on 26 July 1815, dressed in what was to have been her wedding dress: a white muslin gown, with a high "Empire" waist, tied with a satin ribbon. A matching white muslin cap covered her hair. A touch of color was added by her high-laced lilac boots.

When Ann Turner was hanged for her part in the complicated schemes of Frances Howard, Countess of Somerset, to be rid of scholarly Sir Thomas Overbury, she was a leading creator of fashions for the court of James I. She introduced the use of yellow starch in cuffs and ruffs and collars, and prepared and sold perfumes and love potions. She urged fashionable women to discard that awkward Elizabethan leftover, the farthingale. It was also said of her that she was adept at witchcraft, which probably meant that she operated as a closet abortionist to highly placed women. The Countess urged her to procure the poisons that killed Overbury, who was a prisoner in the Tower. Poor Ann Turner must have believed that she was untouchable, living as she did in the confidence of her betters. She, alas, was not the first creature to be beguiled by the seemingly endless power of her connections.

In 1615, Sir Edward Coke, Lord Chief Justice of England, in passing sentence on Ann Turner, turned his bitter wit on the unfortunate young widow. He sentenced her to be hanged "in her yellow tinny ruff and cuff, she being the inventor and wearer of that horrid garb."

According to contemporary accounts, and in spite of the ruling of the chief justice, Ann was dressed very plainly for her appointment with Derrick, the hangman. She wore no makeup or powder in her disheveled blonde hair, appeared pale, and wept throughout the journey to the triple tree at Tyburn as she "scattered money to the poor to pray for her."

Bernard O'Donnell puts forward a different view:

> . . . As she mounted the scaffold at Tyburn Mrs Turner wore a gown whose frills and cuffs were dyed with her famous yellow starch and, not to be outdone, the hangman also donned ruffs and cuffs to the amusement of the great crowd who had gathered for the execution of the woman prisoner. From that day, though, yellow starch ceased to be fashionable. . . .

Justin Atholl suggests that the hangman put on yellow starched cuffs and ruffs, not as further amusement for the crowd, but as a show of gallantry towards the prisoner. Take your pick. There were eyewitnesses who say she wore her famous fashions to her death, and others who say she dressed plainly. Atholl is in complete agreement with O'Donnell and all other latter-day commentators on the question of the fashion for yellow starch. After that day in 1615, nobody would be seen dead wearing it.

Exactly 232 years later, almost to the day, Maria Manning is alleged to have done a similar service for black satin. In fact, Maria or Marie Manning has gone down in history as "the woman who murdered black satin." Hers is a sordid story of greed and cold-blooded murder. A foreigner in service as a lady's maid in England, Swiss-born Maria murdered her lover, Patrick O'Connor—aided and abetted by her husband—and buried his body under the flagstones in the kitchen of their Bermondsey house, in South London. When arrested, after trying to flee the country, Maria and Frederick George Manning tried to blame each other through the Old Bailey trial, which Maria enlivened by her appearance every day in memorable flowing black satin dresses with white lace ruffles at the cuffs and primrose-colored gloves. Foolishly, Maria believed that because she had been in service to the nobility and had actually been in the presence of Queen Victoria, no jury would be able to convict her. How wrong she was. And how surprised. She shouted "Shame!" at the black-capped judge in the act of sentencing her to death, and hurled at the bench a bouquet of rue and other herbs—a protection against jail fever—lying on the edge of the prisoner's dock. After sentence was pronounced, the two were

Marie Manning is less imposing in this modeled figure, taken from Madame Tussaud's Archives. But in November 1849, many thousands, including Dickens, turned out to see her and her husband hanged. By wearing a black satin dress on the gallows, Marie is reputed to have made that material and color immediately unfashionable.

removed to Horsemonger Lane Gaol, to await the coming of Mr. Calcraft, the hangman.

When that day, 13 November 1849, arrived, all London was there to see. The crowd was numbered at thirty thousand. In front of the door of the jail, the rabble congregated, hawking last dying confessions, oranges, and other refreshments for the rowdy lower classes who had come to see a married couple turned off. Nor were the upper classes a whit less blood-thirsty. They had rented every room, roof, and window facing the jail and had invited their friends to make a party of it. Grandstands were erected opposite the prison. Entrepreneurs arrived every hour with toys to hawk, religious screeds, and denunciations of foreigners. The police had to be sent for to deal with the crowd. Confectioners prospered. Wicker picnic hampers were stuffed with good things to eat and drink and hoisted to vantage points. In a word, the scene was Dickensian, and the eponymous writer was there himself, with his biographer no less, to see these two fellow creatures executed.

The expert on what happened on the scaffold is a lawyer and writer from Cleveland, Ohio, named Albert Borowitz. His book, entitled *The Woman Who Murdered Black Satin,* is the current Bible on the unfortunate couple. He has sifted all the contemporary authorities and even investigated the claim made in his title. Since she had become somewhat more Junoesque during her confinement, he tells us, she removed padding from her dresses in places where she now could do the job herself. Borowitz is a mine of information. He tells how Maria refused to wear cotton stockings to her death, when there was a perfectly good pair of new silk ones at hand, which she put on with great care. She had also provided herself with new undergarments for the occasion. On the eve of her execution, Maria burned her bustles in the fireplace of her cell. Before being pinioned by Calcraft, she, with the help of the attending physician, had a black silk handkerchief tied over her eyes and a black lace veil over her head.

It dawned a chilly autumn morning, and at least some of the disorderly conduct of the rabble might be put down to encouraging circulation in the feet and legs. Here is Borowitz's description of the last minutes of the Mannings:

> . . . Then it was nine [o'clock], and shortly afterward the jail procession, to the tolling of the prison bell, emerged from a small door . . . at the east end of the roof. . . . Fred was wearing a black suit, and his shirt collar had been loosened for the convenience of Mr Calcraft. . . . Marie, dressed in a handsome black satin gown, followed him with firm strides and did not exhibit any signs of agitation. When she approached the scaffold . . . Calcraft proceeded to draw a white nightcap over [Fred Manning's] head and to adjust the rope. In the meantime, Marie had mounted the scaffold, and when she took her place under the gallows beam, she did not tremble but stood "as fixed as a marble statue." Perhaps her firmness communicated itself at last to Fred, for he leaned over in Marie's direction as far as the rope would permit and, whispering something, held out his pinioned hand to her. One of the turnkeys brought Fred's hands into contact with those of his wife, and the couple took their final leave of each other. . . .
>
> Calcraft put a nightcap over Marie's head and then the noose; the scaffold was cleared of all occupants but the Mannings. . . . An instant later Calcraft withdrew the bolt and the drop of the scaffold fell. According to some accounts it appears that the hangman for once had done his work well and that the Mannings died almost without a struggle; "at least," said the *Daily News*, "there was far less muscular action than is usual."

Dickens admitted to what he called the "attraction of repulsion" that public executions had for him. He was so revolted by the morbid roistering in the streets that led up to the Mannings' execution that he immediately wrote a letter to *The Times* protesting the public spectacle:

> . . . When the two miserable creatures who attracted all this ghastly sight about them were turned quivering into the air, there was no more emotion, no more pity, no more thought that two immortal souls had gone to judgement, no more restraint in any of the previous obscenities, than if the name of Christ had never been heard in this world, and there were no beliefs among men but that they perished like beasts.

Dickens ended this eloquent letter saying that he did not believe that "any community can prosper where such a scene of horror and demoralisation as was enacted this morning outside Horsemonger Lane Gaol is presented at the very doors of good citizens, and is passed by unknown or forgotten." He had trouble forgetting it himself, however. He wrote elsewhere that the image of the hanging figures in Horsemonger Lane remained with him some time after the event. The figures still dangled in his imagination:

> . . . the man's a limp, loose suit of clothes as if the man had gone out of them; the woman's a fine shape, so elaborately corseted and artfully dressed, that it was quite unchanged in its trim appearance as it slowly swung from side to side. . . .

Dickens had rented "a whole roof and back kitchen" in a house overlooking Horsemonger Lane Gaol. From his observations of Marie Manning at her trial and execution, he fashioned a memorable character for *Bleak House*. Mademoiselle Hortense, a violent French maid, was also a murderess. The author made good use of his research. She was finally brought to justice by the redoubtable Inspector Bucket.

Following this execution a lively newspaper debate occurred between abolitionists and those who wished to retain the death penalty. Dickens sided with the moderates, believing that it would be easier to end capital punishment once it was swept from the street. Of course there was also grumbling about the newspaper space given over to the fashionable clothes that Maria Manning picked to be hanged in.

The question of Maria's black satin dress rustled in the background, and, as we have heard, black satin went out of fashion the moment Maria fell through the gallows trap and didn't recover for many years. Ah, that black satin dress! How it manages to sweep the hard facts of history, the pros and cons of the issues, to the sidelines with a swish and rustle of silk.

There is no question that Maria caught the imagination of all of literate Britain. Even the Carlyle and Ruskin households were on tenterhooks awaiting the latest revelations from the press. *Punch*, the satirical paper with a serious edge to its humor, especially where it touched the question of capital punishment, exploited Maria Manning to the hilt. Under the heading FASHIONS FOR OLD BAILEY LADIES, they printed the following fashion notes:

> At the elegant *réunion* on the occasion of the late *Matinée Criminelle* at the Old Bailey, the lovely and accomplished Lady B——— carried off *"les honneurs,"* by her lovely *Manteau à la* MANNINGS, trimmed with *ruche en gibbets*, and *têtes de mort bouffonées*. The neck is surmounted with a running cord, *à la* CALCRAFT, which finishes in a *noeud coulant* in satin, under the left ear. . . . With the *chapeau* is worn a *bonnet de pendue*; this sweet cap can be arranged so as to cover the whole face, and is likely to be thus worn during the approaching season.

Some time after the double hanging, *Punch* returned to Maria's black dress. In a cartoon depicting criminals talking in Madame Tussaud's Chamber of Horrors, a female criminal is saying, "I've a nice black satin dress I've only worn once."

As Albert Borowitz mentioned earlier, there was nothing peculiar in the costume itself. Similar dress might have been seen anywhere in Britain or in America in November 1849. When Donald Nicoll, who was sheriff of London and Middlesex at the time of the Mannings, wrote his account of the case, he said: "After this it was useless for linendrapers to advertise black satin to be sold at even half their cost, as the material remained upon their shelves till Mrs Manning was forgotten." Bernard O'Donnell says that it took nearly thirty years for black satin to recover from the damage wrought by Maria Manning.

Borowitz observes that none of these commentators cite contemporary sources when they pass on this bit of lore to us. So, it seemed a sensible idea to him to take a look at them himself. After assiduously examining fashionable ladies' magazines immediately after the autumn of 1849, he finds that black silk and black satin stand high in the list of what was being worn in court circles and elsewhere in polite society. He looked at advertisements for fabrics in *The Illustrated London News* dating from before the Mannings trial to several years afterwards and found that the material was still highly recommended and the prices firm. At the Great Crystal Palace Exhibition held in 1851, there were several awards made to the makers of black satin both from Britain and from the Continent. In spite of the stories, it would appear that the wearing of black satin went on after Maria Manning's death much as it had gone on before. As Borowitz himself says:

> In light of this evidence, admittedly scattered, that black satin had not vanished completely from the London fashion scene, what can we make of the traditions attaching to Mrs Manning's dress and its powerful influence? When the "murder mania" of early and mid-Victorian England is considered, it seems at least as likely that the dress of a famous murderess would inspire a fashion as destroy it. Certainly *Punch* thought so and counted on Mrs Manning to be a trendsetter. In a satirical letter entitled "Old Bailey Ladies" published immediately after the trial, a young woman writes a friend her enthusiastic fashion notes from the courtroom: "MRS. MANNING was very nicely dressed, indeed. When I looked at her, I thought the jury must find such a black satin gown not guilty—but they didn't. . . ."

Borowitz goes on to say that the only new fashion created by a murderer, as far as he knows, is the short top hat. It was invented when the original Great Train Robber, Franz Mueller, cut down his victim's hat to get rid of his name firmly attached to the inside. But who remembers Franz Mueller? And while one can only applaud Albert Borowitz's fascinating revelations, is Maria Manning going to proceed through history as the "Woman who didn't murder black satin?" I wonder.

CHAPTER FOURTEEN

Hangman's Pay

"In connection with this subject I should like to point out that in asking for the office of executioner to be made a recognised and permanent appointment, I am not suggesting any new thing, but merely a return to the conditions in force not more than fifteen years ago. . . ."

—LETTER TO CAPITAL PUNISHMENT COMMITTEE
BY JAMES BERRY, EXECUTIONER

Before Calcraft, a hangman's pay was difficult to calculate. An executioner had to depend upon the largesse of his victims, which might come to a sovereign or more from wealthier clients, but less or nothing from the poor, who tended to be in the majority. There were perks, of course: the hangman collected the clothes of all his victims and some hangmen took to selling off lengths of rope, claiming that they were from the ropes upon which celebrated criminals had died. In the second decade of the nineteenth century, the authorities took upon themselves the obligation of paying the hangman, since men and women about to be hanged have other things to think about and not full use of their hands for holding coins. The ritual of having the victim pay the executioner—a venerable one, possibly related to paying Charon, the ferryman, who conveys the dead across the river Styx—was replaced by having the state pay the executioner. From that time a hangman's pay was one pound a week. During Calcraft's long tenure, he received one guinea a week—one pound one shilling—with a special fee of a guinea for each execution. When he performed in other parts of the country, he got ten pounds a head or neck. This arrangement came to an end when Calcraft reluctantly retired. Thereafter, each hangman had to negotiate a fee with the sheriff of the county requesting his services. If there was no willing hangman, the sheriff, as we have seen, was required to do the job himself.

The American executioner Robert G. Elliott wanted to make a million dollars through his function as agent of death to many of the eastern state prisons. He was paid $150 per client, which was better than Mr. Pierrepoint, in Britain, who didn't make much more at hanging than Calcraft, or the complaining Mr. Berry. The latter devoted a full chapter in his book

My Experiences as an Executioner to "Hanging: From a Business Point of View." He says that he became an executioner "to obtain a living for my family by an honest trade."

> I consider that if it is right for men to be executed (which I believe it is, in murder cases) it is right that the office of executioner should be held respectable. Therefore I look at hanging from a business point of view.

Berry was a good businessman in the full Victorian tradition. After his first job, a double execution in Edinburgh in 1884, Berry solicited testimonials from the attending officials in order to scare up more work of the same sort. Here is one of them:

City Chambers, Edinburgh,
1 May, 1884.

> We, the Magistrates who were charged with seeing the sentence of death carried into effect, on the 31st March last, on Robert F. Vickers and William Innis, in the Prison of Edinburgh, hereby certify that James Berry, of Bradford, who acted as Executioner, performed his duties in a thoroughly efficient manner; and that his conduct during the time he was here was in every way satisfactory.
>
> George Roberts, Magistrate
> Thomas Clark, Magistrate.

During his career Berry collected ten pounds per drop, plus expenses, which were often difficult to collect after the work was done. He claimed five pounds when the criminal was reprieved. Only on a last-minute reprieve would he claim expenses. Berry was a stickler for having things in writing. He demanded a written order from the sheriff to authorize him to carry out an execution. This practice is at odds with normal offhand British practice of not sending down from the courts a specific written authorization to carry out the sentence of death. In Berry's time and earlier, the order for an execution was a note written by hand on the list of cases heard during a given series of trials.

Across the English Channel, M. Deibler, and the other French headsmen, received varying rewards for their work. When you consider the fact that the work isn't everyone's café crème, that a certain amount of social ostracism is involved, as well as inconvenient hours of work, it is gratifying to see that happy arrangements were in force through a fair swathe of French history.

This was not so in the penal colonies, such as the infamous Devil's Island. Here the convict executioner, who decapitated a fellow inmate, was given ten francs, a couple of bottles of vin ordinaire, and a tin of sardines! Much earlier, the executioner was part of the interlaced traditional agreements we call feudalism. His place was spelled out from time to time in documents like the one installing the first of the Sansons as the Executioner of High Works in Paris in 1688. The royal signature at the bottom was that of the Sun King himself, Louis XIV. The contract is quoted in Georges Lenotre's book, *La Vie à Paris pendant la Révolution*, and given in translation in Alister Kershaw's *A History of the Guillotine*:

> Louis, by the grace of God King of France and Navarre, to all those who shall see these presents, greetings! By order of our Court of the Parliament of Paris, the eleventh August of the present year, it having been ordained for the reasons hereinafter set out that Charles Sanson known as Longval shall alone fulfil the office of Executioner of High Justice in our city, provostry and viscounty of Paris . . . and added under the counterseal of our Chancery, in respect of the said office and its tenure, future exercise, enjoyment and use by the aforesaid Sanson, to the rights of levy in the fairs and markets of our said city . . . products, gains, revenues and emoluments, such and similar as have well and properly been enjoyed by the incumbents of like offices; to wit enjoyment of the house and habitation of the Pillory of *les Halles*, its appurtenances and dependencies, without let or hindrance for whatsoever cause, and furthermore the right to exact from each merchant bearing eggs on his back or by hand one egg, from each saddle-load two eggs, from each cart-load a *demiquarton*, and from each basket of apples, pears, grapes and other produce whether arriving by land or by water in boats carrying the same load as a horse one *sou*; for each laden horse the same amount and for each cart two *sous*. . . .

The document goes on at some length to spell out what Sanson might expect to collect from such items brought to market as green peas, medlars, hemp-seed, walnuts, chestnuts, butter, cheese, fish, oranges, lemons, oysters, brooms, and so on. He also had the right to collect flour and grain from grain merchants, coal from coal merchants, and rope from rope-makers, naturally. These traditional rights, called *havage*, brought into the executioner's coffers, Lenotre estimates, 60,000 *livres* a year. To this add another 6,000 straight salary and you have an impressive total of 66,000 *livres* per year, or roughly £2,640 a year, which would be around $13,200.

Sanson's provincial cousins naturally had to be satisfied with less, but they were able to collect it on market days in the same way. When the Revolution came, however, the feudal system was swept away with the monarchy and the aristocrats. Although the Revolution kept headsmen sweating as never before, burdened with more heads to crop than during the worst royal tyranny, the *bourreau* often went unpaid, or his assistants did. The Revolution broke up the traditional families of executioners just when it had most use for them.

To compensate the headsmen for their beggarly treatment by the democratic reforms, the state agreed to pay for the transportation of the guillotine, and to allow the executioners to run a gambling house or, as at Arras, have exclusive rights to the carcasses of dead horses left in the streets. Further, officials turned a blind eye to the trade in ointments and unguents prepared from the corpses of the executed criminals. The superstitious were always after charms, aphrodisiacs, and cures of one kind and another. An inch or two of rope used in a hanging was highly regarded as a painkiller for a victim of toothache.

Headsmen across France protested to the revolutionary powers for redress: their old economic base had been swept away, and the new one was imperfect and feeble. Many an executioner was forced out of business. Jean-Louis Desmorets wrote an impassioned letter from Lyons demanding justice from the minister of justice, reminding him of his thirty-six years of blameless service on the scaffold. When the fledgling republic at last got around to the problem, it assessed payment at one level for cities with a population range between 300,000 and 100,000, and other rates for cities and towns with smaller populations. It was a head-count with a very practical genesis. By then, of course, because of the heavy traffic of the Terror, headsmen were being borrowed by cities and towns with a backlog of condemned prisoners, from neighboring cities who had found a way of keeping their *bourreau* in business.

Later governments [writes Alister Kershaw] were even less generous in their treatment of the headsman. In 1832, the Paris incumbent was receiving the shamefully small sum of 8,000 francs for his services, and his provincial colleagues were paid salaries which dwindled from 5,000 francs for Lyon to 4,000 francs for Bordeaux and Rouen, and so down to 2,000 francs for towns with a population of less than 20,000. In 1849, M. de Paris had 3,000 francs lopped off his salary, and in the following year the remainder was, so to say, guillotined of another 1,000. By this time, the doyen of provincial executioners, M. de Lyon, was down to 3,000 francs, MM. de Bordeaux, de Rouen, and de Toulouse to 2,400 each, and the rest just 2,000. . . .

There were further ups and downs, additional humiliations. In the end, they—the survivors—had to be content with free rail travel while on government business and eight francs a day expenses. As Kershaw says: "Eight francs! The *Roi soleil* would have died sooner than treat his servants with such sordid avarice."

At the beginning of the twentieth century, a wave of humanitarianism swept France. The cynical Alister Kershaw calls it a spasm. Nevertheless, one president of the republic after another commuted sentences of death. Reformers also worked for the revocation of the death penalty by removing what remained of the *bourreau*'s income. The celebrated socialist editor of *L'Humanité*, Jean Jaurès, before he himself was felled by an assassin's bullet, voted in a budgetary committee to do away with all remaining allowances traditionally claimed by the *bourreau*. Anatole Deibler, had he been less dedicated, would have quit then and there, but he soldiered on at a rate of a head every two weeks in a good year until the day of his death. In inflation-ridden France, the thousand francs he was paid didn't amount to much.

Back in Britain, too, the hangman plied a precarious trade. No hangman ever died rich. And the English have always ground the knuckle of thrift into the public service. When in 1305, for instance, the Scottish patriot Sir William Wallace was executed in London, his head and quarters were boiled and tarred and sent to various places to be exposed according to his majesty's pleasure. His head was placed on London Bridge, where it stayed until it disintegrated; the rest of him went to Newcastle, Berwick, Stirling, and Perth. The whole catastrophe of drawing, hanging, beheading, quartering, boiling, head displaying, and transportation of the quarters north was accomplished, according to the Chancellors Roll, for no more than three pounds, one shilling, and ten pence.

> Not all hangings were so cheaply done [Louis Blake Duff wrote in 1949]. In Scotland, until a century and a half ago, civic feasts were often held before or after an execution. Thomas Potts who was hanged at Paisley in 1797 cost the town thirty-three pounds, five shillings, three pence ha'penny of which thirteen pounds, eight shillings, ten pence was for the civic feast and something over a pound for entertaining the executioner. The festive gatherings were held at Paxton's Tavern and were appropriately known as "splicing the rope."

The high cost of hanging! Jane Jameson, who murdered her mother near Newcastle, was executed on the Town Moor. She was taken to the Moor in a cart, which was occupied by a turnkey. In the cart was her coffin upon which she sat. By each side of the cart walked five porters with javelins and twenty constables with staves. Now for the accounts:

	£	s	d
The hangman.	3	3	
Cart and Driver		15	
Mourning coach.		15	
Joiner's bill for scaffold	8	5	3
Joiner's special allowance.		6	

This comes to a total of thirteen pounds, four shillings, and thru'pence for stitching up Jane Jameson in style.

For many centuries the Scots found their own executioners. From the nineteenth and through the twentieth century, they relied on the English hangman, and paid him better than he was paid at home. When John Ellis went north to Scotland, he received fifteen pounds for his trouble and expenses over and above that. In his career he must have made about ninety pounds a year for sixteen of his twenty-three years, or about two thousand pounds in all. In spite of this, Ellis complained:

> Hangmen are not paid as they ought to be, and there is no pension. Today the pay is the same as twenty years ago, though the assistant gets a guinea more. But the executioner should have a salary. I have been as long as nine months without an execution to deal with. I have had to carry on another business—I am a barber—because there is no living in it.

It is unlikely that Ellis saw the humor in the thought that there is no living in hanging. Only four other executioners served longer than Ellis. All of them had their ups and downs with an officialdom that only reluctantly recognized their existence. Some, as we have seen, left the service on "a matter of principle," which could be put down to the usual sort of bureaucratic insensitivity and blindness. Albert Pierrepoint got his fees raised from ten pounds a drop to fifteen, with five guineas for his assistant. But that was after ten years of protest. While James Berry may have wished to become a full-time executioner—his notepaper carried the words "Executioner's Office" at the head and his professional card, which he popped into the mail when he heard of a capital sentence being passed, clearly stated: James Berry, Executioner—he had a hard time making it pay. Later executioners

Albert Pierrepoint, last of a dynasty of English hangmen, was also the genial host at his two pubs, the Rose and Crown and Help the Poor Struggler. When asked by a Royal Commissioner how many he had executed, he reluctantly answered, "Some hundreds."

as well as earlier ones had to fill up the gap in family finances by doing other work. Some were cobblers, and in more recent times they turned to barbering and keeping public houses. For many years Albert Pierrepoint was Mine Host at Help the Poor Struggler, at Hollinwood, where his regulars kept curious tourists away from the affable publican. He denied rumors that there was a sign reading "NO HANGING AROUND THE BAR."

The Canadian hangman Arthur Ellis maintained that he was due his fee of $150 (plus expenses) as soon as he got a telegram from the county sheriff asking him to officiate on such and such a day. That way, he expected to be paid, whether the condemned person was reprieved or not. Because of this, he argued, he could look at his work with evenhanded tranquility: "It's my retainer. So it is wrong to picture me gnashing my teeth like a villain in a play when I read of a commutation of sentence."

The American State of Illinois is understandably embarrassed by the amount of money it paid Fred Leuchter for his death machine. While not strictly an executioner, Leuchter passed himself off in Illinois as an

More than 3,000 people watched as two convicted Afghans slowly strangled to death in Kabul in the autumn of 1992. With such a short drop, and the nooses placed so that they slipped to the backs of the necks of the condemned, nothing more merciful was possible. It was reported that the crowd rioted in protest as the struggles continued.

"execution engineer" with credentials that later proved to be false. Leuchter pocketed a bundle of money before he was fired in 1990. But the state continues to use his machine, which is described as a hit-and-miss contraption which may have given John Wayne Gacy, the notorious murderer, a death that even his worst enemies couldn't have devised.

It used to be argued—and it was an argument that stumped many abolitionists—that it was cheaper to kill a murderer than to keep him alive like a fighting cock until he dies of old age. But that is no longer so. It now costs an average of $2.3 million to execute a single criminal. For that amount of cash, the state could buy a lot of beans and grits. The lethal dose of chemicals that those getting "the needle" receive costs around $71.50. The big money goes in legal and administrative fees. In spite of this insane cost, 80 percent of American voters are in favor of capital punishment.

Years ago, there were interesting and subtle pro–capital punishment arguments to be made. Some of them, like the deterrent argument, have evaporated in crime statistics in places with and without the death penalty. Today the gloves are off. Retribution is the reason that most people give for retaining or going back to the rope, the chamber, the needle, or the chair. Retribution is *revenge* moved to a fashionable address. It is a hard argument for those opposed to deal with, because of its apparent honesty, its down-to-earth simplicity, which seems to be supported by Holy Writ. Revenge is a powerful human emotion. It can't be denied that getting even is the best revenge.

But in many of our laws and traditions we have tried to elevate human nature to a higher plane. We try to behave better than we feel we can behave. We call that collective effort civilization. We divide our labor and postpone our gratification in many ways. We have learned and been helped by our best minds to live according to our best instincts. We don't deny that these best instincts are not our only instincts, but in framing our laws we have worked in a tradition of not giving in to the lowest common denominator on every issue. Otherwise why do we have international treaties, engage in collective enterprises, attempt to feed the hungry, and so on. Charity cannot be proved to be a correct response in any situation, but the instinct that knows that it is right and just survives even in these shallow times where we seem to be abandoning whatever does not pay, whatever cannot be justified by a balance sheet.

Another argument against the death penalty is that it debases the society that uses it. Where life is cheap, it gets cheaper. When even the worst of our criminals are put to death, we all become calloused from endorsing it. It becomes easier to kill again, easier to condone euthanasia, the extermination of undesirables of all kinds. Is it any great surprise that the inventor of Illinois's death machine should deny the Holocaust?

The gas chamber and the needle debase the society in whose name executions are carried out. We are all tarred by that brush. In addition, the people who come closest to the actual process of killing murderers are coarsened in self-defense or are disabled in some way by the experience. The law has instructed them to do a brutal, irreversible act, the taking of a human life. They are asked to do their job, asked to suspend their judgement and follow orders. In giving evidence at the Scottish Prison Commission, Dr. James Devon, who had been medical officer in a prison, testified:

> I have never seen anyone who had anything to do with the death
> penalty who was not the worse for it. . . . As for the doctor who must
> be in attendance, it is an outrage on all his professional, as well as his
> personal feelings.

This has proved true, not only for the physicians who must certify death, but also for the guards and warders, the governor or warden of the prison, the other inmates—read Oscar Wilde, Brendan Behan, or Robert Lowell about being in prison while an execution is being carried out—even the executioners themselves, that executions kill a little bit of all who come in contact with one.

When on a St. Paul, Minnesota, scaffold in 1859, Ann Bilansky asked the hangman, a deputy appointed by the sheriff, how he could stain his hands by putting a rope, the instrument of her death, around her neck, the deputy replied, "I assure you that it is only my duty which compels me to do so." At Nuremberg, the trials of the Nazi war criminals instructed us that it is not enough in a free society to follow orders. Each of us has to decide whether or not he or she wants to participate in the killing or to ignore the consequences of our acts.

One last argument against the death penalty as it is used in the United States is the demonstrable fact that it is weighted, as the legal system tends to be everywhere, against the poorer members of the society. In the United States, that tendency unfairly targets black Americans. When a white man kills a black, and when a black man kills a white, the odds of being sentenced to death are different. They should at least be the same. This bias is not lodged in one part of the legal process, but is subtly built in from the moment a suspect is accosted by the police. Even in Canada, a country with relatively good race relations, it is a commonplace for blacks to be questioned about their movements more than other members of the community.

When Edward R. Johnson went to the gas chamber in Parchman Prison, Mississippi, on 20 May 1992, a camera crew had been with him for many weeks and stayed with him to within less than fifteen minutes of his walk to the chamber. In the resulting documentary we heard from the condemned man, his family, his lawyer, his guards, and the warden of the prison. Even the warden, while firm in his belief that Johnson was rightly condemned, still said that there are worse men in the prison than the condemned. He thought that Johnson belonged farther down the list of those who should be put to death. At a press conference immediately after the execution, the warden repeated Johnson's last words which, as always, stressed his claim that he was innocent of the crime for which he had been executed. His lawyer complained that on his way into the judge's chambers, where arguments concerning a stay of execution were to be heard, he had seen the judge's denial already printed out before he had heard a word of argument.

The guards behaved kindly towards Johnson and his family; they made it easy for him. His spiritual comforters sat on his right and his left, holding his hands. For his Last Meal, Johnson ordered shrimp, since he had never eaten shrimp before. The warden explained to Johnson about the process, about having a metal contact taped to his chest for the life-monitoring device, which would be carefully watched outside the chamber.

Modern executions, when stripped of all their ancient associations, would appear to be a peculiar Rorschach test. Just as ordinary people see and report seeing all sorts of shapes and pictures in the ink blots, the advocates of the death penalty see in executions the maintenance of a just society. Abolitionists look at the same evidence and see the opposite. If the revenge that the pro-execution group advocates is pure and proper under the law, why are executioners, in spite of this new openness about the desired ends and purposes that executions serve, still the social pariahs they were six hundred years ago. Why is it that they still hide their names? There must remain deep in the consciousness of the most rabid of the execution fanciers a shred of doubt about what they are advocating, otherwise executioners would be invited out more often, appear on more boards of directors, and be invited to join in groups like Rotary, the Lions, the Elks, and the Chamber of Commerce.

It seems appropriate in a book about executioners to give the last word to Albert Pierrepoint, the long-lived British hangman. After having sent, as he admitted to a Royal Commission on the Death Penalty, some "hundreds" into the hereafter, he concludes his autobiography with the following summation:

> I have come to the conclusion that executions solve nothing, and are only an antiquated relic of a primitive desire for revenge which takes the easy way and hands over the responsibility for revenge to other people. . . . It is said to be a deterrent. I cannot agree. There have been murders since the beginning of time, and we shall go on looking for deterrents until the end of time. If death were a deterrent, I might be expected to know. It is I who have faced them last, young lads and girls, working men, grandmothers. I have been amazed to see the courage with which they take that walk into the unknown. It did not deter them then, and it had not deterred them when they committed what they were convicted for. All men and women whom I have faced at that final moment convince me that in what I have done I have not prevented a single murder.

Bibliography

Anderson, Frank W. *Hanging in Canada.* Calgary: Frontier Press, 1973.

Andreyev, Leonid. *Seven Who Were Hanged.* New York: Avon Books, 1941.

Atholl, Justin. *Shadow of the Gallows.* London: John Long, 1954.

———. *The Reluctant Hangman.* London: John Long, 1956.

Bailey, Brian. *Hangmen of England.* New York: Virgin Publishing. Reprint: Barnes & Noble, 1992.

Beckett, Ray, and Richard Beckett. *Hangman: The Life and Times of Alexander Green Public Executioner to the State of New South Wales.* [Sydney]: Nelson, 1980.

Berry, James. *My Experiences as an Executioner.* London: Percy Lund, 1892.

Bleackley, Horace. *The Hangmen of England.* London: Chapman & Hall, 1929.

Borowitz, Albert. *The Woman Who Murdered Black Satin: The Bermondsey Horror.* Columbus: Ohio State University Press, 1981.

Brian, Denis. *Murderers Die.* New York: St. Martin's Press, 1986.

Brown, George W., David M. Hayne, Frances Halpenny, et al., eds. *Dictionary of Canadian Biography.* vols. I–IV. Toronto: University of Toronto Press, 1966–79.

Byron, George Gordon, Lord, *"So Late into the Night." Byron's Letters & Journals.* vol. 5. Edited by Leslie A. Marchand. London: John Murray, 1976.

Calcraft, William. *The Groans of the Gallows, or the Lives and Exploits of William Calcraft and Nathaniel Howard, the Living Rival Hangmen of London and York.* London: 1855.

Charlesworth, Hector. *Candid Chronicles.* Toronto: Macmillan of Canada, 1925.

Croker, John Wilson. *History of the Guillotine.* London: John Murray, 1853.

Delarue, Jacques. *Le Métier de Bourreau.* Paris: Fayard, 1979.

D'Israeli, I[saac]. *Curiosities of Literature.* London: George Routledge & Sons, 1866.

Duff, Charles. *A Handbook on Hanging.* London: John Lane, The Bodley Head, 1928.

Duff, Louis Blake. *The County Kerchief.* Toronto: Ryerson Press, 1949.

Dumas, Alexandre. *Celebrated Crimes.* Translated by I. G. Burnham, vol. vii. Philadelphia: George Barrie & Son, 1895.

Elliott, Robert G. *Agent of Death: The Memoirs of an Executioner.* London: John Long, n.d.

Faber, John. *Great Moments in News Photography.* New York: Thomas Nelson & Son, 1950.

Fiske, John. *Witchcraft in Salem Village.* Boston: Houghton Mifflin & Co., 1923.

Fetherling, Douglas. *Travels by Night.* Toronto: Lester Publishing, 1994.

Friedland, Martin L. *The Case of Valentine Shortis.* Toronto: University of Toronto Press, 1986.

Gammage, Bill, et al., eds. *Australians*, 10 vols. [Sydney]: Fairfax, Syme & Weldon Ass., 1987.

Gatrell, V. A. C. *The Hanging Tree.* Oxford: Oxford University Press, 1994.

Gaute, J. H. H., and Robin Odell. *The Murderers' Who's Who.* Montreal: Optimum Publishing Co., 1979.

Gittings, Robert. *Young Thomas Hardy*, London: Penguin Books, 1975.

Hecht, Ben. *A Child of the Century.* New York: Simon & Schuster, 1954.

Henry, Brian. *The Dublin Hanged.* Dublin: Irish Academic Press, 1994.

Heppenstall, Rayner. *French Crime in the Romantic Age.* London: Hamish Hamilton, 1970.

Herzen, A. I. *My Past and Thought.* Moscow: Academy of Sciences, 1956.

Hibbert, Christopher. *The Road to Tyburn.* London: Longmans Green & Co., 1957.

Hinckeldey, Christoph, ed. *Criminal Justice Through the Ages.* Translated by John Fosberry. Rothenbug ob der Tauber: Medieval Crime Museum, 1981.

Hughes, Robert. *The Fatal Shore.* New York: Alfred A. Knopf, 1987.

Hume, David. *The History of England.* London: Jones & Co., 1826.

Hustak, Alan. *They Were Hanged.* Toronto: James Lorimer & Co., 1987.

Johnson, Robert. *Death Work: A Study of the Modern Execution Process.* Pacific Grove, Calif.: Brooks/Cole Publishing, 1990.

Keneally, Thomas. *The Playmaker.* New York: Simon & Schuster, 1987.

Kershaw, Alister. *A History of the Guillotine.* New York: Barnes & Noble Books, 1993.

Klein, A. M. "Portrait of an Executioner" in *Short Stories.* Edited by M. W. Steinberg. Toronto: University of Toronto Press, 1983.

Lachance, André. *Le Bourreau au Canada sous le régime français.* Québec: Cahiers d'histoire, Société historique de Québec, 1966.

Lane, Brian. *The Encyclopedia of Cruel and Unusual Punishments.* London: True Crime, Virgin Books, 1993.

Laurence, John. *A History of Capital Punishment.* London: Sampson Low, Marston & Co., n.d.

Lawes, Lewis E. *Life and Death in Sing Sing.* Garden City, N.Y.: Star Books, Garden City Publishing, 1928.

Lenotre, Georges [pseud.]. *The Guillotine and Its Servants.* Translated by Mrs. Rodolph Stawell. London: Hutchinson, [1929].

Loomis, Stanley. *Paris in the Terror.* New York: Avon, 1973.

Lustgarten, Edgar. *A Century of Murderers.* London: Eyre Methuen, 1975.

McDade, Thomas M., ed. *The Annals of Murder: A Bibliography of Books and Periodicals on American Murders from Colonial Times to 1900.* Norman: University of Oklahoma Press, 1961.

Marks, Alfred. *Tyburn Tree: Its History and Annals.* London: Brown, Langham & Co., 1908.

Mencken, August. *By The Neck: A Book of Hangings.* New York: Hastings House, 1942.

Michelet, Jules. *Satanism and Witchcraft.* Translated by A. R. Allinson. New York: The Citadel Press, 1939.

Mitchell, Edwin Valentine, ed. *The Newgate Calendar.* Garden City, N.Y.: Garden City Publishing, 1926.

Naish, Camille. *Death Comes to the Maiden.* London & New York: Routledge, 1991.

Nash, Jay Robert. *Almanac of World Crime.* Garden City, N.Y.: Anchor Press/Doubleday, 1981.

———. *Look for the Woman.* New York: M. Evan & Co., New York, 1981.

———. *Murder, America: Homicide in the United States from the Revolution to the Present.* New York: Simon & Schuster, 1980.

O'Donnell, Bernard. *Should Women Hang?* London: W. H. Allen, 1956.

———. *The Old Bailey and Its Trials.* London: Clerke & Cockeran Publishers, 1951.

Parry, Edward Abbott. *The Overbury Mystery.* New York: Charles Scribner's Sons, n.d.

Pierrepoint, Albert. *Executioner: Pierrepoint.* London: George G. Harrap & Co., 1974.

Potter, John Deane. *The Fatal Gallows Tree.* London: Elek Books, 1965.

Robertson, John Ross. *Old Toronto: A Selection of Excerpts from Landmarks of Toronto.* Edited by E. C. Kyte. Toronto: Macmillan of Canada, 1954.

Roughead, William, ed. *Trial of Mary Blandy.* Edinburgh & London: William Hodge & Co., 1914.

Rumbelow, Donald. *The Triple Tree.* London: Harrap, 1982.

Sanson, Henry, ed. *Memoirs of the Sansons.* London: Chatto & Windus, 1881.

Schama, Simon. *Citizens: A Chronicle of the French Revolution.* New York: Vintage Books, 1989.

Schmidt, Franz. *A Hangman's Diary.* Ed. & intro. Albrecht Keller, trans. C. Calvert & A. W. Gruner. London: Philip Allan & Co., 1929.

Scott, George Ryley. *The History of Capital Punishment.* London: Torchstream Books, 1950.

Sharpe, J. A. *Crime in Early Modern England: 1550-1750.* London & New York: Longmans, 1984.

Shaw, George Bernard. *Man and Superman.* London: Penguin Books, 1954.

Sifakis, Carl. *A Catalogue of Crime.* New York: Signet, New American Library, 1979.

———. *Encyclopedia of American Crime.* New York: Facts on File Inc., 1982.

Starkey, Marion L. *The Devil in Massachusetts.* New York: Alfred A. Knopf, 1949.

Stead, Philip John. *Vidocq: A Biography.* London: Staples Press, 1953.

Symons, Julian. *A Pictorial History of Crime.* New York: Bonanza Books, 1966.

Told, Silas. *An Account of the Life and the Dealings of God with Silas Told.* London: Gilbert & Plunner & T. Scolleck, 1785.

Van Loon, Hendrick Willem. *Van Loon's Lives.* New York: Simon & Schuster, 1942.

Wilson, Patrick. *Murderess.* London: Michael Joseph, 1971.

Zola, Émile. *Germinal.* Translated by Havelock Ellis. New York: Vintage Books, Random House, 1994.

Periodicals and Newspapers:

Altschuler, Stuart. "The killer who deserved a fate worse than death." *The Wall Street Journal.* Reprinted in *The Globe and Mail,* 7 June 1994.

Appleby, Timothy. "The vengeful society." *The Globe and Mail,* 18 November 1995.

Anderson, Kurt, et al. "An eye for an eye." *Time Magazine,* 24 January 1983.

Atwood, Margaret. "Marrying the Hangman." *The Capilano Review,* Spring 1975.

Darbyshire, Neil. "Britain's last hangman dies." *The Daily Telegraph,* 2 November 1994.

Davies, Hugh. "Prisoner will pray for swift end to life." *The Daily Telegraph,* 7 April 1995.

Dobbs, Kildare. "Travels in Law." *Lawyers Weekly,* 16 February, 1996.

Haughton, The Rev. Samuel. "On Hanging, Considered from a Mechanical and Physiological Point of View." *Philosophical Magazine,* July 1866.

Jenkins, Nicholas. "Dirty needle." *The New Yorker,* 19 December 1994.

Jerrold, Douglas. "The Gibbet-Cure" and other selections from *Punch, or the London Charivari,* 1849–1850.

Langley, William. "At death's door." *The Sunday Telegraph.* London, 2 April 1995.

Partridge, Frances. "Watching them die." *The Spectator.* London, 9 April 1994.

Acknowledgment of Sources

The following material is reprinted with permission:

From Margaret Atwood, "Marrying the Hangman," originally published in *The Capilano Review* (Spring, 1975), by permission of the author; From Brendan Behan, *The Complete Plays of Brendan Behan* (London: Eyre Methuen, 1978), by permission of Reed Consumer Books Ltd.; from Albert Borowitz, *The Woman Who Murdered Black Satin* (Columbus: Ohio State University Press, 1981), by permission of the author; from G. W. Brown, et al., eds., *Dictionary of Canadian Biography*, vols. I-IV (Toronto: University of Toronto Press, 1966–1979), by permission of the publisher; from Albert Camus, *The Stranger*, trans. Stuart Gilbert (New York: Vintage, Random House, 1954), by permission of the publisher; from Douglas Fetherling, *Travels by Night* (Toronto: Lester Publishing, 1994), by permission of the publisher; from Martin Friedland, *The Case of Valentine Shortis* (Toronto: University of Toronto Press, 1986), by permission of the publisher; from W. Gammage, et al. (eds.), *Australians*, Fairfax Syme Weldon Associates, 1987, by permission of the publisher; from V. A. C. Gatrell, *The Hanging Tree* (Oxford: Oxford University Press, 1994), by permission of Oxford University Press; from Robert Gittings, *Young Thomas Hardy* (London: Penguin Books, 1975), reprinted by permission of Heinemann Educational, a division of Reed Educational and Professional Publishing Ltd.; from Robert Hughes, *The Fatal Shore* (New York: Alfred A. Knopf, 1987), by permission of Alfred A. Knopf Inc.; from Thomas Keneally, *The Playmaker*, copyright © 1987 by Serpentine Publishing Company Proprietary, Ltd. Reprinted with the permission of Simon & Schuster; from A. M. Klein, "Portrait of an Executioner" in *Short Stories*, ed. M. W. Steinberg (Toronto: University of Toronto Press, 1983), by permission of the publisher; from Donald Rumbelow, *The Triple Tree* (London: Harrap Inc., 1982), by permission of the publisher; from Bernard Shaw, *Man and Superman* (London: Penguin Books, 1954), by permission of the Society of Authors on behalf of the Bernard Shaw Estate; from Hendrik Willem Van Loon, *Van Loon's Lives* (New York: Simon & Schuster, 1942), by permission of the estate of Hendrik Willem Van Loon; and from Émile Zola, *Germinal*, trans. Havelock Ellis (New York: Vintage, Random House, 1994), by permission of the publisher.

The following images are reproduced with permission:

Page 2: An Execution (1803)/Thomas Rowlandson/Museum of London/Bridgeman Art Library, London; *12*: by permission of the British Library; *30*: from C. Whitehead, *Autobiography of a Notorious Legal Functionary* (1836), by permission of the Syndics of Cambridge University Library; *33*: by permission of the Fotomas Index; *47*: by permission of the Museum of London; *51*: by permission of the Syndics of Cambridge University Library; *55*: by permission of the British Library; *56*: by permission of the British Library; *57*: by permission of the Hulton Picture Library; *62*: by permission of the Mary Evans Picture Library; *89*: by permission of the Mary Evans Picture Library; *92*: by permission of the York City Art Gallery; *100*: by permission of the Hulton Picture Library; *104*: by permission of Brown Brothers Stock Photos; *119*: by permission of Express Newspapers; *123*: by permission of the Hulton Picture Library; *129*: by permission of the Hulton Picture Library; *136*: by permission of the Hulton Picture Library; *141*: Albrecht Dürer, *Christ on the Cross with Mary and Saint John*, Rosenwald Collection, © 1996 Board of Trustees, National Gallery of Art, Washington; *143*: by permission of the Mary Evans Picture Library; *181*: by permission of Charles Skilton Ltd.; *196*: by permission of the Mary Evans Picture Library; *203*: by permission of Wide World Photos; *232*: courtesy of Madame Tussaud's Archives, London; *243*: by permission of "PA" News; *244*: by permission of Reuters/Archive Photos.

Index

Note: Page numbers in **boldface** indicate an illustration or caption.